LIBRARY OF NEW TESTAMENT STUDIES

419

formerly the Journal for the Study of the New Testament Supplement series

Editor

Mark Goodacre

A POETIC DISCONTENT

Austin Farrer and the Gospel of Mark

ROBERT TITLEY

t &t clark

Published by T&T Clark International
A Continuum imprint
The Tower Building, 11 York Road, London SE1 7NX
80 Maiden Lane, Suite 704, New York, NY 10038

www.continuumbooks.com

British Library Cataloguing-in-Publication Data
A catalogue record for this book is available from the British Library

ISBN: 978-0-567-28321-4 (hardback)

Typeset by Free Range Book Design & Production Limited
Printed in Great Britain by the MPG Books Group, Bodmin and King's Lynn

CONTENTS

ABBREVIATIONS

Below is a list of abbreviations used for Farrer's writings. The reader will easily be able to infer other abbreviations from the full references in the main text or in the bibliography.

Finite and Infinite	*Finite*
The Glass of Vision	*Glass*
A Rebirth of Images	*Rebirth*
A Study in St Mark	*Study*
St Matthew and St Mark	*Matthew*
A Short Bible	*Short*
Said or Sung	*Said*
Love Almighty and Ills Unlimited	*Love*
Saving Belief	*Saving*
A Science of God?	*Science*
Faith and Speculation	*Speculation*
A Celebration of Faith	*Celebration*
The End of Man	*End*
Interpretation and Belief	*Interpretation*
'A Return to New Testament Christological Categories'	'Categories'
'On Credulity'	'Credulity'
'History and the Gospel'	'History'
'The Inspiration of the Bible'	'Bible'
'An English Appreciation'	'Appreciation'
'On Dispensing with Q'	'Dispensing'
'Revelation'	'Revelation'
'On Looking Below the Surface'	'Surface'
'On Religion, Natural and Revealed'	'Religion'
'St Mark'	'St Mark'
'Inspiration Poetical and Divine'	'Inspiration'
'Mary, Scripture and Tradition'	'Mary'
'The Painter's Colours'	'Colours'
'Infallibility and Historical Revelation'	'Infallibility'
'The Brink of Mystery'	'Brink'
'Gnosticism'	'Gnosticism'
'The Mind of St Mark'	'Mind'

Letters and other writings of Farrer reproduced in Philip Curtis'
biography
A Hawk Among Sparrows   *Hawk*

PREFACE

The roots of this book lie in my doctoral research in the 1990s on Austin Farrer's biblical scholarship. During its germination there have been many people to thank.

Those who hear my subject's name can be largely divided into to two groups: some say, 'Mmm, Farrer', in the manner of Homer Simpson when faced with anything edible; and the rest just ask, 'Austin who?' I was in the latter camp until – now Archbishop, then Professor – Rowan Williams responded to my musings about wanting to wrestle with the ideas of a single thinker by suggesting Farrer's as a mind well worth getting into the ring with. As the then Chaplain of Whitelands College, Putney, I found the Principal, Dr David Peacock, and the Governors to be generous with both funding and time to get my research off the ground; and when I went on to be Vicar of the parish of All Saints, West Dulwich, I was blessed with understanding parishioners.

My present work requires the wearing of two hats, as Director of Ordinands in the Anglican Diocese of Southwark, and as a Canon of Southwark Cathedral. At seminars with newly ordained clergy I have aired Farrer's thoughts about the nature of inspiration in the Bible, and their spirited responses have confirmed that his scriptural thinking still has bite. My two bosses, the Bishop of Southwark, the Right Reverend Dr Tom Butler, and the Dean of Southwark, the Very Reverend Colin Slee, agreed (in fairly short order) to my having sabbatical leave in the summer of 2008, and that proved to be crucial in bringing the project to fruition. During my absence a fine team – Margaret Jackson, Geoff Mason, Sue Hoad, Sue Maree, Annie Kurk, Delbert Sandiford and Jane Speck – tended the vocational vineyard; and my clergy colleagues at the Cathedral – Michael Hart, Anna Macham, Andrew Nunn, Bruce Saunders, Colin Slee and Jane Steen – serenely grafted into their own work the duties I would have had there. Jane is another two-hat-wearer, and as Director of Training in the diocese she also helped me set up the sabbatical. Once my professional Sabbath had started, Professor Richard Burridge, Dean of King's College, London, whose acclaimed work on the genre of the Gospels will be a vigorous presence in what follows, was immensely helpful in an extended conversation about the state of play in Markan studies. I thank them all.

I have failed to find a single horticultural metaphor with which to do justice to Professor Leslie Houlden. Newly ordained, I was sent to him to Read Books with, and Leslie then turned from mentor to supervisor as the Farrer project began. Since then, he has continued to be a deft waterer of seeds and pruner of shoots, gifted with the knack of sending a note – always gracious and with a friend's pointedness – at just the right time to prompt a further spurt of growth. Leslie was Farrer's successor as Chaplain and Fellow at Trinity College, Oxford, and has brought not just a profundity of knowledge but also a critical friendship to this work. I owe him a very great deal.

My thanks go also to Professor Mark Goodacre for saying Yes to the book, to Dominic Mattos and the T&T Clark/Continuum team, notably Anna Turton, and to Katia Hamza of the Word Factory for getting it into print.

For those who most closely share the writer's life there are thanks of quite another kind. I dedicate the book to James and Julia, and to my wife Caroline, the very best of encouragers.

A word about the title, in which those with a nose for Austin Farrer may scent a quotation. It is in fact a modified quotation, from *The Glass of Vision* (p. 146), where he describes the unease that the reader may feel at the abrupt ending of Mark's Gospel as 'a poetical discontent'. It is a most apt description of the motor propelling Farrer himself in his biblical enquiries and is therefore irresistible as a title, except that – no doubt because fashions of usage have changed in the sixty-odd years since he uttered and then wrote those words – the shorter form, 'poetic', seems to sit better. Any distinctions between the two are still pretty porous, but – twenty years before Farrer's words – we find in Fowler's *Dictionary of Modern English Usage* a sense that *poetical* tends to denote the form of poetry and *-ic* the instinct for it; and that the former labels while the latter admires. So *-ic* it is for Austin Farrer and the Gospel of Mark, on this the forty-first anniversary of his death.

Robert Titley
29 December 2009

INTRODUCTION

Isaac Newton was a prolific writer, and is said to have written more words of divinity than of physics, though it was the latter that established his genius. The person who has been described as 'the one genius' that the Church of England produced in the twentieth century[1] wrote and spoke widely as a philosophical theologian, a biblical scholar and a preacher. Nowadays conferences are held on his philosophical work, some of his sermons are still in print, some forty years after his death, and quotations from both of these aspects of his writing have punctuated a fairly recent novel.[2] Austin Farrer's biblical writings, however, were largely dismissed when they were written and have been largely ignored since, so that (for example) *The Oxford Handbook of Biblical Studies* can find room for Jerry Falwell but not for Farrer.[3] My aim is to ask whether, in respect of his work on the Gospel of Mark, this neglect is justified.

We shall approach from three angles, looking at Farrer on Mark as literature, as history, and as Scripture. Farrer remarks that Peter's early beliefs about Jesus were comparatively simple, but that his mature reflections were 'not simple at all' (*A Study in St Mark*, 366), and the latter is certainly true of Farrer's own thoughts. They in turn show that our apparently simple categories, 'literature', 'history' and 'Scripture', are themselves in need of refinement if they are not to confuse. At this stage they simply denote an agenda for discussion.

I shall argue that Farrer's essential hunch about Mark (and other biblical writings) is about their being literary entities, the products of creative, 'poetic' minds, and that in many respects he shows remarkable prescience when his work is viewed in the light of later developments which may be described as part of the emergence of a 'literary paradigm' in Gospel interpretation. In particular, I hope to show that a conversation with Farrer's work has something to contribute to the continuing debate about whether – and, if so, how – to take account of authorial intention in reading a text, and about what significance – if any – can be given to statements about what a text 'means'. To that end we shall make a number of extended comparisons between Farrer and more

1. See Richard Harries, *Genius*, ix. See also Basil Mitchell's 'Austin Marsden Farrer', in Farrer/Houlden, *Celebration*, 13).

2. Susan Howatch, *Absolute Truths* (London: Harper Collins, 1994, 9 and all chapter headings thereafter).

3. J.W. Rogerson and Judith M. Lieu (eds), *The Oxford Handbook of Biblical Studies* (Oxford: Oxford University Press, 2006).

recent critics: in the literary section, first Frank Kermode, then the trio of David Rhoads, Joanna Dewey and Donald Michie (where we shall also look at a critique of Farrer by his contemporary, Helen Gardner); and in the historical section, Mary Beavis, Richard Burridge, Kermode again and David Carr. In particular, I hope to show that awareness of the historicality of the act of reading a narrative may ease some present difficulties over interpretation.

I shall also argue, however, that Farrer's writings suggest a person always conscious of being a Christian scholar, a public servant of the church working on a scriptural text, and that on occasion this burden clouds his judgement; that it leads him to conclusions about the evidential value of Mark as 'history' which are bolted on to his literary observations and not organic developments from them; that it makes him insufficiently critical in considering Mark's canonical identity; and that it forces him into distinctions within the realm of inspiration brought about by the assertion of orthodoxy rather than by the deployment of argument. Nevertheless, I think we shall see enough in his wider theological convictions to show how his insights into the Bible and its texts might be rescued from obscurantism.

Farrer's is a thoroughly theological reading of Mark, aimed at deepening Christian faith, and he never lets us forget his credal presuppositions. Since there is no such thing as a 'presuppositionless' interpreter, however, we should see him in this respect as a salutary example, for while objectivity must be an interpreter's ideal, it can be a mask to disguise the 'tendency' of the critic who wears it.

We have two major texts of Farrer's to examine: his 1948 Bampton Lectures, published as *The Glass of Vision*, and his *A Study in St Mark* (1951). Other works, notably his second look at Gospel interpretation, *St Matthew and St Mark* (1954), and several lectures, articles and sermons, will also be significant. Though Farrer's first published piece was biblical,[4] it is his philosophical work of 1943, *Finite and Infinite*, which is the crucible for the Bampton Lectures. In all that follows, therefore, we should keep in mind that Farrer's biblical scholarship represents a major campaign in what is nevertheless a larger theatre of operation: the exploration of God's action in the world, and (in particular) the way in which divine and human activity are related. This means that we must at times give attention to Farrer the philosopher.

Part I of this book is an exposition of the *Glass*, which is the foundation of his work on Mark. Avowedly an essay about poetry and inspiration, it sets before us authorial creativity and the scriptural identity of Mark, but also treats of the Bible as a set of writings purporting to tell of event as well as of incorporeal image, as Farrer urges us to see the enfleshment of images of God in the historical person of Jesus as the summit of revelation.

---

4.   'A Return to New Testament Christological Categories', 1933.

This brief Part I therefore serves as an introduction to each aspect of our enquiry. In the much longer Parts II and III, *A Study in St Mark* will generally be at the centre of the stage, as we consider the categories of 'literature' and 'history' respectively. Awareness of the third category, 'Scripture', pervades Farrer's work, and it will surface frequently in our investigations. A short Part IV will therefore be sufficient to consider it in its own right.

Farrer deserves praise for openness about his aims and presuppositions as a student of Mark. I should be similarly open. I approach Austin Farrer as a Christian myself, one of whose concerns is to explore the usefulness of Mark's Gospel, critically appropriated and in all its aspects, within the life of the church. But I hope that what follows will not appear to be what Farrer himself called 'servile ecclesiasticism' (*Finite*, v) to someone who does not share my starting point.

PART I

FOUNDATIONS

THE GLASS OF VISION

[T]he sense of metaphysical philosophy, the sense of scriptural revelation, and the sense of poetry ... These three things rubbing against one another in my mind, seem to kindle one another, and so I am moved to ask how this happens.

The Glass of Vision, ix

In the Preface to *The Glass of Vision*, Austin Farrer describes his Bampton Lectures for 1948 as an exercise in examining the relation between those three things 'rubbing against one another' in his mind (*Glass*, ix). In the lectures we can find in brief compass the character of his thoughts, or the seed of those thoughts, about the questions it is our task to probe: the Gospel according to Mark as literature, history and Scripture. Farrer's field in the *Glass* is wider than that, of course. He touches on the distinction between metaphysical and scientific thought, he asks about the nature of divine disclosure and poetic inspiration in various forms, and when he turns to the Christian Bible (it is very much in this sense that he views not just the New Testament but also the Jewish Scriptures) he has as much to say about the prophecy of Jeremiah and the Revelation of John as about the Gospel of Mark. Moreover, in the case of Mark, it is Mark as Scripture that is foremost in his mind. Paying some attention to the broader scope of his thought here, then, will help us to keep a sense of direction in the more narrowly focused work which is to follow. We begin with a brief summary of the whole cycle of lectures before attempting any evaluation, in order not to interrupt the flow of his case; whenever I am doing anything other than offering a précis of Farrer's own words I shall indicate this clearly. An evaluation of his argument will follow, which will leave us with a set of questions to take up subsequently.

Chapter 1

The Lectures

In these eight lectures Farrer is concerned with the disclosure of divine truth. Human perception of God, for Farrer, can be derived from God's natural revelation, in those aspects of the world which by their nature speak of God as we perceive them, and from supernatural revelation, by which God effects special disclosure. This latter God does through the human understanding, not overwhelming it but supernaturally extending (or inspiring) it to receive revealed images, rather as the poetic mind fixes upon a rich symbol to evoke multiple echoes in the reader's mind. Natural revelation acts both as a preparation for the other sort, and as a check upon what purports to be supernatural revelation. The heart of God's supernatural revelation is Jesus Christ: he embodies the controlling images and offers the prime interpretation of them (or rather, he remints them, for images like 'David' or 'Lamb' are taken up from existing Jewish faith and derived from Jewish Scripture). In Jesus divine word and deed speak to one another. It is the purpose of the inspiration of the apostolic minds, in and through which the New Testament issues, both to bear witness to Jesus' deed and word, and to develop the revelation of images which he inaugurates.

The common ground between a poet and a prophet like Jeremiah (or an evangelist like Mark) lies in the presence of constraint upon their activity. The poet is constrained only by the broadest notions of the task and manner of poetry, while prophecy concerns being a mouthpiece of God, yet the prophet's receiving of images 'which live as it were by their own life and impose themselves with authority' resembles poetic inspiration, the poet's sense of how the form and content of a poem 'ought' to develop (*Glass*, 113, 121). Indeed, prophecy uses poetry – 'an incantation of images' – as a 'method of divination' (*Glass*, 128f). Biblical writing is poetic, therefore, insofar as the writers share with poets the 'technique of inspiration', a 'felt inevitability' about their work (*Glass*, 129).

To illustrate the 'quasi-poetical' movement of images which he sees in the New Testament (*Glass*, 132), Farrer offers a reading of the closing verses of Mark's Gospel and the well-pondered question whether the Gospel ends, or merely ceases, at the last authentic verse, 16.8: 'I wish to show that the sort of criticism of most use for getting to the bottom of the New Testament is often more like the criticism we apply to poetry than we might incline to expect' (*Glass*, 136).

He advises against the easy but unfalsifiable solution to the puzzle of the final ἐφοβοῦντο γάρ (ephobounto gar) which is offered by positing some accident or, say, the sudden arrest of the author, pen poised. How then are we to proceed if we ask whether, on the evidence we have, Mark could have decided to end his Gospel there? '[W]hat do you mean by "could"? Some sort of a psychological difficulty, no doubt, is intended. Could he have felt that this was the proper place to stop?' (*Glass*, 137). That 'could' stems not from doubts about the logical possibility of such an ending. No, if we are uneasy with the ending, it is an aesthetic unease, a sense that the ending lacks 'poetic inevitability ... St Mark has built up in our mind strong poetic expectations: we feel them to be disappointed by his conclusion, and we cannot believe that such a writer could have written so ill' (*Glass*, 138).

This inevitability Farrer tries to show on thematic grounds: the flight of the frightened women is a fitting closure to the theme of human perversity in the face of the divine, which begins with a woman anointing Jesus – as she thinks, for glory – in preparation for burial; continues with the disciples' promising to die for Jesus, and then fleeing while he remains to die for them; with the priests' condemning him, to preserve – but in fact to overthrow – their priesthood; with Pilate's crucifying Jesus as a pretender to a rule that is but a shadow of the rule that is actually his; and with Joseph's offering of a tomb for the one death cannot hold. Finally, the women come 'to embalm the already risen God ... The mere rustling of the hem of his risen glory, the voice of the boy in the white robe, turns them to headlong flight: "and they said not a word to anyone, for they were afraid". Do we stop there or do we go on? I think we stop' (*Glass*, 140).

Farrer then extends his case on grounds of wording, drawing parallels between the closing passage and the sequence from the anointing at Bethany to the arrest. Both mention a *woman* (or *women*) with *ointment*, and the prophecy of Jesus going ahead into *Galilee*. The giving of the sacramental body is echoed in the preoccupation with the physical body, and both feature a *linen cloth* ('the youth in the garden is stripped of one, the sacred body is wrapped in one') and 'a lad ... clad in' some named garment. Both episodes speak of misunderstanding and perversity, and the firm ending of the first in the flight of the disciples 'prepares us to find a firm ending' to the second, in the flight of the women (*Glass*, 141f). This short cycle of perversity gathers up a longer cycle, containing such misunderstandings as when Jesus enjoins silence after a healing and everyone broadcasts it (*Glass*, 142f). Finally Farrer resolves the 'fine linen' motif (the boy's shirt in Gethsemane, and Joseph of Arimathea's winding-sheet) typologically. The disciples are asleep on duty and so deserve stripping, the punishment of dozing Temple-guards, while other moments echo the Joseph narratives in Genesis: the fleeing, shirtless youth recalls Joseph fleeing Potiphar's wife; Joseph of Arimathea begs to bury Jesus as his namesake asks to bury his father; and the fear of the women reflects the fear of Joseph's brothers at his self-revelation (*Glass*, 143–145).

The main objective, says Farrer, is the demonstration not that he has the right answer to the question of the ending of Mark but that his is the *sort* of approach to that question, the approach of literary criticism, which should be made, for it examines the root of our unease, which is 'a poetical discontent' (*Glass*, 146). In this excursus Farrer claims to have detected the play of secondary images (the Joseph motifs, for instance) under the pressure of the great images in what he now describes as 'St Mark's poem' (*Glass*, 146). 'Poetry and divine inspiration have this in common, that both are projected in images which cannot be decoded but must be allowed to signify what they signify of the reality beyond them.' (*Glass*, 148)

Chapter 2

EVALUATION

Our immediate aim here is to examine Farrer's Bampton Lectures as they bear upon the Gospel according to Mark as literature and as history. We must first note that, despite his sensitive literary antennae, this is not quite Farrer's point of entry. Revelation is his theme, both in Mark and in the rest of the Bible, so much of what he offers us is under the heading of 'Scripture'.

To read the *Glass* is to overhear a vigorous conversation between two convictions. The Farrer we meet first is neither obscurantist nor dogmatist, but is keen to embrace rational human thought as the gift of God. He thus warms in a Thomist manner to making the case for continuity between human nature and divine grace, and for seeing all talk about God as analogical.[1] He is the friend of natural (or 'rational') theology, and happy to acknowledge that certain phenomena simply impress themselves on the human mind as images of God. In seeing God's self-disclosure as happening through image rather than concept, however, and in allowing that the disclosure may occur to any person who bothers to look, Farrer is investing in a potentially under-regulated business. When he likens prophecy to poetry, it is the fertility of poetic images that he stresses, and he is firm in saying that metaphors for God cannot be directly checked against their object (*Glass*, 76, 120). How then can all this coexist with – or rather be contained within – the rather more controlled environment of Christian orthodoxy?

---

1.   The lines of *Finite and Infinite* are visible beneath the surface of Farrer's argument here. Though in his earlier book he refers to Aquinas and Thomism only occasionally (*Finite*, vi, 42, 207, 241, 267, 270, 274, 279), the presence of Aquinas is pervasive. Farrer's observation in the Preface is significant:

> The Thomists possess the true principles for the solution of the problems of rational theology and above all the problem of analogical argument ... [so despite their failings] ... there is nothing for it but to re-state the doctrine of analogy in a credible form, and this is our endeavour here. (*Finite*, vi)

To meet this objection he makes a distinction, which we shall meet repeatedly and in different guises as we examine his later work. It is the key to his understanding of the books of the New Testament (certainly of Mark) and of the way they should be read. We see it in his fifth lecture, as he distinguishes between natural and supernatural images.[2] The former are worldly things which speak of God by being congruous with, or participating in some faint way in, that attribute of God which they evoke; they are part of a 'pattern of being we simply meet', they are 'just there' (*Glass*, 94). The latter are parabolic images, which we could never infer or guess at if they had not been revealed. Though he does not make this wholly clear, Farrer surely cannot regard all parabolic images as supernatural, as when a poet deploys an image which has no part in what the poet seeks to depict, but is just an adventitious and helpful analogy: an instance might be Donne's conceit 'the spider love', or the sermon in which Farrer himself says 'we are of the race of moles', craving the presence of human company and of God as often as the mole needs worms (*Said*, 113). In the *Glass* he is undoubtedly speaking of much more privileged disclosure, as in the case of the revelation of God as Trinity. Nothing spontaneously speaks to us, he says, of the Trinity, though we may see shadows of it everywhere once God has disclosed the reality to us; symbols of the Trinity are not 'just there' in the way that, say, the human moral sense is 'there' and so speaks to us of divine justice (*Glass*, 94). This distinction introduces a much greater element of control just where most is at stake, for it is what he calls the 'principal' or controlling images (*Glass*, 111) that he classes as parabolic and revealed. But how far does this distinction stand up?

For one thing (to take Farrer's own example) talk of God as Trinity does (the Third Person apart) draw on the *natural* image of the family, or of its male members anyway. For another, this is a 'revealed' image which does not drop from the sky, for we can trace the lines of its historical development. Is it not after all shaped in response to – *inter alia* – the presence of Jesus, the eyewitness memories, the stories about him, a 'pattern of being we simply meet' which *is* 'just there'? Since Farrer argues that the heart of the *revealed* images of Christianity lies in Jesus' application of archetypal, *natural* images to himself (*Glass*, 109 cf 102f, 105), it is no wonder that the border between them becomes difficult to defend. There are signs here of pre-critical special pleading.

Farrer is happy to see God active in the impression that natural images make upon the human mind, shaped by God to receive them, and happy also to see what he calls supernatural revelation as occurring by the enhancement and not by the abolition of human capacities. Thus far his

---

2.   Note again the Thomist echoes. Cf the Preface to *Finite and Infinite*, where Farrer invokes Aquinas' distinction: 'We have, then, to be ready to draw the ancient line between rational and revealed theology' (*Finite*, v).

scheme is able to account quite elegantly even for something so remarkable
as embryonic trinitarian imagery in the New Testament, without invoking
the category of 'revealed' image as he describes it. If we play Farrer's
hand for him, we can show writers in collaboration with God (as all
writers are, in some sense or to some extent) meditating upon the unique
icon of Jesus, who provides both the 'primary action' and the 'primary
interpretation' (*Glass*, 41). If, working with Farrer's incarnational view
of Jesus, we call that icon 'supernatural' and 'revealed', then what the
apostles come up with will be 'supernatural', because of the quality of
that which is 'just there' before them. God's activity can remain of a piece
with the activity implied for inspiration in its wider sense (though Farrer
never states what his scheme heavily hints at, that God is in some sense
inspiring Milton as well as Mark), while the genuine innovation in this
case, the reminting of images, can be adequately explained by the unique
conditions produced by Farrer's Jesus. He, after all, *incarnates* the images
of God.[3]

Farrer could leave it at that, with the apostles working (much, as he
says, in the way that any Rabbinic Jews might upon the Torah (*Glass*,
109)) to draw out the implications of Jesus. Indeed, he directly confronts
the possibility of the 'sheer occurrence' of Jesus being enough to effect
revelation, but he rejects it: 'Christ's existence' is useless to us 'unless we
are enabled to apprehend the fathomless mystery which his manhood is'
(*Glass*, 40). The difficulty here is not with Farrer's insistence that embodied
revelation in Christ is worthless unless it is apprehended – it must be so,
otherwise revelation becomes an uncommunicated communication – nor
is it with the agency of God, once we consent to proceed within a theistic
framework. It is rather with the *quality* of apprehension required, which
he has already described as 'supernatural thinking of a privileged order'
as Christ's interpreters are 'supernaturalized by the Spirit of Pentecost'
(*Glass*, 35, 41). To the supernatural revelation of certain images,
embodied in Jesus, we must now add a further moment of revelation,
'the Spirit of Christ moving the minds of the Apostles' (*Glass*, 109), to
tell us what it all means. That 'privileged' overplus looks like a move
closer to a doctrine of inspiration-by-conferment and away from the
enhancement-doctrine he has already espoused, as well as resembling the
very duplication he rebuts in considering a 'divine dictation' account of
scriptural inspiration (*Glass*, 37). Farrer's objection there is that Jesus'
life and work is made otiose if it is to be followed by verbally inerrant
documentary revelation; but, on this reckoning, is the embodiment of

3.   As the physicist John Polkinghorne says of the natural sciences: 'Changing
circumstances can lead to totally unexpected effects' (*One*, 75). This more economical
scheme also accords with Farrer's view of cosmology: 'God not only makes the world, he
makes it make itself' (*Saving*, 51). See also Farrer's *Science*, esp. 39–69. For an approach
similar to that which I describe, see Ruth Page, *The Incarnation of Freedom and Love*
(London: SCM Press, 1991, 46f).

the images of God in Jesus strictly necessary, if it is to be followed by a second moment of divine disclosure in the minds of the apostles which is qualitatively different from that enjoyed by a poet or any other sort of writer? Though Farrer loyally declares his convictions about the necessity of a core of Christian origins embodied in the historical life of Jesus (e.g. *Glass*, 41), what necessary thing does incarnation effect? Why (to use Louis Mink's distinction) do we need a 'story lived' by Jesus when we are to have a 'story told' under the conditions Farrer sets?[4] We shall return in Part III to the place in Farrer's work on Mark of the contingent events surrounding Jesus, and in Part II we shall consider the effects of such scriptural privilege on Farrer's reading of Mark. Meanwhile, we must note something else, without which Farrer's scheme is incomplete.

Farrer wishes us to agree that believing minds such as those of the New Testament writers cannot look at the sheer occurrence of Jesus and apprehend the mystery by the diligent use of natural faculties, unless they are inspired in an utterly special manner. But will their Christian successors recognise the 'sheer occurrence' of such inspired interpretation among the pile of early documents which will be candidates for inclusion in the New Testament canon? Do we not now need a *third* phase of inspiration to ensure the right reception of this inspired interpretation, to get it safely into Holy Scripture? Nowhere in the *Glass* does Farrer address the question of how these writings *become* Scripture, apart from the bald remark that '[i]f the biblical books had not been taken to express the apostolic mind, they would not have been canonized' (*Glass*, 53). Indeed, the canon as a providential given is an *a priori* of his whole enquiry.[5]

In his fundamental case for the divine enhancement of human capacities, Farrer lays before us a pattern of double agency which is rich, deep and subtle,[6] and when he likens the Bible to poetry he suggests a God of consistency and of generous sympathies, influencing poet and prophet alike. But even as he acknowledges the similarities, he will not

4.   Louis O. Mink, 'History and Fiction as Modes of Comprehension', *New Literary History*, 1, 1970, 57f. We find the same criticism of Farrer in John Barton's 1988 Bampton Lectures:

> The supernatural injection of revealed knowledge which is attributed to Scripture can, if we are not careful, make everything apart from itself unnecessary in the economy of salvation. As long as we have the Bible (it seems) Jesus need not really have existed, for it is the text that reveals the truth about God, not Jesus himself as he actually lived and died and rose again. Farrer, of course, was far from believing that ... [but showed] what now seems perhaps an excessive concentration on revelation as the major category for understanding the Bible. *People*, 37f

5.   See Part IV.

6.   But see J.N. Morris, 'Religious Experience in the Philosophical Theology of Austin Farrer', *Journal of Theological Studies*, NS, Vol. 45, Part 2 (October 1994), 569–92. Morris argues that Farrer's scheme is essentially subjectivist.

say that biblical material is distinctive simply because of the direction of the writers' attention to a unique subject. Something makes him 'fence off'[7] the expression of central Christian imagery from the expressive work of the poet.

It is a fence we shall meet many times, and it protects Farrer's own devotion to the Bible as sacred and miraculous (*Glass*, 36). Such is the place it occupies for him in Christian knowledge of God that it seems to require of him the belief that it contains some unique element quite absent from any other writing. It is as though someone were so entranced by the beauty of a diamond that they could not believe it had the same chemical constituents as coal. Farrer's canonical fence certainly cuts across the enticing tract of country he opens up in his presentation of biblical writings as thoroughly *literary* documents. His sketch of the poetic mind at work in the last verses of Mark, his appreciation of the polyphonic character of poetic writing, and his simultaneous insistence upon fidelity to what the writer wants to say (e.g. *Glass*, 46, 124) place him firmly in the middle of the ground disputed in current debates in biblical studies over the intention of the author, the sovereignty of the text, and the extent to which texts should be read as 'wholes'. Part II will consider further his contribution to these debates. His worked example of the end of Mark's Gospel exposes most of the main features, and we shall look at it again when Farrer returns to those verses in *A Study in St Mark*.

In a series of lectures springing from a mind occupied with philosophy, scriptural revelation and poetry, we should expect there to be some attention to the historical aspect of Christian origins, but that it should not be dominant. Such proves to be the case.[8] In Lecture III he pins his allegiance on historical event as the heart of Christian faith, but reminds us that event is dumb without interpretation. But later he raises the question whether event is dumb even *with* interpretation, when he briefly alludes to the inability of 'ancient books' to bring us into contact with any minds other than the mind of the author (*Glass*, 55).

---

7.   The phrase is Farrer's own (*Glass*, 52).

8.   Even so, we might have expected more attention in these lectures to questions of history, at least a nod towards some of the then current objections to easy assumptions about 'getting back to Jesus', and about the exportability of biblical images from one cultural setting to another. As a reader of German, Farrer might be expected to have known a book like Troeltsch's *Die Absolutheit des Christentums* (1929), which addresses both matters. There is not much evidence in the *Glass* of an interest in the Quest of the Historical Jesus and its hazards. A letter to his father from as early as 1931 might shed light: in it he praises Brunner's *The Mediator* for offering a robust transcendentalism 'without denying any of what the History of Religion people [Troeltsch included?] can genuinely allege' (*Hawk*, 79). This suggests no deep sense – at *that* stage at least – of the problem of the accessibility of the past. This is in contrast to his keen sense in these lectures of *philosophical* objections to his thesis.

Here too he is touching on what will in time become a well-contested dispute, for his observation leads to the general question of whether a narrative (like Mark) can ever be genuine historiography, and not just a self-referring text. This is really an overspill of the literary-critical debate about authors, for if a text cannot even be a window into the writer's intentions in presenting events, it certainly cannot be a window upon the events themselves. While the question may be posed for any so-called 'historical' narrative, it gains greater keenness when put to the text of Mark's Gospel, if it indeed displays the literary artifice which Farrer imputes to it.

Part of that artifice lies in the realm of typology, which Farrer is confident of seeing at work in the mind of the author of Mark (and of the Apocalypse). Though we take Farrer's point about access to minds beyond the author's, and decline to pre-empt the debates mentioned above, we may at least consider the possibility that if we can know anything of a writer's intention it is that the writer (usually) expects what is written to be intelligible to those who read or hear it. The presence of typology therefore implies a typological competence in the people for whom the author writes (though Farrer has little to say in these lectures about audiences), and may point, if we can first establish the required cultural continuity, to a typological mentality among the people *about* whom the author writes. Farrer's insights, if they carry conviction, might then serve to illuminate not only primitive Christian writings but also the actions of those participating in the historical events which give rise to the writings. Typology will return when we look at the *Study*, and we shall explore its implications for Christian origins in Part III.

Finally, we must consider the place of Farrer's work in the whole arena of biblical studies, and our way in is provided by the crucial distinction within the *Glass*, which he describes by his favourite pair of words, 'natural' and 'supernatural'. The distinction belongs firmly within a theistic framework, and for some readers of his lectures that will lie on the other side of a wide chasm which separates the theistic from the 'secular' frame of reference that is taken for granted in many aspects of modern biblical studies. Just as they might question, say, the differentiation of general and special providence by asking whether there was such a thing as providence at all, so they might have similar reservations about this talk in the *Glass* of God's natural and supernatural activity. Farrer is aware of this, concedes that theistic belief may turn out to be just a hardy superstition, but asks his readers to assume the hypothesis that God exists in some realist sense (*Glass*, 80f). He has every right to do this, especially in a series of lecture-*sermons* such as the Bamptons, and we see here early evidence of Farrer's constant willingness to be candid about his fundamental presuppositions (or most of them, anyway). What should we infer, however, about Farrer's perception of the audience to which his work is addressed? What status does he give to his work – and what status can it be given – in a wider, pluralist field of discourse? What *respect*, to put it bluntly, does he accord the guild of biblical scholars who might be expected to form an important part of his readership? Are Farrer's biblical writings, in the end, no more than exercises in 'servile ecclesiasticism' (*Finite*, v)? This question will resurface repeatedly in the following pages.

Chapter 3

SUMMARY OF THE MAIN QUESTIONS RAISED BY
THE GLASS OF VISION
FOR FARRER'S TREATMENT OF THE GOSPEL
ACCORDING TO MARK

As literature:

- How much can be maintained of Farrer's account of poetic creativity, in the light of the subsequent critique of authorial intention?

- If authorial intention *is* still accessible, how much need it be the constraint upon interpretation that Farrer holds it to be?

- How far does Mark's Gospel admit of the literary-critical analysis advanced by Farrer? In particular, how far can it be regarded as a literary whole, or as a 'poem'? And how far can his typological reading be pressed?

- What is the effect on Farrer's reading of Mark of his conviction that it is an instance of privileged inspiration?

As history:

- Farrer locates two historical moments in his account of revelation: the embodiment of images in Jesus, and the apostolic witness (including the composition of Mark). How necessary is the former to his scheme and what is achieved by this 'grounding' of the images in Jesus?

- How well-founded are Farrer's assumptions about the accessibility of the historical Jesus, especially given his intensely literary idea of Mark?

- What are the implications of Farrer's claim that events alone do not 'mean' anything? And of his observations about the opacity of texts?

- Do his thoughts about typology have any bearing on the study of Christian origins?

As Scripture:

- What are the implications for the formation of the canon of Farrer's estimation of canonical texts?

In Parts II and III we shall not treat these questions systematically, but discussion of them will emerge from interaction with authors who have themselves discussed Farrer's work or, more often, dealt with similar issues as they have come to be perceived in the years since Farrer wrote.

PART II

MARK AS LITERATURE

[A] book is the expression of a living mind like our own, and we can never be satisfied until we have understood from within the movement of thought which produced it.

A Study in St Mark, 35

Introduction

In Part II we seek to describe and evaluate Austin Farrer's approach to the Gospel of Mark chiefly through the literary analysis he advances in *A Study in St Mark*. That book is the second of the two major texts of Farrer's on Mark that we are considering closely (though other work of his will also come into view), and it will furnish the bulk of the material for this part of our enquiry and for the next two as well, when we look at Mark as history and as Scripture. Since Farrer himself describes the *Study* as 'an essay in literary analysis', it is fitting that we should meet the book first in these, our 'literary' chapters (*Study*, vii).

We shall begin by filling in the story of Farrer's work between the writing of our other chief text, *The Glass of Vision*, and this one. We shall then examine Farrer's literary approach in the *Study*. Our treatment will be illustrative rather than exhaustive, since the aim is to examine his method, not to offer a full-dress alternative reading of Mark. We shall, however, make a close reading of his first three chapters, since they offer us the essence of his interpretative creed and practice. Moreover, since a number of Farrer's critics (whom we shall meet later on) have generally neglected detailed appraisal of his work in favour of generalised dismissal, it will be important for our critique to proceed from a grasp of the particularities as well as of the sweep of his work. Since the *Study* is a large piece of writing, we shall evaluate his arguments as we go, examining the degree of success Farrer's analysis attains within its own terms, and the character of Mark as Farrer sees it. We shall then turn to the significance of Farrer's picture of Mark for wider concerns, listening for resonances and contrasts between Farrer's writings and those of several exponents of the 'literary paradigm' in Gospel studies. This will lead us to some general conclusions both about the value and flaws of Farrer on Mark and about the present state of literary strategies for reading the Gospels. A reader of this text might wonder what I mean by 'Mark': the text of the Gospel, or the person who wrote it? Farrer himself, on the strength of the prefatory quotation above, seems keen to merge the two. I shall generally use the name Mark to denote the text of the Gospel; on occasions when I use it to refer to the author, I shall make this clear.

From Glass *to* Study

Farrer ends *The Glass of Vision* with a picture of divine inspiration uniting the process of poetic image-making and the subject of metaphysics' analogical discourse (that is, God), and the biblical writers as inspired to project these images in what they write. His first sustained application of this proposal was to come in a book published the following year.

A Rebirth of Images: The Making of St John's Apocalypse (1949) takes up hints from the *Glass* about the book of Revelation and develops them into a comprehensive study of its composition. Farrer sees Revelation as the creation of a powerful Christian mind, working in many ways as a poetic mind works; the author's mind is also an inspired mind, which makes Revelation also the creation of God. We can see that the kaleidoscopic book of Revelation is the most congenial of the books of the New Testament to Farrer's programme: it purports to be the work of a single person and to be the fruit of inspiration, and the briefest examination reveals its complex, riddling nature, its debt to images in the Old Testament and its innovative treatment of them. Here if anywhere in the New Testament is a case of some sort of literary artifice at work.

More of a challenge would be an attempt to apply his method to one of the Gospels, and here there stood in Farrer's way at least three obstacles which the book of Revelation did not present. First, the texts of two of the Gospels, Matthew and Mark, make no reference to their author (cf Lk. 1.1–4, Jn 21.24). Secondly, academic study of the Gospels in the 1940s and 1950s was deeply imbued with the spirit of *form criticism*, which saw all the Gospel texts, or at least the Synoptics, as agglomerations of pre-existent gobbets of tradition, partly preserved, partly moulded by early Christian communities; there was little space here for the living mind of an author, space only for what Farrer would depict as a 'colourless compiler' (*Study*, 7). Thirdly, popular reading of the Gospels had long seen them as in some way transparent upon the events of history; even form criticism held out some promise of access to reliable historical traditions behind the texts, and the historical origins of Christianity were for the great majority of believers (Farrer included) an indispensable testimony to Christian truth. Would not the existence of a genuine author, a Gospel-*maker* (however guided by God's inspiration), render the history much more inaccessible? These challenges Farrer took up in *A Study in St Mark*.

Chapter 4

A STUDY IN ST MARK

I ... am committed to the claim that I have found in St Mark's Gospel a pattern of
which St Mark was in some measure conscious, and which in any case shaped his
story as he wrote it. I take so much to be a true discovery and not a speculation.

A Study in St Mark, v

In this chapter we examine closely the Preface and introductory Chapter I
of the *Study*, which set the tone for all that follows. This will help us keep
an impression of Farrer's whole conception when we move on to look at
its parts. We then consider Farrer's next two chapters, which will give us
the essential workings of his scheme.

A. Preface and Introduction *(A Study in St Mark, v–29)*

In the Preface to *A Study in St Mark*, Farrer's key to the composition of
Mark is what he believes to be a dominant rhythm in Mark's thought,
expressed in cycles of material centred on healing miracles, which extend
and progressively clarify the revelation of Jesus, culminating in his
passion and resurrection. The *Study* is thus 'an essay in literary analysis,
not in historical learning ... Its concern is with the sentences St Mark
writes and the mental processes they express' (*Study*, vi).

Farrer encourages us to divide his book into several sections. After
the introductory first Chapter, Chapters II–VI set out his thesis, with VII
as an appendix concerning the ending of the Gospel. Chapters VIII–X
discuss the implications of the thesis for the historical value of Mark, XI
and XII apply the thesis to the question of Messianic secrecy, XIII–XV
extend the thesis by enquiry into three particular topics (the miraculous
feedings, the apostles and tribal symbolism), and XVI considers the
date of writing. Following Farrer's advice we shall begin by examining
those chapters in which the essential thesis is set out (I–VII). Aspects of

Chapters XIII–XV will come into our comparison of Farrer's work with that of other and later exponents. Chapters VIII–X await our discussion of Farrer's view of the Gospel as history.

As we turn to Farrer's first chapter, we quickly see the close cohabitation in his thought of the literary and the inspired aspects of the Gospel, but also his insistence upon its evidential value as history. So evident are these that, at the risk of poaching from later discussions, we shall do well to pause over them here; otherwise we shall have a distorted view of the character of the *Study* itself, as Farrer seems keenly sensitive in these early pages to the objections a traditional believer might have to his project. Signs of the difficulties implicit in Farrer's position begin to appear quickly as well, so it will also be helpful to make some evaluation before moving on to a brief sketch of his overall thesis. We shall then examine significant aspects of it in detail.

Farrer begins by endorsing the historical value of Mark. Mark's priority is important, he says, for the history of Christian origins, and 'bare history is of inestimable importance'; the four Gospels differ, and so to say that all are equally historical, 'if by history we are meaning a correct account of the whole pattern and order of Christ's public life', is to say that none is very historical (*Study*, 1f). Farrer urges the importance of the interests of the enquirer in the choice of questions put to the text: Farrer himself is interested in 'four little first-century narratives' because he is a Christian, and his faith leads to the seeking of some 'treasure of historical truth' in Mark (*Study*, 2). Those who have sought to see the author as a historian, offering a connected account of the sequence of events in Christ's life, have fared badly, however; little better is the condition of those who have seen Mark as a quarry for raw historical data, '*disjecta membra* of simple unadulterated tradition', for the *membra* themselves have a history (which the form critics try to reconstruct) and – as he will proceed to show – the text reveals the signs of considerable 'constructive activity' on the part of the author (*Study*, 5). In support of this claim Farrer invokes the work of R.H. Lightfoot, in his *History and Interpretation in the Gospels* (1935) and *Locality and Doctrine in the Gospels* (1938), and offers a prescient description of what will come to be known as redaction criticism: 'in making the traditional anecdotes illustrate theological topics under which he [Mark] has grouped them, he has had to modify their traditional wording a good deal, so as to make their connexion with those topics more evident' (*Study*, 5f).

Like Lightfoot, Farrer is seeking another ordering principle behind Mark's sentences and paragraphs than that of historical linkage; whatever peril it appears to bring to the historical value of the Gospel, the solid gain of Lightfoot's approach is that it restores to the reader of Mark the sense of encountering 'a living Christian mind'; this is for Farrer a more credible position than that of groping after the 'colourless compiler' who peeps out between the interstices of the form critics' *pericopae*

(*Study*, 7). Once we allow the possibility of a theological interpretation of the text, we cannot, in Farrer's view, pursue the 'quarrying' method of historical enquiry, in which we 'shoulder St Mark out of the way and lay our hands on his materials'; instead we must assume a 'docile state of mind', content 'to examine the pattern that is there, instead of looking for a preconceived type of pattern which is not there', willing to pay attention to what Mark himself wishes to tell us; we may even find that the evangelist's 'theological' or 'symbolical' telling of the story, while not conforming to our own ideas of historical enquiry, may yet yield 'a genuine history which is communicated to us through the symbolism and not in defiance of it' (*Study*, 7). And pattern there is, for Farrer: the text of Mark is before all else a unity, 'a genuine, and profoundly consistent, complex act of thought ... if we sift this complex unity to the bottom, and master it as fully as we can, we may find that it speaks history to us' (*Study*, 7f).

How then does Mark's 'living Christian mind' work? It is subject to 'double control': '[h]e was controlled by the traditional facts about Jesus Christ and ... by the interpreter Spirit who possessed his mind' (*Study*, 7). Mark is a Christian writer, and so would not expect the latter control to derogate from the former. Farrer, as a Christian himself, has no such fear either, and nor should his readers: 'Now we are Christians too ... As scholars we endeavour to understand and to distinguish the effects of the two controls in the evangelist's work; and as historians we shall refer the working of the Spirit to the story of the Church, but the facts about Christ to the story of our redemption' (*Study*, 8). Farrer assumes Markan priority and so, since we have none of Mark's sources, 'it is only by the right analysis of St Mark's narrative that we are to arrive at the simple facts' (*Study*, 9). The right analysis of the narrative entails for Farrer the risky venture of trying 'to become, as far as that is possible, St Mark in the act of Gospel-writing, through an effort of carefully guided imagination' (*Study*, 9). Once again he feels bound to reassure that this will not impugn the value of Mark as history: the enquiry will not deny it any more than would attention to the design of an eagle's wing tend to deny the importance of the atmosphere in keeping the bird airborne (*Study*, 10).

After disposing of what is in his view the erroneous testimony of Papias to the writing of Mark (we shall look at this passage (*Study*, 10–21) in Part III), Farrer turns to repulse a putative counter-attack upon his earlier remarks. Farrer says, disarmingly, that he has no quarrel with form criticism in its attempts to reconstruct oral traditions about Jesus behind the Gospels. The form critics in turn, however, must not be allowed to object to his project, because it is not demonstrably clear that the text of Mark is (as they argue) a compilation of pre-existent paragraphs, while it *is* demonstrably clear that the text is a connected whole; the form critic should cede first place to the 'interpreter' of the Gospel, and the interpreter should not assume *a priori* that article of faith from the form-critical creed which says that Mark is a concatenation of largely self-sufficient paragraphs, for this assumption could seriously distort the view of the whole. Farrer believes that there is less than meets the eye to the claim that the different paragraphs of the Gospel have (as they do indeed appear to have) an autonomous, anecdotal nature; this need only mean that the author chose to write in an anecdotal style, as well he might if looking to Old Testament prophecy (or, if Revelation is typical, to Christian apocalyptic) as any sort of model. No, '[e]very sentence of a book is formulated by the mind which writes the whole' (*Study*, 22).

Evaluation

Our present concern is with Farrer's view of Mark as a literary entity, but we have noted how, throughout an Introduction to what will indeed be a literary enquiry, he repeatedly looks over his shoulder to an imagined believer who keeps objecting that the historical foundation of faith will crumble under Farrer's analysis. So far, however, he betrays no sign of seeing the need to hold up what he will say to the scrutiny of the unbelieving enquirer, or even to that of the believer seeking some objective estimation of Christian origins and literature. We find ourselves immediately in the world of 'Inspiration', 'Spirit', and of Farrer's own Christian belief, for he writes as though it really has not occurred to him to ask how such ideas can possibly have any currency in open scholarly discourse. Later I shall argue more fully that what we see here are the beginnings of a disabling confusion in Farrer's work, the shadow side of the unity of Christian and scholar which many found so compelling in his person. This credal bias we shall see to be most damaging in *A Study in St Mark* while Farrer is seeking to defend Markan historicity, but we shall also see it obtruding into his literary analysis, and swerving his judgement at more than one point.

It is not as if Farrer is commending a kind of Barthian fideism,[1] which would doom any attempt to place even the tiptoe of his believing discourse on the ground of the unbelieving world, for he has (as we have seen in *The Glass of Vision*) a cherished place for the work of human reason. This makes his blind-spot here puzzling, not to say ironic, since he displays it while gently but deftly disparaging the ideological bias he sees in the form-critics' historical enquiry into the Gospels, and in his urging us to come to the documents with innocence, content to be shown what is there. A secular literary critic would find much bias in Farrer's own assertions, such as when he says of Mark that 'the control of the Spirit is visible and evident' (*Study*, 9). A few 'observations' like this

---

1. For Farrer on Barth see p. 174, note 16, below.

might lead such a person to place all that Farrer writes in illuminated quotation marks.

Is further conversation impossible, then, between Farrer and his colleagues 'over the border'? When we come to consider the continuities between Farrer and later exponents of literary enquiry into the Gospels, I shall argue that the picture need not be so bleak. What if Farrer's terminology were broadly convertible (losing a little in the exchange, as always happens in such transactions) into currency which was legal tender outside his own credal territories? Can we, for instance, read for 'the control of the Spirit' something like 'narrative design'? If we can, Farrer's work then becomes (in more modern terms) a rather elaborate form of composition criticism,[2] and there could follow some fruitful exchanges. All this, however, awaits an examination of how Farrer seeks to achieve the objectives he sets himself in Chapter I of the *Study*, and whether he succeeds.

B. *The Overall Thesis of* A Study in St Mark

Farrer is convinced that the seemingly artless succession of paragraphs which make up the Gospel according to Mark is anything but that. At the start of Chapter II he twists a favourite metaphor of form criticism to say that the beads on the string that make up the Gospel are not only carefully arranged in an order, but that 'perhaps each bead is carved by the jeweller for the place it is to occupy in the row' (*Study*, 30). For him, shape is given to the composition of Mark – and he denies that he has found '*the* shape' (*Study*, 30) – by the healing miracles. These he sees as divided into four 'blocks', three of which have a further healing miracle 'annexed' to them. Each block and each annexe is the heart of a 'cycle' of material. An annexe belongs with its block, and the respective block-cycle and annexe-cycle together make up a 'double cycle'. There are ten cycles – and so five double cycles – in all. Each cycle and double cycle evolves out of its recent predecessors and especially out of its immediate predecessor. The Gospel thus treats of a limited number of themes of Jesus' ministry and revelation, whose principle is that of healing; successive cycles work over these themes again and again, and at each stage there is some

---

2.   Stephen Moore's definition in his glossary in *Literary Criticism and the Gospels: the Theoretical Challenge*: 'As used in recent gospel studies ... it denotes a holistic variation of redaction criticism in which the gospel itself ... viewed rigorously and persistently in its entirety, becomes the primary context for interpreting any part of it.' (*Challenge*, 179). It is a useful term for denoting an approach that is distinct within redaction criticism, not only as described above, but also in its greater emphasis upon authorial creativity and its lack of interest in abstracting some conceptual 'theology' from the narrative. Its use seems to have faded, however. For instance, the glossary in the more recent *Mark & Method* does not mention it, despite Moore's editorial involvement (Anderson and Moore (eds), *Method*).

mutation and some advance. The total effect is a spiral of clarity and intensity, culminating in the resurrection of Jesus, the greatest healing of all. The cyclical form has theological force: 'Christ's action, according to our evangelist, constantly expresses the essentials of the Gospel, and the essentials of the Gospel are always the same' (*Study*, 34). Farrer also sees a large-scale cyclical pattern: 1.14–6.56 is the 'little Gospel', which prefigures the end and is fulfilled in 9.2–16.8 (*Study*, 146f, 152–55). Finally, he discerns in the terminal sections of the last four cycles, what he calls 'paracycles', which themselves tend to behave like complete cycles (*Study*, 175–77).

It will be helpful to set out here Farrer's analysis of the verses of the Gospel (apart from the paracycles).

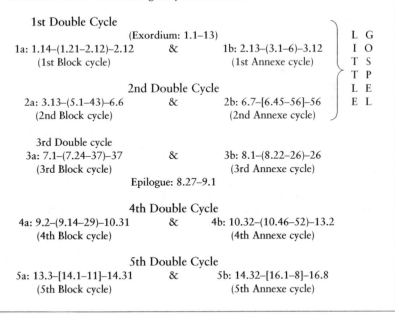

References '1a' and so on (which are not part of Farrer's own classification) are a concise way of denoting the position of each of his cycles in the whole: e.g., 2b is the second cycle in the second double cycle.

References in round brackets denote a healing block or annexe; those in square brackets are passages which, while not in themselves accounts of a healing, 'do duty' – in Farrer's words – for a healing story in his scheme.

1st Double Cycle
        (Exordium: 1.1–13)
1a: 1.14–(1.21–2.12)–2.12   &   1b: 2.13–(3.1–6)–3.12
   (1st Block cycle)   (1st Annexe cycle)

2nd Double Cycle
2a: 3.13–(5.1–43)–6.6   &   2b: 6.7–[6.45–56]–56
   (2nd Block cycle)   (2nd Annexe cycle)

3rd Double cycle
3a: 7.1–(7.24–37)–37   &   3b: 8.1–(8.22–26)–26
   (3rd Block cycle)   (3rd Annexe cycle)
        Epilogue: 8.27–9.1

4th Double Cycle
4a: 9.2–(9.14–29)–10.31   &   4b: 10.32–(10.46–52)–13.2
   (4th Block cycle)   (4th Annexe cycle)

5th Double Cycle
5a: 13.3–[14.1–11]–14.31   &   5b: 14.32–[16.1–8]–16.8
   (5th Block cycle)   (5th Annexe cycle)

LITTLE GOSPEL

Figure 4.1: The Double Cycles

As this plan begins to hint, a hallmark of Farrerian exegesis is complexity. In examining it we must avoid giving what would be in effect an alternative close reading of the text of Mark, since our interest is primarily methodological, yet we must do justice to the subtlety of Farrer's scheme and to the concentration on detail upon which his method rests. Fortunately, Farrer himself suggests the best samples for analysis, in highlighting the role of the healing stories and in presenting his first double cycle as programmatic for the structure of the whole Gospel. We shall therefore examine these most closely of all, before proceeding to a rather briefer survey of the remainder, though with more minute attention to Farrer's treatment of that final Markan crux, the ending of the Gospel.

C. *The Healing Miracles* (A Study in St Mark, 30–52)

In Chapter II of the *Study* Farrer analyses the sequence of healing miracles, which is the kernel of his scheme. He divides the miracles into those which are 'positive' – acts of healing which restore the full vigour of healthy life – and those which are 'negative' – acts of exorcism or cleansing of ritual impurity, which remove some malign presence or excluding condition (*Study*, 39). With regard to the latter healings, he believes that Mark might well have thought in terms of Jesus' ministry bearing the power of both water (negative) and spirit (positive), as promised by John the Baptist and inaugurated at Jesus' baptism. This leads him to his contention that Mark's narrative proceeds by what he calls 'self-developing series' (*Study*, 46): for instance, the rites of purification for leprosy and vaginal haemorrhage prescribed in Leviticus required water-purification (and they appear in consecutive chapters, 14 and 15), so the leper healing, the first of the two Markan healings requiring cleansing (1.40–45), would easily lead in his mind to the second, the issue of blood (5.25–34). 'All we need to claim is that the first easily evokes the second in the mind of a Bible-reading Jew' (*Study*, 46).

Farrer sees in the restorative healings a more elaborate self-development. He identifies an 'annexe' attached to all but the second block: that is, a restorative miracle linked to the last miracle of the block (which is in each case also restorative). Each of the resultant pairs contains a type of healing answering to one or more items in the list of vital powers in Psalm 115 (verses 4–8) which the gods of the heathen are said to lack – '[t]hey have mouths and speak not, eyes have they and see not ...'; together these powers denote the full attributes of healthy, God-given human life (*Study*, 40, 48). Mark achieves a 'climax' by deploying them in ascending order of nobility, moving from 'motive powers' (in hands, legs and feet) to 'sentient powers' (in eyes and ears) (*Study*, 49). A further line of development emerges if we see how each block contains a healing at the request of a parent, culminating in the final block with the healing of 'the son of the father' (9.14–29, *Study*, 51).

The first block (1.21–2.12) contains two pairs of healings, each with one positive and one negative: a man with demons and Peter's mother-in-law, a leper and a paralytic; it is a prelude to the climactic second block (5.1–43), which begins with the exorcism of Legion and itself culminates in the composite sequence of the healing of the woman with the haemorrhage sandwiched within the raising of Jairus' daughter. Farrer sees in the restorations a dominant theme of resurrection, most evident as the girl is raised from death. All this looks forward to the raising-up of Jesus, the last and greatest healing miracle of the Gospel. The second block has no annexe: it interrupts the vital-powers sequence because it 'presents us with the resurrection of the whole person, which admits of no supplementing' (*Study*, 49).

The third block (7.24–37) continues the crescendo as the themes of the three miracles of the second block are all condensed into the first of its two miracles, the healing of the Syrophoenician child: Legion was possessed, the haemorrhaging woman was impure, and Jairus' child was healed at the request of her parent; now a possessed child is healed at the request of an impure (because Gentile) parent. This leaves the second miracle of this block, the healing of the deaf mute, to resume the vital-powers sequence. Together with its annexe (8.22–26) it establishes the healing of the senses, and looks forward to the resurrection of Jesus, just as the healings of the 'less noble' motive powers looked forward to the lesser resurrection of Jairus' daughter (*Study*, 49). The third block is almost consummated by the single miracle of the fourth block, the healing of another deaf mute child, though this time one who is possessed. This healing (9.14–29) thus fuses the purificatory theme of exorcism with the restorative theme of the healing of vital powers. Farrer sees more resurrection motifs here – the boy falls 'as dead' – yet because the child raised is not actually dead, the climax is denied in deference to the apical moment of the whole book when Jesus himself is raised from the dead (*Study*, 51f).

Evaluation

Can the complex internal workings of Farrer's scheme, and the alleged Old Testament references, be sustained? And even if we allow an internal consistency in Farrer's theory, could Mark the author conceivably have *designed* the Gospel thus? If he did, how much of it could he have intended to be discernible to the reader (the virgin reader, or the returning reader), or the *hearer* of his work? Conversely, are these irresponsible questions even to ask? And if questions of authorial intention are not actually irresponsible, do they really matter, and need they detain any reader not inclined to pursue them? All these touch on issues of current literary-critical interest, and they will occupy us in the later pages of Part II, while the question of Mark's original audience will be something for us to examine in Part III. For the moment we shall concentrate on an intrinsic critique, though even then we will not be able to escape some of these wider considerations. Farrer shows the flow of Jesus' healing ministry in Mark coursing, we might say, down a narrowing channel, so that the current becomes more and more intense. There appear at the moment to be some awkward boulders in the way, though Farrer will try to remove some of them, or at least justify the eddies they create.

The first difficulty arises with his categories of healing. The healing of the paralytic in 2.1–12 is inconvenient, for while he classes it as 'positive', it is linked with forgiveness of sin, which is fairly negative, surely? Then there is his case for the water/spirit categorisation he employs, which he offers as part of his impressive claim for Old Testament echoes in Mark's healings. He makes a good case for Elisha's cure of Naaman underlying Jesus' healing of the leper (2 Kgs 5 cf Mk 1.40–45), and for a link between the lowering of the dead man into the sepulchre of Elisha and the lowering of the paralytic through the roof to Jesus (2 Kgs 13.21 cf Mk 2.1–12). He sees Mark having the texts 'in mind' as he writes his own, and goes on to argue a connection between the sons Elijah and Elisha raised at mothers' request, and the child-for-parent healings in Mark: Jairus' daughter, the Syrophoenician's daughter, and the epileptic son (*Study*, 47). He is less convincing in claiming a similar background for the reverse case of the raising of Peter's mother-in-law, though he says that in this 'series' Mark sees Jesus' healings 'on the background of the Old Testament type for all such stories' (*Study*, 50f). Is it not pushing things a little to say of Mark that '[s]on-in-law and mother-in-law remind him of mother and son' (*Study*, 51)? And how do water and spirit fit into these patterns of allusion? Farrer offers the distinction only as a suggestion, but we must assume that it is the best he can offer; and in the exorcisms, one of the two categories of healing the 'water' genus subsumes, it offers nothing like the richness of Old Testament background he finds in the other healings. Water is well-attested in the Old Testament as a medium of purification (e.g. Lev. 13–15 *passim*; 2 Kgs 5.1–14, Ps. 51.2,7), and it is a potent element at other moments, from the Red Sea to the Jordan, yet there is very little to connect it with exorcism, apart perhaps from a few references to the crushing of Rahab and Leviathan (e.g. Isa. 51.9, Ps. 74.14). This is partly because there are so few demons in the Hebrew Scriptures to be exorcised. Would, therefore, such a water/spirit framework (and here we move into historical concerns) suggest itself to a first-century 'Bible-reading Jew'? Extra-canonical Jewish literature might give Farrer more material, but as we shall see in Part III, he is generally quiet about Jewish literature outside the canon.

Secondly, what grounds are there *within the text* for these classifications and motifs? Though Farrer does not say as much, the best way for Mark to denote which of his healings were purificatory and which restorative (and so harbingers of resurrection) would be to use defining words. What, then, if such words are sometimes not there? The absence of a καθαρός (katharos) derivative in a purification (as in the healing of the haemorrhage 5.25–34) is no great problem, since everyone would know about the need to cleanse such ritual impurity. In the case of the restorations, however, their affinity to resurrection is not self-evident, and it is for Mark to show that these are resurrection motifs, which he can only do by the words he uses, in particular by using ἐγείρω (egeirō), ἀνίστημι (anistēmi) or a derivative. It does not help Farrer that such a word twice does not appear (the deaf mute and the blind man, 7.31–37, 8.22–26) and twice appears before – that is, not as a *result* of – the healing (the withered hand and the second blind man, 3.1–6, 10.46–52). If Mark does dominate his material as Farrer suggests, then these absences are a puzzle. His best defence is to say that Mark preserves much of the wording of inherited *pericopae*, but this blows him towards what he sees as the treacherous shoals of form criticism.

Thirdly, the exorcisms. Farrer is correct to say that they 'form a class by themselves' and cannot easily be confused with other sorts of healing (*Study*, 50). What is not obvious from his treatment of them, however, is that they constitute a 'self-developing series', which is what Farrer's scheme requires. Though Legion in the second block (5.1–20) is a bigger challenge to Jesus than the lone demon in the first (1.21–28), Farrer makes nothing of the stress of the text upon the multitudes of demons in the Gadarene demoniac. The third block then reverts, anticlimactically, to a single demon with the exorcism of the child, and although this story has the added impressiveness of a 'distance' healing, it is performed on a female at the request of a female; and since Farrer reminds us that the ancients considered the male sex the nobler (*Study*, 51), this too lessens the sense of crescendo. True, in the healing of the epileptic son, we have a final exorcism (Farrer wants us to see it as a restoration too) which is an all-male affair, but the overall effect of this series is blurred. If we extend Farrer's definition of self-development that 'the first easily evokes the second' (*Study*, 46) and apply it to the exorcisms, it is not clear that these healings meet the requirement. Oddly, Farrer despatches all discussion of the place of these healings in his scheme in one short and cursory paragraph (*Study*, 50).

Fourthly, the 'blocks and annexes'. Farrer argues that the sequence they create is that of a crescendo in four stages, with the 'healing' of Jesus in the resurrection as a consummation (*Study*, 52). He sees Mark opting for a number of healings which, when added to the resurrection, will give a total of fourteen, twice the golden number and so very satisfying. A simple sequence of reduction such as 5 : 4 : 3 : 2 : 1 will yield a total of fifteen, however, so Mark's expedient, says Farrer, is to use a less obvious sequence of 5 : 3 : 3 : 2 : 1. At the second stage the three miracles

are made up of Legion (5.1–20), and the composite healing of Jairus'
daughter and the woman with the haemorrhage (5.21–43), which can be
counted as two healings to give the required total, or as one to provide the
early climax which he will later explain by his Little Gospel hypothesis.
Nevertheless, the composite story remains awkward within the sequence.
Why, then, does Mark need to build his crescendo so elaborately? His
choice of thirteen healings argues no historical constraint, Farrer is clear
about that (*Study*, 182f), so Mark could (we presume) have exercised a
Johannine economy, and offered just six healings plus the resurrection,
to give a bold sequence of 4 : 2 : 1; this would still yield a golden total
of seven. The elaboration Farrer explains by the Mark's chasing of two
other objectives, an exposition of the vital powers sequence in fulfilment
of Psalm 115, and (as he will later argue) the matching of the number of
persons healed by Jesus to the number who are called (*Study*, 68f). He
will claim that the latter can be counted as twelve or thirteen, depending
on whether you include Levi as a thirteenth Disciple (*Study*, 80f), and
later still he will link the double healing of daughter and woman with
the double tribe of Joseph: if Joseph is split into Ephraim and Manasseh
the tribes of Israel can also be numbered as thirteen (*Study*, 328). But
for now, we must be patient! Farrer consistently prefers complexity to
the admission that there is incoherence in the Gospel's structure, or that
the writer's creative hands are tied by circumstance. The result is not
unworkable but certainly inelegant, for all its ingenuity and despite the
elegance of Farrer's own rhetoric in commending it: 'the evangelist begins
from multitude ... The principle of the pattern is a movement towards
unity ... The resurrection of Jesus is all things together, it is seeing eyes,
open ears and a praising tongue, for it is the life of the world to come'
(*Study*, 52).

If we look at the 'annexes' alone (3.1–6, 8.22–26, 10.46–52), they tend
further to obscure the lines of Farrer's scheme. As restorations, they come
under Farrer's category of spirit-healing, yet their resurrection character
is muted, as none of them refers to the person, once healed, being 'raised
up'. Though they cannot be there purely to fulfil the Psalmist's notions of
the full vigour of the healthy body, there appears to be something in the
'vital powers' sequences. In linking it too closely to Psalm 115 Farrer sets
himself too great a task, since there is no hint in Mark of the last attribute
in the psalm's list, the sense of smell, and for Farrer to say, as he does,
that smell is no life-or-death matter for good Christians, does not remove
the inadequacy of a less-than-complete parallel. It would be sufficient to
say that there was a common idea of what constituted physical vigour (an
idea shared with Psalm 115 and other parts of the Old Testament, like
Psalm 135 and Isaiah 35) and that Mark wanted to show Jesus bringing
this about (*Study*, 48). Most interesting is the way Farrer sees Mark
spiritualising these attributes in 8.18 and relativising physical wholeness
at 9.43–48. In effect, Jesus is saying that people may have the equipment

to discern (fully-working ears and eyes) but cannot use it (does he thus hint that physical healing is not enough, but is symbolic of a greater healing?), and he then actually advocates physical handicap – 'if your hand offends you, cut it off ...' (9.43–47) – if that is the price of 'entering into life'. Farrer presents the paradox well: 'It is most striking that a Gospel based upon the scheme of the healing of the whole man in all his members should thus provide its own antithesis' (*Study*, 49).

On the matter of sight and discernment, Farrer does not develop the suggestive fact that only the demons seem at first to know who Jesus really is ('I know who you are...' 1.24; also 3.11, 5.7). We might add, in support of Farrer's case, the significance of the last person to be healed, Bartimaeus: in calling him 'Son of David' he not only 'sees' – while still blind – who Jesus is, but also follows him (becomes a disciple) once his physical sight returns; he shows the way you can 'see' in both senses (10.46–52).

Our final point is more limited. If we look now at the second and third blocks, how much real similarity is there between the trembling woman with the haemorrhage and the witty Syrophoenician? The former hardly 'thrusts' herself on Jesus, and (if we reserve judgement on what Farrer will say about tribal typology) it is hard to see why she need be there at all. We have seen that the twice-seven symbolism requires some squashing of the sequence, but would not the anticipatory function of the raising of Jairus' daughter (as the climax of the Little Gospel) be better served by its being combined with an annexe-type restorative healing, 'drawing into itself all dualities of partial powers' as Jesus' resurrection will do (*Study*, 52)? The purification theme is, after all, already present in Block 2 in the healing of Legion. As it is, the woman appears as a schematic embarrassment, for some reason requiring Mark to embed her in another story. She might, of course, have come to him already embedded, so that he feels unable to remove her, but that is a chasm of textual pre-history into which Farrer refuses to look.[3] An alternative is that Mark interpolates her healing to make some point within the composite story itself, such as to demonstrate Jesus' willingness to address immediate need, or his freedom from the constraints and anxieties of the time-bound and death-fearing. Indeed, in this unusual paragraph the most vivid effect is the drama created by the delay, the distraction of Jesus from an acute case by a chronic one. It is odd that Farrer, in a chapter devoted to healing miracles, does not mention this dramatic force at all, though he will, characteristically, mention the numerical motif (a twelve-year-old girl, and a twelve-year-old illness, *Study*, 328). As with the Legion of demons, we sense that a rather donnish sophistication is blinding him to some of the almost crude effects which the text creates.

---

3. He will use the term 'chasm' himself in describing the pitfalls of this approach (*Study*, 369).

This close interrogation of Farrer's analysis of the Markan healing miracles has been to raise questions suggested by this part of his scheme as a preliminary to a consideration of the general sweep of his argument. Our probing boils down to the repeated posing of this question: 'would Mark have arranged things thus if his mind was working somewhat as Farrer suggests?' Of course, it may be not so much that Farrer's approach is wrong as that his particular proposals will not stand, either in detail or in substance. Or it may be that, in finding him wanting, we are not so much undermining this particular attempt of Farrer's as supporting the case of those who are convinced that any attempt at 'getting inside the head of the author' is futile anyway, and that such a project is in truth no more than a disguise for the ineluctably creative business of interpretation. We shall see.

D. *The First Double Cycle* (A Study in St Mark, 53–78)

Mark 1.1–2.12 (1a) and 2.13–3.12 (1b)

We come now to our second piece of close examination, as we consider Chapter III of the *Study*. There Farrer establishes the other half of his main thesis. He leads us first through what he sees as the alternating short paragraphs of the 'exordium' (1.1–14) into the longer alternations which will complete the first cycle (1a), and then into the fully cyclical material of Cycle 1b; together they will comprise the First Double Cycle. Again, some fine attention to these verses will be valuable, for it is here that Farrer establishes the cyclical model; he tells us at the end of the chapter that what will follow this first double cycle will be essentially more of the same. As in his survey of the healing stories, Farrer will listen for the Gospel's themes and its rhythm, tracing the text's references both to the Old Testament and to itself.

He describes the start of Cycle 1a as a complex of prophecy announcing Good News brought by a messenger, in which Mark cites Isaiah but draws on Exodus and Malachi as well. Mark, according to Farrer, here follows the synagogue tradition in prefacing the prophecy with the text of the Torah to which it most closely corresponds, but he also deliberately fuses Exodus with Malachi: Exodus sends a messenger before Israel, Malachi sends one before the Lord, and Mark sends one before Jesus. Mark therefore sees in Jesus both Israel and the Lord, and (by virtue of his name) a new Joshua to lead God's people to the true Promised Land. This use of Malachi hints at the nature of the messenger whom Mark will reveal, for the closing verses of Malachi promise the return of Elijah and so suggest that Mark's messenger, John the Baptist, will be he. The prophetic voice in the wilderness becomes John in the wilderness, the promise of Elijah's return is embodied in John dressed and feeding like Elijah, and the identification of the Baptist with Elijah tells us in turn of more to come, for Elijah is the forerunner of the Day of the Lord.

John confirms this by speaking of one to come who will baptise not with water but with the Holy Spirit. His own prophecy is then fulfilled by the arrival of Jesus. Jesus, the 'Anointed' and 'Son of God' (1.1) is now baptised, and his baptism becomes an anointing with the Spirit (as Isaiah 9.1–7 foretold) and a revelation of his sonship. John also foreshadows Jesus in another way, for Jesus is a second and greater John, with a superior baptism and fed in the wilderness not on locusts but, like Israel, on 'supernatural bread' (Farrer omits to say that Mark never mentions 'bread'); and if a second John, so a new and better Elijah (*Study*, 59).

In laying out Farrer's typological observations we have moved into his description of how Mark's text develops 'rhythmically' within itself. The overlap is proper, because Farrer sees both as exercises in fulfilment: as Mark writes, it is not just a matter of arranging material to demonstrate fulfilment of certain Old Testament texts:

> An interlocking pattern of refrain-words emphasized the continuous drawing out of the sense, and how the matter grows under the evangelist's pen out of the suggestions contained in what he has written already. As 'message' is taken up in 'messenger', so is the first 'prepare' in the second; the voice in the wilderness suggests John in the wilderness, and so on. St Mark's tendency is to write short passages which are rounded and complete, and yet provide rich material for further development. (*Study*, 57)

Farrer sees this at work in the short rhythm of small paragraphs in vv. 1–15, but also in longer rhythms which govern the general sweep of the story, all guided by the principle of fulfilment. For instance, he detects a rhythm carrying the text from the private to the public: Jesus' commissioning as he comes up out of the Jordan waters and his wrestling with Satan in the desert are private mysteries; presently we see him publicly calling disciples out of the water where they fish (much as Elijah called Elisha from the plough), and doing open battle with demons in the synagogue; all is ringed by the refrain-word 'Galilee' (*Study*, 63f).

How then do these rhythms extend through the ensuing paragraphs? Surveying the Gospel up to 3.12 (the end of the first double cycle), Farrer detects two forces at work, the tendency of each paragraph to echo the last-but-one, and the movement of a group of paragraphs towards a single story which distils their essence. Once again, it will be helpful to see this in a diagram. The verbal echoes are in italics or Greek script, though Farrer confines himself to the English text; all the other information appears in Farrer's own analysis.

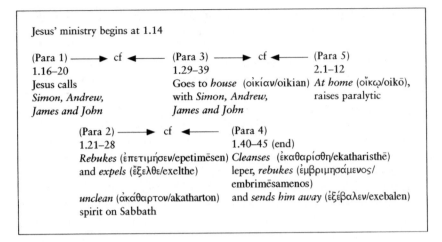

Figure 4.2: Alternation

All the above is in Cycle 1a. The distillation embraces 1a and 1b.

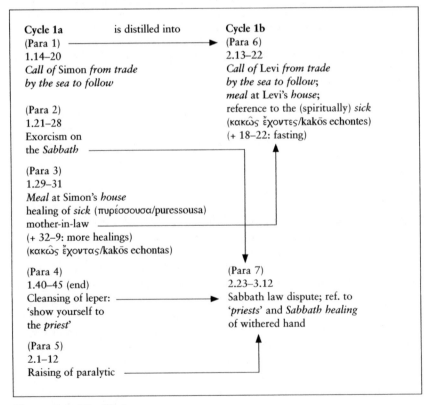

Figure 4.3: Distillation

In this chapter we also find some typological analysis similar to that in the healings chapter. For instance, Farrer now suggests Moses' sign of the leprous hand as a type for the leper cleansed and the hand restored (Exod. 4.6f cf Mk 1.40–45, 3.1–12, *Study*, 77f). Farrer concludes his schematic analysis like this:

> St Mark's total rhythm is now in step with the healing pattern which we studied in a chapter by itself. It looks as though each block of healings, and each annexed healing, is going to be the heart of a separate cycle ... If the beat of the rhythm does not keep changing ... we shall have a more straightforward phenomenon to describe. (*Study*, 78)

Evaluation

Farrer's argument for a pastiche of prophecies in the opening verses has been confirmed by similar examples of this practice, for instance at Qumran (e.g. in 4Q *Florilegium*), and the overlapping of characteristics between Elijah, John and Jesus is genuinely complex. If for a moment we consider Mark's original setting, the array of expectation surrounding Elijah probably would have caused many associations to come to the minds of a first-century audience. Similarly, he makes a good case for the principle of fulfilment which seems to drive the text, both as it 'caps' the Old Testament and as it develops its own momentum in the refrain-like way which Farrer describes. We shall see this happening on a grander scale when the overlapping of Elijah/John/Jesus reappears in later cycles (6.14f, 8.27–30, 9.2–8). When Farrer comes to the longer rhythms of these two cycles, however, there are some inconvenient 'off' beats, and we shall concentrate on these.

First, there is the condensing passage 2.13–22. The Levi story can indeed be seen as a neat distillation of the call of Simon by the sea and the scene at Simon's house (1.16–20, 29–31), though in the latter there is only the implication, in the woman 'serving' them, that they are having a meal. The dispute over fasting, however (2.18–22), does not sit so comfortably with Levi, and is not necessary to help condense 1.16–20 and 29–39. Farrer proposes the link that eating on the 'wrong days' (fast days) belongs with eating with the 'wrong people' (Levi and friends), but this is weak (*Study*, 71). The fasting passage actually feels quite free-standing, unless it goes with what immediately follows it, another food dispute, with which it has a stronger link, that of days of religious obligation, whether for fasting or for rest (2.23–28). Farrer himself says the transition to this passage is 'perfectly smooth' (*Study*, 72).

Secondly, there is the raising of the paralytic in 2.1–12. We have already seen it causing some problems for Farrer's positive/negative categories in the healings, and now it provides an unexpected third course for 2.23–3.12 to digest. This latter passage fails to distil it except in the most general sense that it maintains the healing theme and takes up the theme of dispute between Jesus and the religious authorities. Farrer does not even offer this much in defence of his case, but merely says, with Procrustean briskness, that the paralytic story is added 'for good measure' (*Study*, 70). In fact, this story could go at least as well with the Levi episode, which immediately follows it, where it would serve to condense a key element which it has in common with the scene at Simon's house (1.16–20), the emphasis on 'raising'. The paralytic story also has the 'house' motif in v. 1, ἐν οἴκῳ (en oikō), which is stressed in the healing of Simon' mother-in-law and in the Levi passage, but absent from the 'base' paragraphs with which Farrer links it (1.21–28 and 1.40–45), and from the condensing passage into which he seeks to distil it (2.23–3.12). Indeed, all three of these 'no-house' passages revolve around the *synagogue*, a feature which becomes even more pronounced if 1.39 is transferred from the scene at Simon's house to the leper story.[4] If we transfer this verse, we can follow principles similar to Farrer's, and have this more balanced, three-stage model:

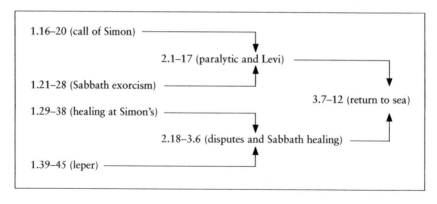

Figure 4.4: A Three-stage Model

This scheme disturbs Farrer's division into two cycles, but it is this very division that has produced the strains we have detected. It does, however, leave his first four 'base' paragraphs intact, except for the transfer of 1.39. It removes the awkwardnesses described above and preserves Farrer's principle that paragraphs should generally be of comparable length (see *Study*, 78). Verses 2.1–12 now join the Levi story in the first condensing passage (2.1–17); this passage combines the themes of food, healing and sins/sinners, the last eliciting the question to Jesus, 'who do you think you are to forgive sins?' The difficult verses 18–22 join the other ritual disputes in the second condensing passage (2.18–3.6); this

4. As the paragraph-break in Nestlé-Aland, Edn 27, suggests.

passage combines the themes of food, healing and holy days (especially the Sabbath), the last eliciting the question to Jesus, 'Why do you behave thus?' Both condensing passages therefore end with a pregnant question about Jesus. The brief concluding paragraph takes us back to the sea, where the action began with the calling of Simon, gathers together people from all over the region (including the areas in which Jesus has ministered), summarises Jesus' healing activity, and provides the answer to the 'Who?' and 'Why?' questions, as the demons say to Jesus, 'you are the Son of God'.

The first aim of this exercise has been to show some difficulties with Farrer's analysis, particularly concerning the internal rhythm of the text, which lessen the overall force of his thesis; if he is unable to establish a clear double cycle here at the programmatic start of the Gospel, then he has only a shaky foundation for what follows. The second aim has been to show how the text is susceptible of variations under Farrer's essential method. He is astute in detecting resonance and correspondence, yet more than one plausible scheme can be 'discerned' to orchestrate what he detects. If his intention is to 'get inside the mind of St Mark' (*Study*, 27), how elusive is that mind! This raises again the suspicion of something inescapably creative about Farrer's work, though he would insist that as it was for Mark, so it is for him: his business is 'not creation but obedience' (*Study*, 54).

E. The Second and Third Double Cycles (A Study in St Mark, 79–107)

Mark 3.13–6.6 (2a) and 6.7–56 (2b); 7.1–37 (3a) and 8.1–26 (3b)

The rhythm, according to Farrer, is now established. Henceforward we can proceed more rapidly. In Chapter IV he describes his next two pairs of cycles: 2a is a 'block' cycle, centred on the healing block 5.1–43; 2b is an 'annexe' cycle', though vv. 45–56 do not contain a conventional annexed healing. 3a is a block cycle centred on healings in 7.24–37, 3b an annexe cycle centred on 8.22–26. Farrer proceeds as follows.

Cycle 2a: Mark 3.13–6.6 (A Study in St Mark, 79–88)
The cycle begins, as the others have, with a call-narrative. Farrer's argument is that each cycle is modelled on its predecessor but shows some mutation from it. The opening cycles are dominated by the cardinal Christian themes of calling and healing, and so in 1a Mark balances the call of Peter and his three companions with the healing of Peter's mother-in-law and three others, and in 1b the call of Levi with the healing of the man with the withered hand. Now in 2a the calling theme is wrapped up by the naming of all twelve disciples – that is, eight new names (Mk 3.13–19), balanced by eight healings, distributed through the Gospel up

to Chapter 10 – and Jesus is again entertained (as by Simon and then by Levi in 1a and 1b), though this time he cannot eat because of the crowds (3.19); this concerns his family (3.20), just as his eating with Levi and friends appalled the Pharisees. Farrer passes very quickly over the Beelzebub controversy (3.22–30); he treats it as a sort of footnote to the anxiety of Jesus' family, which is re-emphasised in 3.31–35. In 1b the incident in the cornfield (2.23–28) came next, and so the parable of the miraculous cornfield with related teaching (4.1–34) has the same position in 2a (*Study*, 79–82).

In 1b the next event was the healing of the withered hand; in 2a it is the healing of the Gerasene demoniac, followed by the raising of Jairus' daughter and the cure of the woman with a haemorrhage (5.1–43). Here the ordering principle for healing material takes over from that for whole cycles: since 2a is a block cycle, it finds the model for its healings not in 1b (an annexe cycle and its overall model) but in the healings in the cycle before that, the block cycle 1a. Mark therefore writes three healings – including the two-in-one composite – to condense the four healings in 1.21–2.12, and then returns to complete 2a along the lines of its immediate predecessor: as the withered hand brought rejection in the synagogue and Jesus' withdrawal (3.1–6), so now the healing of Jairus' daughter precedes rejection in the synagogue of his home town, and Jesus withdraws (6.1–6; *Study*, 82–84).

The healing of Peter's mother-in-law in 1a feeds two antitypes in 2a: Jairus' daughter (for both relatives are raised) and the woman with the haemorrhage (for both are adult women); similarly, the healing of the leper in 1a corresponds to the curing of the haemorrhage, and that of the paralytic in 1a to the raising of the child. Farrer then balances the double antitype for Peter's mother-in-law by arguing that the exorcism in the synagogue, the remaining block healing in 1a, similarly feeds two antitypes in 2a. There are only three healings in 1b, of which two are already allocated as antitypes; Farrer takes the third, the exorcism of Legion, as one antitype to the 1a exorcism, and adds to it the stilling of the storm (4.35–41), which he describes as 'the exorcism of the wind' (*Study* 85). In support of this he points to verbal correspondences between the two – ἀπόλλυμι (apollumi), φιμόω (fimoō), ὑπακούω (hupakouō) – and the identification in 'the Biblical mind' of spirit and wind (*Study*, 85). He argues that, furthermore, the two antitypes clear up an ambiguity in the archetype, in which the man says, with demonic voice, 'Away from us, Jesus [Farrer's translation of 1.24, τί ἡμῖν καὶ σοί; (ti hēmin kai soi?)] ... have you come to destroy us? ... I know who you are ...': in the stilling of the storm it is unambiguously human voices which cry, 'We are destroyed,' and in the Legion story Farrer sees clear separation between the one demoniac – 'away from me, Jesus' (again Farrer's rendering of τί ἐμοὶ καὶ σοί; (ti emoi kai soi?) – and the many demons – 'Legion is my name, for we are many' (*Study*, 85–87).

Cycle 2b: Mark 6.7–56 (*A Study in St Mark*, 88–94)

This annexe cycle, though much shorter, is modelled on its predecessor (2a) but with omissions, most notably the absence of any particular healing miracle. Farrer explains this by saying that there can be no annexed antitype to the raising of the whole person in the story of Jairus' daughter; instead Mark supplies as an antitype to the stilling of the storm in 2a the story of the walking on the water (6.45–52) and a summary statement of a healing expedition (6.53–56).

Like its predecessor, 2b begins with a calling, as the Twelve are sent on a mission (6.7–13); in the calling of the Twelve there was a betrayal motif in the reference to Judas 'who handed him over' (3.19); here the motif is in the fate of John the Baptist (6.14f), and at this point Mark tells the passion story of John, both to echo Elijah's sufferings and to prefigure Christ's passion (6.17–29; *Study*, 92). Once more Jesus and the disciples are prevented from eating by the crowds, again they resort to a boat, and Jesus gives, in the place corresponding to the parable of the multiplied harvest, the miracle of the multiplied bread (6.30–44). Finally comes the walking on the water, reflecting the stilling of the storm, which came immediately after the corn discourses of Mark 4 (6.45–52; *Study*, 88–94).

Cycle 3a: Mark 7.1–37 (*A Study in St Mark*, 94–99)

The emphasis on calling and healing now gives way to healing and feasting, as Baptism gives way to Eucharist, and the focus moves from Jesus' rejection by Israel to his acceptance by the Gentiles. There is now no call narrative, that theme having been exhausted by the call of all Twelve, but again the Pharisees complain, this time at Jesus' failure to observe ritual precautions against impurity; Jesus once more rebuts them, and tells a parable to the crowd (1–23). There then begins the third healing block (7.24–37), including the healing of a Gentile child, which ends not with rejection but with a doxology (*Study*, 94–99).

Cycle 3b: Mark 8.1–26 (*A Study in St Mark*, 99–104)

There is no call narrative (for the same reason as before) and so this cycle begins with the feeding of the four thousand, which corresponds to the feeding of the five in 2b, on which it is modelled (8.1–9). Farrer implies that the four thousand are Gentiles (*Study*, 99). Both feedings are followed by trips on the lake towards Bethsaida in which we hear of the disciples' incomprehension about the loaves (6.45–52 cf 8.14–21), and both lead into healing: a general healing in 2b gives way in 3b to a particular healing, that of the blind villager (8.22–26; *Study*, 99f).

According to Farrer's scheme, these verses should and do also reflect the block cycle 3a to which they are annexed, in that they too include the repulse of Pharisaic questioners (8.11–13 cf 7.6–16) and the attempted enlightening of the disciples (8.14–21 cf 7.17–23). The passage 8.14–21 is a crucial moment: it echoes the sea trip of 2b and, in the 'leaven of Herod', harks back to that same cycle, which was the one in which Herod last appeared; it also refers to the 'leaven of the Pharisees', thus looking back to their conduct in 3a (*Study*, 100–104).

Epilogue: Mark 8.27–9.1 (*A Study in St Mark*, 104–107)

Farrer is not sure whether to make this passage an addendum to 3b or a preface to 4a, but decides on the former. Here Peter's confession at Caesarea Philippi crowns Jesus' restoring of sense and speech in the 'vital powers' healings by ending the disciples' catalogue of failures to hear, see or speak aright in the matter of Jesus' works and words. Just as the blind villager initially sees people as tree-like figures, but then sees people as they really are, so Peter now sees Jesus as the Christ, but needs a second sharp lesson to see the truth about the sufferings of the Son of Man. Like the villager, he is enjoined to silence, and Jesus summons the crowd for more teaching. Up to now, private teaching has followed public teaching, but henceforth the order is reversed (*Study*, 104–107).

Evaluation

In his exposition of Double Cycles 2 and 3, Farrer has a second chance to make virtue of the composite healing (5.21–43), but with the convolutions of single and double antitypes he turns a literary device into an implausible contrivance. He does not clinch his case for what Mark gains by the disturbance his composite passage creates, and he still fails to do justice to the obvious dramatic effect of the passage. More generally, though the resemblances he sees are often clear and persuasive, his connections do not always run with the grain which he claims to see in the text: so, for instance, when he makes the storm-stilling do duty for an exorcism to accompany the Legion story. The association of the sea with evil forces is known in the Old Testament, and others follow Farrer in noticing verbal correspondence between these stories (especially φιμόω (fimoō) at 1.25 and 4.39),[5] but beyond that things become strained. Can disciples be bracketed with demons? Both fear destruction, yet the latter fear the (demonic) wind and the former fear Jesus, who is the scourge of the wind.

The 'exorcism of the wind' brings us again to the exorcisms as a breed. We noticed earlier that Farrer's treatment of them was cursory and the linkage between them weak. Here Farrer contends that the storm and

---

5.   See e.g. Pss 18.16f, 69.14f, 74.13f, 89.9f. For similar interpretations see Nineham, Commentary, 146–148; Schweizer, Commentary, 109; and Hooker, Commentary, 139. For reservations about this, see Collins, Commentary, 378, who leans towards a Galilean setting.

Legion stories resolve the confusion over who speaks, and how many, in the synagogue exorcism of Cycle 1a. Now there need be no confusion at all in 1a, for ἡμᾶς (hēmas, 1.24) can easily refer to the demon and its human host, while the next word, οἶδά (oida), can be the demon speaking for itself. If there is a confusion, it is *introduced* by the Legion story: Jesus says to 'him', αὐτῷ (autō, 5.8) – and grammatically this should refer to the man, though contextually it refers to the demon – 'come out of the man, *you unclean spirit*'; 'he' then says 'Legion is *my* name' – the word is μοί (moi), not ἡμῖν (hēmin), unambiguously singular – 'for *we* are many'. All this brings from Farrer a rhetorical tour de force: 'So long as the demons possess one man, their number is concealed, and they pass under a single name, but in their vain attempt to escape destruction ... a regiment of Satan's host is visibly displayed' (*Study*, 87). His eloquence hardly clarifies, however.

The healing summary in 2b (6.56) just about works as an annexe healing, especially since it includes the motif from the haemorrhage story of people touching Jesus, but this makes the presence of the walking on the water (6.45–52) very puzzling. In a place where Farrer has led us to expect an 'annexe' healing, referring to its immediately preceding 'block' healing (the composite story), Mark can only offer us what is neither a healing story nor a story otherwise related to the composite healing.

Nevertheless, schematic difficulties should not be allowed to obscure the helpful connections he make between some passages. In the case of the sower's multiple harvest and Jesus' multiplication of loaves, Farrer's exegesis is very fine: the miraculous word of the parable gives way to the miraculous deed of manifold bread.[6] Equally good is his treatment of the death of John the Forerunner, which gives us a passion narrative to prefigure Jesus' own, and also a link with Elijah. Moreover, Farrer strengthens his case for the interplay of physical and spiritual vision in his interpretation of the man who sees people like trees: his partial sight corresponds to the partial discernment of Peter at Caesarea Philippi.[7] Whatever we may conclude about Farrer's execution or his grand plan for Mark, he is asking cogent questions which throw up 'local' patterning in the text.

---

6. Again, Farrer is in good company, from Augustine onwards, in seeing the four thousand as Gentiles. See Hooker, Commentary, 187.

7. Lightfoot makes a similar case (*History*, 90f).

F. The Last Two Double Cyles (A Study in St Mark, 108–141)

Mark 9.2–10.31 (4a) and 10.32–13.2 (4b); 13.3–14.31 (5a)
and 14.32–16.8 (5b)

These last cycles (*Study*, Chapter V) bring us to the end of Mark's Gospel.

Cycle 4a: Mark 9.2–10.31 (*A Study in St Mark*, 108–117)

The distinctive dual theme of calling and healing had seemed to be exhausted in 2a, but Farrer now sees it returning in the calling of Peter, James and John (just as Jesus called them into Jairus' house) to the mount of Transfiguration (9.2), and in the healing block containing the cure of the epileptic boy (9.14–29). To this is now added teaching, private teaching at Capernaum (9.30–49), public teaching beyond the Jordan (10.1–16). The model for the former is Caesarea Philippi in the Epilogue to Cycle Three, where Jesus also puts a question: there Peter, arrogant and human-minded, denounces the need for the Son of Man to suffer; now, as worldly disciples argue over who is the greatest, Jesus enjoins servanthood and humility by bringing a child among them. In the public teaching, Jesus stands where Moses did, across the Jordan: Moses delivered the Deuteronomic Law and left 'Jesus' (that is, Joshua) to complete his work; Jesus the Christ, as the new Lawgiver, overrules him on divorce and repeats the private teaching on the significance of children. The requirements of Jesus' Law are summed up in the story of the rich young man (10.17–31).

Cycle 4b: Mark 10.32–13.2 (*A Study in St Mark*, 117–127)

The controlling theme is the approach and entry into Jerusalem. Like 4a, this cycle has a calling, as the disciples are summoned to go to the city (10.32–34), and a dispute over status, as the sons of Zebedee ask for the places to right and left of Jesus which we know to have been vacated by Moses and Elijah (at the Transfiguration, 10.35–45), and a healing miracle, that of Bartimaeus (10.46–52). Since public teaching in Jerusalem is to follow, we expect there now to be private teaching as in 4a, but instead we have the triumphal entry into Jerusalem (11.1–11). This is because the need for private teaching is superseded by Bartimaeus' public confession, in contrast to the blind villager in 3b and Peter at Caesarea Philippi, who are made to be silent. Now comes the public teaching, in the Temple courts, and – *inter alia* – it rehearses the Deuteronomic teaching beyond the Jordan in 4a: on marriage (against the Sadducees, 12.18–27), on loving God unreservedly (the good scribe, 12.28–34), and on wealth (the bad scribes, and the widow's mite 12.38–44).

Cycle 5a: Mark 13.3–14.31 (*A Study in St Mark*, 127–133)

The cyclical form continues, though there are no more healings. It begins with an apostolic scene – though not a calling – as the four original disciples ask about the End (13.3f). As with the thrones for James and John, Jesus replies that what they seek is not his to give; to both requests all he can promise is suffering (13.5–37). The anointing at Bethany (14.3–9) does duty for a healing block: as Bartimaeus hailed the king, so now the woman enacts the regal anointing. The Last Supper (14.17–31) is the antitype to the Temple episode in 4b: Jesus and his presence in the sacrament are the new Temple. Both 5a and 4b end at the Mount of Olives.

Cycle 5b: Mark 14.32–16.8 (*A Study in St Mark*, 133–141)

Farrer readily agrees that the passion narrative existed in substantially its present form before Mark wrote his Gospel, and sees in it the germ of all that precedes it. In it there are two themes only: calling and healing, and we now see that all the calling has been to the passion, and that all healings have been anticipating the Resurrection (*Study*, 133f). In Gethsemane Jesus calls the Three (14.32–4); as for healings, the anointing at Bethany was a substitute healing, and now the final attempt at anointing (16.1f) will also be a sort of substitute, and a belated one; the healing – the Resurrection – has already happened (*Study*, 134f). Further correspondences with Cycle 5a follow: as the so-called Markan apocalypse in 5a referred to a shortening of the times (13.20) – that is, a halving of the apocalyptic tradition of the Week of Oppression to three and a half days – so Mark's passiontide in 5b is itself three and a half days long (*Study*, 137–9); as Jesus' apocalypse requires them to 'watch' (13.23, 37), so he himself watches in Gethsemane (14.35–42, *Study*, 140); as he told them they would not know the time of coming (13.35: late, midnight, cockcrow, early), so Peter and the others are variously unprepared in the garden late that night, at midnight at the arrest, at cockcrow by the high priest's house, and early at the Praetorium, where Jesus faces Pilate alone; finally the women who come early to the tomb are no better prepared for what awaits them there (14.37–42, 50, 66–72, 15.1, 16.1–8, *Study*, 140f).

Evaluation

We find here further intricate forcings of the text and implausibilities, especially the casting of the Bethany anointing as a quasi-healing, when it is additionally seen by turns as a coronation and a burial act (*Study*, 129f, 137). We also sense special pleading when Bartimaeus vetoes further private teaching, and when the once-suppressed themes of calling and healing spring up again. Nevertheless, Farrer produces here some of his most attractive interpretation. He suggests, most notably, that in the conduct of the disciples during the passion narrative Mark provides exegesis and fulfilment of the prophecies in Jesus' apocalypse of Chapter 13.[8] In the case of the times to be watchful – 'late' – 'midnight' – 'cockcrow' – 'early' – it almost works perfectly: only the absence of a reference to 'midnight' at the time of the arrest (14.41) denies Farrer a complete trick. The concept of prophecy and fulfilment may even shed light on the puzzling reference to the young man leaving his coat as he flees Gethsemane: when the time of the Abomination comes, says Jesus, let not someone in the field even turn back for his coat (13.16 cf 14.51f; *Study*, 141). This passage brings from Farrer one of his tersest pieces of eloquence:

> Christ dies now in himself; at a later day he will suffer in his apostles. For the present it is not theirs to die. The young man puts off his *sindon* and escapes alive. Christ is destined, at this season, to wear the *sindon* alone. The Arimathaean wraps him in it; it is his shroud. (*Study*, 141)

We return below to the fleeing young man, when we discuss the ending of the Gospel.

When he considers the Transfiguration, Farrer makes a fine case for the way in which we might see how it recapitulates the initial call of the disciples, raising them up to a new level of revelation, and how two of them at least are quite unequal to the experience, as they ask to fill Moses' and Elijah's now empty places (*Study*, 156f). We should note, however, that Jesus first calls four disciples in Galilee, but takes only three up the mountain; this denies Farrer the last degree of correspondence.

G. *The Prefigurative Sense* (A Study in St Mark, 142–171)

In Chapter VI Farrer elaborates on his claim that there is a prefiguring Little Gospel, whose climax is the raising of Jairus' daughter, comprising the material in Cycles 1a to 2b: two double cycles and eight healings (eight being the number of resurrection, on the first day of a new week). The last two double cycles, 4a to 5b, must therefore be modelled on the first two, as well as each being modelled on its predecessor (*Study*, 142–146). Farrer will maintain his belief, however, that the passion narrative itself is not written in order to 'square' with any of its antecedents, but that the opposite is the case (*Study*, 168).

In seeking to demonstrate the pattern of model and antitype between the Little Gospel and the *dénouement* of the whole Gospel, Farrer adduces many parallels between the first two and last two double

8. Lightfoot had had similar thoughts in *The Gospel Message of St Mark*, which appeared in the year before the *Study* (*Message*, 48–59). On p. 51 he acknowledges his debt to *Farrer* for part of the argument!

cycles. These include the following: the calling of the Four in Galilee
and the Transfiguration (1.16–20 cf 9.2; *Study*, 155–7); the crisis in the
Synagogue at Capernaum over the healing of a 'withered' hand, and the
protracted crisis in the Temple, which includes the story of the 'withering'
of the fig tree (3.1–6 cf 11.12–12.44: the first passage uses ξηρός
(xēros), the second the passive of ξηραίνω (xērainō; *Study*, 158–163));
Jesus' dissociation from his family in Galilee and the betrayal within
families warned of in the apocalypse (3.31–5 cf 13.12f; *Study*, 165f);
the shallow-rooted believer withering in the face of 'oppression', and the
need for endurance in the face of 'oppression' in the apocalypse (4.1–20,
the parable of the sower, cf 4.17: both use the word θλίψις (thlipsis),
otherwise absent in Mark; *Study*, 166); and finally in this selection, the
miracle of the loaves and the walking on the water 'like an apparition
from the dead' (φαντάσμα (fantasma), 6.49), and their fulfilment in Last
Supper and Resurrection (6.35–52 cf 14.22–25, 16.1–8; *Study*, 168f).

Evaluation

Farrer's exegesis of the Transfiguration returns as one of the hinges of
his proposal for the Little Gospel. Overall, he makes a persuasive case
for prefigurative 'coding' (not Farrer's term) in the early chapters of
Mark, though it feels a little overdriven when Farrer calls a pattern of
such hints 'a complete Gospel' in its own right (*Study*, 147). The least
effective piece of alleged foreshadowing is the bracketing of the walking
on the water and the Resurrection, a link which also serves to support
his arguments over the ending of the Gospel (see below). It is what he
sees as the apparition-like character of the two episodes which makes
Farrer draw them together, though this leads him to go beyond Mark in
Matthaean style and call an 'angel' what the evangelist calls, in a rather
this-worldly way, a 'young man' (*Study*, 169 cf 16.5).[9] Also, the key
to the final scene is the *absence* of Jesus: 'he is not here ... he has gone
ahead of you'; Farrer admits this (*Study*, 169), but it is still hard to hear a
strong echo, in the young man's words, of Jesus' own from the water, 'Do
not be afraid, it is I' (6.50, θαρσεῖτε (tharseite) cf 16.6, μὴ ἐκθαμβεῖσθε
(mē ekthambeisthe)).

H. The Ending *(A Study in St Mark, 172–181)*

Farrer now (Chapter VII) considers the problem of the ending of the
Gospel, Mark 16.1–8. As in the *Glass*, he allows the possibility of a lost

9.   Though Mark might have found some warrant for calling an angel a νεανίσκος
(néaniskos). Hooker, who describes the figure as 'recognizably an angel', finds suggestive
references in 2 Macc. 3.26, 33 (Commentary, 384).

last section, but places the burden of proof on those who cannot believe that Mark the evangelist finished writing where the authentic verses of our Mark leave off. This inability, which in the *Glass* he described as coming from poetic discontent, he now puts down to 'a supposed psychological impossibility', that no Christian could end so ambiguously as to leave the reader with the fleeing speechless women of 16.8, and that not even Mark could end a book with the abrupt and virtually ungrammatical γάρ (gar; *Study*, 173). Farrer cites Lightfoot's catalogue of similar Greek usage, which he gives in *Locality*, but happily agrees that such evidence does not remove the abruptness: 'no one denies that St Mark ends abruptly. The question is whether he may not have meant to' (*Study*, 173).[10]

This is the moment to return to Farrer's earlier treatment, in the *Glass*, of what he here calls the 'poetical effectiveness' of Mark's ending (*Glass*, 136–146, *Study*, 174). We noted it in Part I, reserving it for closer examination here. Farrer, we recall, sees in the women, who are enjoined to spread the good news but flee speechless, the fitting conclusion to Mark's theme of human perversity, a theme already established in the sequence from Bethany to Gethsemane: an inappropriately intended anointing, disciples' vainglory, the topsy-turvy power games of the priests and of Pilate, and even Joseph's misplaced generosity in offering a tomb. This theme, says Farrer, Mark reinforces by verbal echoes ('women', 'ointment', 'Galilee', 'body', 'linen cloths'); finally, the flight of the disciples at the arrest prepares us for the flight of the women at the end. In particular, Farrer seeks to unpick a peculiar knot of correspondences between the Arrest, Burial and End of the Gospel. We can tabulate them thus:

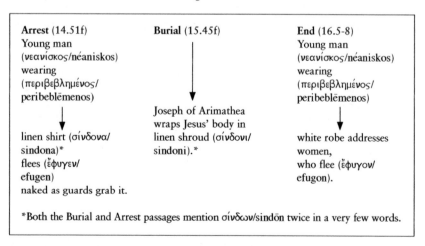

Arrest (14.51f)	Burial (15.45f)	End (16.5-8)
Young man (νεανίσκος/néaniskos) wearing (περιβεβλημένος/ peribeblēmenos)		Young man (νεανίσκος/néaniskos) wearing (περιβεβλημένος/ peribeblēmenos)
	Joseph of Arimathea wraps Jesus' body in linen shroud (σίνδονι/ sindoni).*	
linen shirt (σίνδονα/ sindona)* flees (ἔφυγεν/ efugen) naked as guards grab it.		white robe addresses women, who flee (ἔφυγον/ efugon).

*Both the Burial and Arrest passages mention σίνδων/sindōn twice in a very few words.

Figure 4.5: Arrest, Burial and End

10.   Farrer's reference to Lightfoot, typically, is not specific. It is to *Locality*, 1–48. See also *Message*, 80–97. Hooker adds to Lightfoot's lists Menander, *Dyscolos*, 437f (Commentary, 391).

Mark must intend some symbolic linkage, says Farrer, and Farrer's solution, we recall, is typological. First, he brings in the punishment of stripping which was set for Temple guards caught, as the disciples are, asleep on duty. Secondly, he invokes the patriarch Joseph, who both completes the resolution of the puzzle of these passages and also provides the key to the wider aspects of the question whether Mark intends to end so oddly. Joseph is the type for his namesake from Arimathea, in that each seeks the body of someone precious to them (in the case of the more ancient Joseph, it is his father); he also provides a second model for the fleeing young man, for he too flees, from Potiphar's wife (*Glass*, 144f). Finally, we come to the boy at the tomb:

> Joseph was stripped, first by his eleven false brethren, then by Potiphar's wife: he was buried in prison and believed by the eleven to be dead. But in due course he appeared to them as though alive from the grave, clothed in a robe of glory as the man of the king's right hand: he said to them, 'I am Joseph.' But his brethren could not answer him, for they were confounded. Compare the women, confronted not, indeed, with the new Joseph in person, but with one who wears his livery, and unable to speak, for they were afraid. A glance at the Greek Old Testament will show the exactness of the verbal parallel. (*Glass*, 145)

But why does Mark end there, when the Joseph narrative carries on?

> Joseph proceeded to overcome the shame and terror of the eleven who had sold him, and St Mark's readers will know that Jesus is going, in Galilee, to overcome the shame and fear of the eleven who had deserted him: but to include that encounter within his gospel is a thing he cannot do: every sentence in the gospel points a finger towards it, but the poem ends with finality at the words 'for they were afraid'. The rest cannot be written. (*Glass*, 145)

This is the sum of Farrer's case in the *Glass*. In the present chapter of the *Study*, he returns to the Joseph cycle as providing '[t]he most relevant example of a *gar* ending' (*Study*, 174). He now 'glances' at the Septuagint on his readers' behalf, and softens his claim for 'the exactness of the verbal parallel' by transliterating the two texts, 'ephobounto gar' in Mark and, in Genesis, 'etarachthesan gar', and simply saying that '[t]he parallel speaks for itself' (*Study*, 173f cf *Glass*, 145). His main task in this chapter, however, is to build some schematic buttresses for his argument that 'the scene at the empty tomb is a final chord which draws together, echoes and concludes the preceding music', and to do this he must 'proceed more scholastically' than in his Bampton Lectures (*Study*, 174).

Farrer finds in the terminal sections of the last four cycles (4a–5b) what he calls 'paracycles', passages which begin to establish themselves as cycles in their own right, though he then says that a cycle tends to become assimilated to its paracycle (*Study*, 174–176). This means that, if he is to demonstrate that Mark intended to end the Gospel at 16.8 (ἐφοβοῦντο γάρ (ephobounto gar)), Farrer must show not only that these closing verses recapitulate the themes of the Gospel as a whole – and he feels that he demonstrated this satisfactorily in Lecture VIII of the *Glass* (*Study*, 174) – but also (and this is where he argues more 'scholastically') that they provide a 'formal' resolution of what now amount to three previous 'endings' in the Gospel, those of:

    (a)   the previous paracycle (14.12–31)
    (b)   the previous cycle (5a)
    (c)   the Little Gospel (Cycles 1a–2b) (*Study*, 176f).

Farrer's demonstration is as follows:

    (a)   the angel at the tomb restates to the women Jesus' own prophecy of 14.26–31, that he would go before them all into Galilee, and the women by their flight enact the first part of that prophecy: 'I will smite the shepherd and the sheep will be scattered';
    (b)   the woman anoints Jesus at Bethany for his burial; the women come to the garden forgetting that what they seek to do has already been done;
    (c)   the walking on the water, a quasi-apparition, is echoed in the angel at the tomb.

(Study, 177f)

Farrer ends with some more meditative thoughts on the inexpressibility of the Resurrection, on Mark's wise reticence about depicting 'the living heart of the World to Come', and the essential unfinishedness of the story: as Jesus sends the apostles forth in mission after the 'resurrection' of Jairus' daughter, so Mark prefigures the broadcasting of the Gospel after Jesus is raised; and since that is still going on as Mark writes, it is best for him to end where he does (*Study*, 179–181).

Evaluation

Farrer's 'formal' case for resolution necessarily re-presents material he has already put before us in a slightly different guise, apart from his last schematic refinement, the paracycle. This last need not detain us; it is a further example of the sort of Markan characteristic Farrer has described at such length before, and it prompts the same mixture of recognition and suspicion: recognition indeed of resemblances, some of them quite modest, between one passage and another; suspicion at a scheme whose sometimes painful and tenuous intricacies become oppressive as Farrer lays one on top of the other.

    Farrer is alive here, as ever, to even muted echoes in the text, and he describes very finely the dissatisfaction which the ending of Mark provokes in a modern reader:

> We have discussed the ending of St Mark, not to prove a thesis, but to show what
> sort of argument is appropriate. Such argument belongs plainly to the criticism of
> poetry, that is its *genre*. The further we go into the question, the more clearly we see
> that St Mark's words are shaped by a play of images and allusions of a subtle and
> elusive kind which belongs to imagination rather than to rational construction. It
> may be, after all, that St Mark's ending is not good poetry; that there is a clumsiness
> about it, in spite of all we have said in favour of it. But if it is imperfect, it is still
> poetry, and our dissatisfaction with it (if we still feel dissatisfaction) is a poetical
> discontent. (*Glass*, 145f)[11]

It *is* a poetic discontent we feel, at a story without a proper ending, and
a theological objection to a Christian writer keeping the trump card –
an appearance of the risen Jesus – firmly up the evangelistic sleeve. Of
course, a supposed accident of history like sudden arrest or hungry mice
(Farrer suggests both: *Glass*, 137; *Study*, 173) could remove the problem
by offering the refuge of a lost last page, but Farrer's humour in each case
well expresses the intellectual frivolity of resorting to such an explanation
before all alternatives have been exhausted. Such an alternative must be
found in defending the claim for an ending at 16.8, which can only be
done by what Farrer describes as 'literary arguments' (*Glass*, 138). It
is instructive to compare the words of a much more recent and rather
different critic, Dan O. Via:

> What kind of closure does the resurrection story in 16.1–8 confer on the narrative? In
> what way does it satisfy expectations generated by the text and thereby give the reader
> a sense that the narrative has reached a goal and been completed? (*Ethics*, 50)

Idiom apart, those words might have been written by Farrer nearly forty
years before.

As part of his defence of the ending, Farrer makes a very good case for
the pervasive theme of human perversity, and he identifies an undeniably
fascinating crux in the cluster of motifs around the Arrest, the Burial and
the Ending. Once again, however, we encounter odd bedfellows. Much
earlier in this exercise, we questioned his equation of the disciples crying
out in the storm with the demons crying out at the approach of Jesus, and
we might equally have questioned the plausibility of the healing of 'the
son of the father', the *demon-possessed* boy of 9.17, as a foreshadowing
of the healing – in the Resurrection – of the one already identified as
'Son of the Father' at 1.11 and 9.7 (*Study*, 51). Now we question how
the patriarch Joseph acts simultaneously as the type for such contrasting
characters in Mark as the Arimathean in his request for Jesus' body, the
fleeing young man in his naked flight and the other young man at the
tomb in his glorious apparel (and, by extension, Jesus himself). Even
if the first and third convince, what of the second? When Joseph flees
and loses his clothes it is to *preserve* his honour, while the young man

---

11.   We shall see Frank Kermode take up this theme in relation to 16.8 in 6E below.

(according to Farrer's interpretation) by fleeing *loses* his honour along with his clothes: he becomes a very emblem of the disciples' dereliction of duty (*Glass*, 144). What can Mark gain by using a type in such contrary ways?[12]

It is hard to escape the thought that there is some symbolic significance in the clothing mentioned in these passages, especially in the two double references to σινδών (sindōn), and it is not implausible to say that Mark could not think of Joseph of Arimathea without thinking at once of his older namesake. Can patriarchal and tribal typology ever be far from Mark's mind when he is writing a story in which the *twelve* disciples of Jesus are so prominent? And where in his own Scriptures do twelve tribal personifications appear more vividly than in the Joseph stories? Moreover, there is indeed an echo in the young man's flight from Gethsemane of Joseph's predicament at the mercy of Potiphar's wife – 'And she caught hold of him by his clothes ... and having left his clothes in her hands he fled, and went forth' (Gen 39.12, LXX) – though the reasons for pursuit are predatory in quite different ways, of course. Farrer's case would be stronger, because more consistent, if he did not identify the fleeing νεανίσκος (néaniskos) as a 'negative' figure while seeing the Easter νεανίσκος, as he must be, as unambiguously part of the good news. It is worth asking: if one is a deputy of Jesus, then why not the other? The fleeing youth would then be a 'positive' figure, a prefigurement of the Resurrection: the death-dealing forces try to seize him, but he escapes ἐπὶ γυμνοῦ (epi gumnou), he saves his skin, and leaves them holding the σινδών (sindōn); so, the same forces will be unable to hang on to Jesus, for he will be freed into life, and only the deathly σινδών will remain. The youth in Gethsemane is a hint, when Jesus is apparently at his weakest, that the might arrayed against him is nonetheless doomed. What this interpretation really needs is a mention of the σινδών left in the tomb, rather in the manner of the Fourth Gospel's description, and it suffers from the inconvenient observation that the young man at 14.51 'followed' Jesus. Some such approach will, however, save Farrer's Joseph typology from schizoid characterisation.[13]

Farrer is on considerably weaker ground with his discussion of the final γάρ. The 'glance' at the Septuagint he recommends only confirms the inexactness of the verbal parallel he seeks to draw, and his more modest – almost coy – call in the *Study* to let the parallel 'speak for itself' is significant. We might have the impression in the *Glass* of Farrer's enthusiasm with the motific resemblances leading him to present to his

---

12.   Helen Gardner will make a similar critique. See 6A (pp. 62–72) below.
13.   R. Scroggs and K.I. Groff, 'Baptism', offer another 'positive' exegesis, seeing the stripped young man in the garden and the gloriously apparelled one at the tomb as baptismal motifs.

reader what will at a brief glimpse appear to be a clinching observation, only to hurry that reader on before the awkwardness emerges. We shall see presently how Farrer catches more than one reader of his exegesis.[14]

Overall, Farrer's interpretative rhetoric is most persuasive, but if uncertainty remains about whether Mark intended 16.8 to contain the Gospel's last words, it is because of the fear of anachronism. We can see a modern novelist ending a book with hanging, implicit, teasing words,[15] but what evidence is there that such potent ambiguity would be conceivable in the conclusion of a first-century writing? That, however, is as much a question of 'history' as of 'literature'.

I. The Remaining Chapters of A Study in St Mark

Subsequent chapters treat of the 'historical sense' of Mark (Chapter VIII) and certain limited topics, notably 'secrecy' (Chapter X), the apostles (XIII), bread-symbolism and tribal symbolism (XIV and XV). Aspects of these chapters will surface as we look at other critics of Mark in its literary and historical aspects. For now, we have seen enough of Farrer's thesis to come to some conclusions about it, the methods he employs to establish it, and some of its wider implications for interpretation of Mark's Gospel.

14. See references to Helen Gardner and Hans Hauge in 6A (p. 65, note 2) below.
15. See, for instance, John Fowles' *The Magus*, which ends in just such a way: 'She is silent, she will never speak ... All waits, suspended' (London: Triad/Panther, 1978, 656).

Chapter 5

GENERAL CONCLUSIONS ON FARRER'S THESIS AND METHOD IN *A STUDY IN ST MARK*

> There is no impression I should be so sorry to convey as that St Mark's Gospel is a sort of learned acrostic.
>
> *A Study in St Mark*, 79

In his 'Rabbis, Evangelists – and Jesus', Anthony Harvey's difficulties with the elaborate literary schemes advanced by Farrer and his disciple Michael Goulder in their study of the New Testament can be reduced to one question. 'How', he says, 'can we ever know they are right?' ('Rabbis', 246).[1] While Harvey applies this verifiability test, Goulder himself favours the *falsifiability* test, and so would probably prefer Harvey to ask: 'How can we ever know they are wrong?' In one of his later assaults on the Q hypothesis and related matters ('A House Built on Sand'), Goulder compares biblical study with the natural sciences: in those fields, hypotheses are considered to be valuable

> in proportion to the ease with which they can be refuted or falsified. Thus 'all swans are white' can be refuted by the discovery of a single black swan. A hypothesis which is vague, or elastic, or which claims to account for everything that can happen … is unscientific because we cannot refute it; it is not useful because it does not exclude anything. Useful hypotheses will be clear and specific. ('House', 1f)[2]

He goes on to attack (among others) M.E. Boismard, whose defence of Q invokes seven lost sources. We cannot miss the point: with a theory which is so elastic and luxuriant you can prove anything, for your theory offers no grounds on which it might be falsified. How, then, does *A Study in St Mark* fare under the falsifiability test?

Farrer begins with a 'clear and specific' idea of the ordering principle of the Gospel: it is that of repeating cycles, based on blocks of healings, exhibiting a dual emphasis of calling and healing. What follows, however, shows that nearly a third of the cycles do not conform to this principle.

1. See 6B (pp. 73f) below.
2. Farrer uses the 'black swan' image too (*Love*, 148).

Yet he urges us not to be dismayed: in the absence of a healing story, a summary of healings and a nature miracle (cycle 2b), or the Resurrection (the one 'healing' which is not described, cycle 5b), will do just as well. He tells us that the calling of apostles is a cardinal theme of the cycles, declares it to be exhausted by cycle 2a, but then allows it to appear again in 4a. He tell us that number-symbolism is a key to many conundrums in Mark, but can then find ample significance in the numbers three, three-and-a-half, four, seven, eight, twelve, thirteen and fourteen.[3] Where he finds one paragraph too many, Farrer can say that it is added 'for good measure', and where material is not entirely neat, that Mark happily leaves it to 'shift for itself' (*Study*, 70, 146). When one of Farrer's rules of composition is overturned he can say that a rule is only in force until something else supersedes it.[4] Faced with his endlessly supple theories, where would we have any hope of finding in the *Study* one of Farrer's 'black swans'?

Farrer, like his protégé Goulder, was a doughty opponent of Q. In what is his best-known piece of biblical scholarship, 'On Dispensing with Q', Farrer attacks the attempts to solve the Synoptic Problem with lost-source hypotheses, and does so on much the same lines as those Goulder will follow. He argues that they trespass against the principle of economy, inventing what they do not have while ignoring what they do have, the extant texts of the three Gospels themselves ('Dispensing', esp. 87f). Now it is with a similar sense of trespass that we watch Farrer on Mark, trying to account for everything which one of those texts presents. Each time the material proves recalcitrant, Farrer can rummage and find an explanation, a case for an exception. What he offers is often no less plausible in itself than anything that has gone before, but once added to all the other exceptional cases, it also adds to the impression that what Farrer is giving us is, despite himself, less an interpretative tool than an

---

3.   Examples are:

Three: groups of three people point to resurrection on the third day (*Study*, 146f).
Three-and- a-half: the halving of the apocalyptic week of oppression and the number of days in Mark's passion narrative (*Study*, 139).
Four: the fourth person healed is carried by four friends (*Study*, 146). Farrer offers no extrinsic symbolism for this number (Irenaeus has not yet pronounced on four Gospels for the Four Winds!).
Seven: a Jewish golden number, and length of a week (*Study*, 144f).
Eight: the eighth day is the day of the Resurrection, and first of a new week (*Study*, 145).
Twelve: the number of the tribes and of the apostles (*Study*, 144, 317–347).
Thirteen: Christ heals thirteen persons in Mark, the tribes add up to thirteen if Levi is counted seperately (*Study*, 305–308).
Fourteen: twice seven; Christ is the fourteenth person 'healed' (*Study*, 144).

4.   As when Bartimaeus' public confession before Jesus' public teaching in Jerusalem overturns the principle of 'private before public' (*Study*, 122).

administrative one, a way not so much of discerning how things are as they are (and even possibly why they are as they are) in the Gospel of Mark, but of organising what is there to his own mental satisfaction.

If his scheme fails to convince, it is not on the formal ground that it is false (how can we prove that Mark did *not*, more or less consciously, set himself rules and then, more or less severely, bend them?), but rather on aesthetic grounds. Something which at first appeared elegant becomes progressively more hedged and cumbersome and even oppressive in its elaboration, so that we are finally reluctant to think of an author's mind *wanting* to work to such a scheme, or naturally producing such a pattern. Even if we shun all talk of intentionality, any aesthetic unease we may feel at Mark's jagged ending (the 'poetical discontent' described in the *Glass*) is matched by our unease at the end of the *Study* when Farrer has tried so hard to show the 'shapeliness' of the Gospel, and the Gospel has failed to co-operate. He does not demonstrate that 'felt inevitability' which is the core of his case in the *Glass* for the poetic character of inspiration (*Glass*, 129, 146; *Study*, 30).[5]

In reading Farrer we may feel we detect some hint of anxiety on his part at the obscurity of it all, as when he says that 'we fear that we shall not be believed' (*Study*, 100). Farrer's remedy is sometimes to talk of Mark's mind as 'inspired', and sometimes to suggest that he is laying out patterns of which the author can barely have been aware. Notice how Farrer's claims to intimacy with the Markan mind fluctuate through the book:

I have found in St Mark's Gospel a pattern of which St Mark was in some measure conscious ...

[We seek to] become, as far as that is possible, St Mark in the act of gospel-writing ...

Some system or other expresses the direction of his conscious intention, other systems spontaneously arise in the working out of his plan; the shapely mind of itself produces shapely works. (*Study*, v, 9, 30)

The workings of the inspired mind are endlessly complex ... Naturally we are not pretending to describe what St Mark saw himself doing ... We are not psychologising St Mark, we are describing the phenomena in the text. (*Study*, 100f)

We have examined the cyclical rhythm ... not so much to prove a thesis, as to enter (if we can) into the movement of the evangelist's mind. If we have in any degree thought his thoughts after him, then our trouble has not been in vain. (*Study*, 142)

These facts do not show, of course, that St Mark thought out an elaborate scheme of cycles and paracycles, but simply that the rhythm in which he moved was doubling itself in the last part of his Gospel. (*Study*, 177)

5.   Cf James D. Watson's account of the discovery of the structure of DNA: 'The structure was too pretty not to be true' (*The Double Helix*; London: Weidenfeld & Nicholson, 1968, 124). We do naturally suspend disbelief before claims that reality is beautiful.

Pejorative as 'psychologising' sounds, what does it mean if not trying to think another person's thoughts?

Farrer attempts to produce an exhaustive account of the patterning of the text (and what is that if not trying 'to prove a thesis'?), only to have his model shuffle and stumble as it tries to dance to the tune of the material it seeks to interpret. We have registered similar unease with the ramifications of some of Farrer's typological exegesis, as with the confusing use to which Mark seems to put the Joseph stories. The sense of contrivance grows when we see Farrer setting himself some further, rather churchly, requirements, as when he is determined to see the proper progression for the admission of Gentiles from exclusion through Baptism to Eucharist, almost as though the Gospel were a confirmation course (*Study*, 298). At the same time, Farrer's thoroughgoing interpretation is ill-equipped to discern what seems to be so obvious a feature as the dramatic effect created by the delay of Jesus' arrival at Jairus' house.[6] This raises questions about the genre of Mark's Gospel, and whether Farrer's decision to treat it as a species of poetry (rather than as, say, a kind of novel) is sound. We return to this in Part III.

On the other hand, who can deny that there is some link to be made between twelve disciples and twelve tribes, or that there must be some principle of selection underlying the number of healings narrated in Mark? And have we not noted a number of points of penetrating insight, like the connections Farrer makes between the parable of the sower and the feeding of the multitude, and between the Transfiguration and the sons of Zebedee? If for a moment we can anticipate our discussion of subsequent developments in literary theory, we can make much of Farrer's work, provided that we are content to note his insight into various small narratives in Mark while acknowledging that there is a wider indeterminacy. We may also pick up the multiple echoes, both within the text and between this text and other texts, to which Farrer alerts us, while yet protesting to him that they often baffle and often contradict one another. It is in Farrer's attempt to give an overarching account of meaning and significance that we lose him. We are describing here a limited case of the suspicion of 'metanarratives', and pointing to what is, in a gentle form, a deconstructive appropriation of the text of Mark, noting how it builds and then undermines both rhyme and reason.[7] In the *Glass*, Farrer himself is at one point open to such a possibility. He argues that we must approach Mark's ending in a poetic frame of mind, even though it may turn out to be 'imperfect poetry'; we take him to mean here that the Gospel may in the end fail to attain complete resolution,

6.   For even more elaboration on the Jairus/haemorrhage passage, see his kaleidoscopic Chapter XV, 'Tribal Symbolism' (*Study*, 317–347, esp. 328). See also 7F (p. 98) below.

7.   Francis Watson describes metanarratives as '[t]heories offering a comprehensive account of significant reality' (*Open*, 3); see further Jean-François Lyotard, *Postmodern*. On deconstructive readings, see 12D (p. 158, note 17) below.

and so still leave us with the indeterminate and the discordant. By the time of *A Study in St Mark*, however, such caution has gone. Mark is now 'an inspired masterpiece', and the imperfection belongs only to the interpreter (*Study*, 3).

Any strictures of ours should not obscure the achievement of Austin Farrer in presenting, as early as 1951, a picture of a Gospel as a literary organism. The case for the presence of patterning withstands his faltering exposition of it, and he finds many points at which the literary-critical shoe will later pinch the feet of Gospel critics. We remember that in 1963 Dennis Nineham was happy to say of Mark's Gospel that 'it consists of a number of unrelated paragraphs set down one after another with very little organic connexion, almost like a series of snapshots in a photograph album' (Commentary, 27). He did not see fit to alter those words in a revised edition as late as 1969. In that light, *A Study in St Mark* emerges with flaws, implausibilities, but also far-sightedness, not least in its very well-aimed critique of form criticism.

Two instances of Farrer's topicality may be emphasised at this point. First is his openness about his motives in studying Mark. Spurning the studied mask of scholarly disinterest, he confesses to being a Christian, and once we know this, we can more easily allow for it in evaluating him. This is in contrast to most biblical scholars, and also to a secular critic we shall consider below: Frank Kermode's *The Genesis of Secrecy* remarks on Farrer's piety but says little of Kermode's own presuppositions.[8] It is not only believers who bring *a priori* beliefs to their reading of a text, for there is no such thing as motiveless interpretation, so *why* do scholars think it worthwhile to study such texts, reasons of salary apart?[9] Secondly, Farrer is (by today's standards) disarmingly frank about the status of his enquiry, which is grounded in his belief in the text as the product of an authorial mind. We do have here a criterion of falsification, even if it is a very hard one to apply in practice, for another intentionalist reader of Mark might conclude that what Farrer sees in the text of Mark cannot be plausibly derived, even in a semi-conscious way, from the mind of a first-century writer (we leave out of account Farrer's inspirational Spirit, for here Farrer does over-insulate himself). Once again he puts his presuppositional cards on the table, to the great advantage of his readers. This places an onus upon readers of Farrer to establish the status of their own observations about Mark and about him. So when I have described Farrer's interpretation as a 'success', as 'penetrating', or as containing

8.   See Kermode, *Genesis*, 72, and 6E (pp. 76–81) below.
9.   Stephen Moore's *Challenge* is also vulnerable here. He is justly taxing on other scholars about their presuppositions, but less willing to submit his own position to 'theoeconomic analysis' (*Challenge*, 38), beyond the question of investment in certain *methods*. This leaves unanswered the question of what his goals are. For the need to declare aims and interests, see further Morgan and Barton, *Biblical*, 5–16, 204f; Brett, 'Things', 357f; and Fowl, 'Ethics', 379–381.

'insight', what do I believe Farrer's success to be? What is he penetrating or seeing into? Is it the mind of the author of Mark? Or that of a member of Mark's original audience? Or do I mean that Farrer is discerning some transcendent 'meaning' which is independent of any mind, unless it be the mind of God? Or am I simply saying that I, perhaps because of *my* Christian motives in reading Mark, simply like what Farrer says about him? These are questions which will repeatedly return during the rest of this enquiry.[10]

Postscript:
Second Thoughts – St Matthew and St Mark

Our life is a continual repentance.

Matthew, 1

A Study in St Mark did not receive wide acclaim. One reviewer, Vernon McCasland, dismissed Farrer as an allegory-obsessed, latter-day Alexandrian, 'an Origen *redivivus*' (Review, 201f). Four years after the *Study*, Farrer reviewed himself:

> The author of this book (I should say) began from a correct assumption – that St Mark was an able thinker who worked out a plan in composing his Gospel. We may also reckon it to the author's credit, that he made a number of separate observations on pieces of Mark's design which deserve attention. But he failed to bring the pieces together into a convincing unity. His picture of the evangelist shows us a writer keeping several different symbolisms going at once, like a juggler keeping six balls in the air together. We cannot help feeling that it is not the Evangelist who juggles but the interpreter who suffers from divided vision; he sees as six balls what is really only one ball in different positions and catching the light from different sides. When he begins to feel qualms about the psychological credibility of what he describes, the author takes refuge in mystery, invoking the intrinsic fertility and complexity of imaginative inspiration. We are willing too to agree that this consideration has been in general too little applied by modern interpreters of the Gospels, but we are unwilling to accept it as an entire substitute for common sense. The author's fault is not that he has enquired too curiously into the inner workings of the Evangelist's mind, but that he has not enquired curiously enough; or that his curiosity has been sustained by too little patience. He who has come only so far as to see the complexity and variety of imaginative thought has not arrived at an understanding of the thinker. It is necessary to persevere until complexity settles and clarifies into unity. (*Matthew*, 2f)

Farrer's *St Matthew and St Mark*, from which these words come, re-examines in much smaller compass the literary patterns of Mark, making several retractions and revisions. He proceeds, however, from the same premises about Mark which informed his earlier study: that the healing miracles determine the structure, which is built round 'a skeleton

---

10. For instance, when Kermode says of Farrer's exegesis of Jesus' arrest: 'This seems to me a fine interpretation' (*Genesis*, 62). See 6E (pp. 76–81) below.

of numerical symbolism' (*Matthew*, vi); that there are strong cyclical characteristics which show passages being modelled on their predecessors (*Matthew*, 203f); that the author's scheme is evolutionary and not entirely pre-conceived (*Matthew*, 27); and that author and audience have a ready facility with number and its symbolic possibilities; the adage that, if lost, you 'stop and count' still holds for him (*Matthew*, 19).

Most noticeable in the new scheme is the abolition of blocks and annexes in favour of a simpler scheme of two series of five healings, plus two (*Matthew*, 32). The total number, twelve, has typological importance, while the distribution is natural for the ancients, whose numerals precluded counting except on hands or abacus, and so rendered everything in tens plus any remainder (*Matthew*, 21, 32). Farrer speaks, therefore, of 'handsful' of healings (e.g. *Matthew*, 33). There is an extra, thirteenth, healing, which is of a Gentile and is fittingly an interloper among the Jewish twelve (*Matthew*, 34f). He divides the Markan healings thus (*Matthew*, 19–35, especially page 23):

1.21–28 demoniac	1.29–31 mother-in-law with fever	1.40–45 leper	2.1–12 paralytic	3.1–6 withered hand	= 5
5.1–20 Legion	5.21 – (25–34) – 43 [▲] Jairus' daughter (Haemorrhage)	daughter 7.24-30 Possessed Gentile child	7.31–37 deaf mute	8.22–26 blind	= 5
			9.14–29 deaf, mute possessed child	10.46–52 blind	= 2
				Total	12

Figure 5.1: Mark's Handsful

To balance these there are twelve callings – or better, the callings of the Twelve, for they are not narrated individually – and Levi's is a thirteenth to correspond to the Gentile healing. He is not a Gentile, but as a tax-collector he is the next worst thing, a renegade Jew (*Matthew*, 35–37).

Farrer claims to have found greater overall simplicity in the Markan pattern; he is certainly more sparing in making his case, but the five double cycles of the *Study* have now spawned five *triple* cycles (*Matthew*, 201–207):

1: (includes first 5 healings)	1.16–34	1.35–2.12	2.13–3.12
2: (includes second 5 healings)	3.13–6.6	6.7–7.37	8.1–26
3: (includes the 'two healings over')	8.27–9.29	9.30–10.31	10.32–52
4: (the Jerusalem ministry)	10.1–19	10.20–13.2	13.3–14.11
5: (the passion)	14.12–31	14.32–15.21	15.22–16.8

Farrer sees further, complex subdivisions in Cycle 5, and concedes that this weakens the case for it to be a triple cycle (*Matthew*, 221).

Figure 5.2: Triple Cycles

There are many revisions of detail in *St Matthew and St Mark*, of which the most significant is perhaps that Farrer now allows the possibility of a lost final sentence for Mark 16, detached to make way for the spurious endings and so lost (*Matthew*, 144–149). This later book, despite the meticulous self-criticism and its recognition of the dangers of using inspired mystery to justify forced exegesis, does not represent a recantation on any significant questions of method. For those unhappy with the *Study* it must have appeared that, in *Matthew*, the contrivances of the earlier book had been changed, not taken away, and it is not surprising that Farrer's critics largely ignore it.

Chapter 6

Austin Farrer and His Critics

I have published some wild expositions of scripture.
Letter to Martyn Skinner (*A Hawk Among Sparrows*, 146)

This chapter will begin by considering a number of scholars who trained their guns on Farrer – one of them, Helen Gardner, delivering a broadside, the rest largely firing passing shots – as well as one or two who were more appreciative, in the years after the publication of his two books on Mark's Gospel. It will then proceed to discuss the treatment of Farrer by the secular literary critic Frank Kermode, who considers Farrer's work approvingly as part of a wider enquiry into the interpretation of narrative. This will form a bridge to Chapter 7, in which we shall begin to conduct as it were a conversation with Farrer and two more recent exponents of literary approaches to Mark. In this present chapter, we shall describe and evaluate criticisms of Farrer's work, and then note any points which throw up questions of wider and enduring concern for literary approaches to the Gospels.

A. Helen Gardner

In 1956 Austin Farrer's presentation of Mark received a sustained attack from a distinguished literary critic. Helen (later Dame Helen) Gardner delivered the Riddell Memorial Lectures of that year under the title 'The Limits of Literary Criticism'; these were later published, with other pieces, as part of *The Business of Criticism*. The second of these lectures, 'The Poetry of St Mark', is a critique of Farrer, with reference predominantly to the *Glass*. Gardner finds the parentage of his approach in the Fathers.

'St Mark's words', comments Dr. Farrer, 'are shaped by a play of images and allusions of the subtle and elusive kind which belong to imagination rather than to rational construction.' It will be noted where the images come from. The Christian Fathers were concerned to defend the ancient Scriptures as the revelation of the one God and Father of the Lord Jesus against Marcion and the Gnostics. For this reason they looked everywhere in the Old Testament for types and figures of the New, to bind together the two Covenants. Today the process is in a sense inverted, in that it is the New Testament which is being interpreted through the Old. A literary criticism which sees narratives as organisations of symbolic images sees everywhere in the New Testament the images of the Scriptures on which the writers' imaginations had been nourished from childhood. How else should these writers express their belief that the God of Israel had indeed visited and redeemed his people except through images coloured by the memory of the images of his great deliverances of old? ('Poetry', 112)

Her concern, then, is more with the extrinsic, typological aspect of Farrer's analysis than with what he says about the innate rhythms of the text. Farrer, she says, sees the Gospel as 'a great effort of symbolisation', in which patterns of lesser images finally cohere in a total structure of meaning, all of which is embodied in material containing typological allusion to the Old Testament and hidden senses; Farrer, she says, would have us see the finding of 'esoteric meanings' and of pervasive traffic from the Old Testament, not as an aberration of the Alexandrian Fathers but as part of the air breathed in the world which produced the New Testament ('Poetry', 112–114). Gardner is familiar with all three of the essays on Markan interpretation Farrer had produced by then, the relevant parts of the *Glass*, the *Study* and *Matthew*. She notes the 'considerable modifications' in the last work but shows no sign of being moved by them, no doubt because they mainly concern the internal scheme of the Gospel rather than typology, and because they bring no great repentance on questions of method. Her opposition to Farrer can be resolved into four areas: the status of the Gospel as a historical narrative, the alleged presence of typology, the accessibility of meaning in the text, and the ethics of his analysis ('Poetry', 121). The first and last aspects are more the concern of other parts of this enquiry; the remainder we examine here.

Gardner is generally unhappy with the extent to which Farrer is wedded to typology, and she challenges the assumption that Mark could only have thought in an allegorical way (of which she sees typology as a sub-species). We have clear evidence, she says, of allegorical thinking in other parts of the New Testament, and the writers signal unambiguously that this is what they are doing, as Paul does with the two sons of Abraham (Gal. 4.22–24). How likely is it, then, that the author of Mark would engage in so much symbolism yet leave it all implicit? How likely that the allusions would be so clear to his readers that Matthew, for instance, would not need to clarify elaborate number symbolism? How likely, on the other hand, that Mark's symbolism defeated all readers (Matthew included) until the twentieth century and Austin Farrer ('Poetry', 119f)? Like Farrer, Gardner speaks of the 'mind' of the author of Mark as an

organ in principle accessible to the modern critic, although by 1956 there
were voices questioning this (Wimsatt and Beardsley published their
influential article 'The Intentional Fallacy' in 1946). Gardner herself
alludes to what she believes to be the 'reckless' position of those whom
she takes to assert:

> The meaning is there because I have demonstrated its presence. Whether the author
> intended or not is something we can never know. He is not here to be cross-examined,
> and if he were he might well refuse to add to what he has written. ('Poetry', 113)

To this extent, however, she approves of Farrer's enquiry:

> A conception of how St Mark, a Greek-speaking Jew of the first century, would have
> thought is present, as well as a conception of how the human mind operates. The
> object of the enquiry is how St Mark thinks. We are to arrive at a meaning which he
> would have recognized as what he meant. ('Poetry', 113)

Despite Gardner's caution, she and Farrer stand together in seeking the
goal, 'much scoffed at', of the writer's intention ('Poetry', 120). Her
disagreement with Farrer is over what sort of a mind it is that produces
the intention. As we listen to Farrer and his antagonist, let us assume for
now that enquiries about the authorial mind are admissible. Questions
about the viability of authorial intention as a goal of interpretation will
arise naturally out of what they each say.

A particular focus of Gardner's argument over typology concerns
Farrer's treatment of the ending of Mark, specifically his claims about
Mark's use of the Joseph stories. If, she says, in the 'rag-bag of memories'
in Mark's mind, certain ideas about Joseph of Arimathea, Joseph the
patriarch, the traditions about Jesus and vaguely similar episodes in
the Joseph stories got 'hooked together', then Farrer's contention is fair
though uninteresting; if, however, he suggests that Mark consciously
models his narrative on the Joseph stories, Farrer becomes incredible
('Poetry', 120f). Gardner surveys Farrer's three Joseph parallels: Joseph
fleeing Potiphar's wife (cf the young man fleeing in Gethsemane), Joseph
asking leave of Pharaoh to bury his father (cf Joseph of Arimathea)
and Joseph appearing to his brothers (cf the women at the tomb). Why,
she asks, if Mark is consciously modelling his narrative on Genesis, is
he happy to present them in what is (for Genesis) the wrong narrative
order? And can he be content that the motives for flight are quite
different: Joseph runs to save his honour, while the young man (according
to Farrer's interpretation) by running loses his? 'Conscious literary
influence', she says, 'does not work like this' ('Poetry', 121).[1]

The verbal leg to Farrer's Joseph theory does not convince Gardner
either, though here she concedes too much, taking at face value Farrer's
misleading words that 'a glance at the Greek Old Testament will show

---

1.   See 4H (pp. 47–53) above.

the exactness of the verbal parallel' between Mark 16.8 (ἐφοβοῦντο γάρ (ephobounto gar)) and Genesis 45.3 in the Septuagint ἐταράχθησαν γάρ (etarachthēsan gar), 'Poetry', 111 cf *Glass*, 145).[2] She allows that an unconscious reminiscence of Mark's about the brothers' amazement at recognising Joseph could have 'dictated the actual words he used to describe the amazement of the women'; but this, she says, is 'purely verbal' ('Poetry', 120f). Gardner notes the distinction, which she feels she may be accused of blurring, between authorial intention and the way 'his mind works', but she suspects that in a study like Farrer's both are being sought at once; and the latter, if it can only be looked for in the finished work and not in a writer's working papers, is a real 'will-o'-the-wisp' ('Poetry', 120).

Her attempted rebuttal of Farrer in his own terms is in support of her general unhappiness with his whole project. What she seeks and cannot find in Farrer is an awareness of that sense of 'happening', of 'actuality', in Mark's narrative which is so evident to other readers of the Gospel; what she does find (and worries over) is the too-ready assumption about the 'ways of thought' of Mark's world ('Poetry', 118). In the first case, she feels that exegesis like Farrer's

> leaves an impression of intellectual frivolity, as if the critic were concerned with anything and everything except what mattered to the writer and what mattered to his readers ... I am quite certain that I have been in contact with the mind and imagination of Dr Farrer ... I have very little sense, after reading him, of having come nearer to the mind and imagination of St Mark. ('Poetry', 121)

In the second case, she finds Farrer's work to be typical of an approach to literature which is 'often oblivious of, and impatient with, the historical' ('Poetry', 123): 'Whoever wrote the Gospel of St Mark was a man, not a disembodied imagination. He was writing a work in which his readers would find things able to make them "wise unto salvation"' ('Poetry', 123).

Farrer, she admits, sees Mark as being 'controlled' by the facts (*Study*, 8); but what if we believe that what Mark writes 'are facts'? Will not Mark's imagination be full of those facts and the wonder of them? Will he then be 'merely respectful' of them and meanwhile go about the business of obscure allusion ('Poetry', 123)? Gardner concedes that Farrer himself relegates much of his interpretation to the second division of importance, and distinguishes between things like Joseph typology and Markan fundamentals, the 'great images', such as 'the figure of the Son of Man ... the ceremony of the sacramental body ... the bloody sacrifice of the Lamb ... the enthronement of the Lord's Anointed' (*Glass*, 146).

2.   See 4H (pp. 49, 52f) above. Hans Hauge, a Gardner enthusiast who endorses her misgivings about Farrer, makes the same error, compounding it by apparently thinking that both women and brothers actually speak, the former quoting the latters' words ('Sin', 116).

Gardner quotes this passage, but is unimpressed: 'the central image of a human life and death seems to have disappeared' ('Poetry', 123).

Evaluation

Austin Farrer mounted his own defence against Helen Gardner in his paper of 1959, 'On Looking below the Surface'. Some aspects of this paper we consider here. As we have noted, some of what Gardner says concerns Mark in its historical aspects, but these thoughts of hers are not entirely detachable from our present concern with 'Mark as literature', and it will be one contention of the whole of this enquiry that the historical and literary aspects of a text are finally inseparable. There will therefore be some 'historical' discussion in the next few paragraphs. We should note at once an unclarity in Gardner's remarks. Is this sense of 'happening' she finds in Mark a sense of 'Goodness, it's so true to life' which might come across from a vividly written novel, or is it a sense of the text actually referring to real events? (These are crude, even naïve terms, but they make the distinction.) Her elliptical mention of 'the facts' suggests the latter, as does a passage in the closing words of her lecture, in which she offers 'a prime historic fact ... that for centuries Christian emotion directed towards the historic person of Jesus Christ ... has found in the Gospels the strength of its own conviction that "Christ walked on this earth"' ('Poetry', 126). She also says, however, that '[t]he same sense of historical reality ... inheres in works of art' ('Poetry', 124), and although she does not say what she has in mind, it does not sound like works of historiography. All that Mark need do to satisfy Gardner's stated requirement, then, is to produce a history-like narrative, which might nevertheless be pure fiction.[3] Nowhere does Gardner offer any criteria for historicity which Farrer's exegesis might be seen to flout, and Farrer is quite fair in suspecting her of a pre-critical yen for the days before the form criticism of 'Schmidt and Dibelius': it is precisely the same difficulty, that of giving a 'plain biographical answer' to explain the arrangement of Mark's material, that leads Dibelius in one direction and Farrer in quite another ('Surface', 58).[4] The question of fictive but

3.   In her Norton Lectures of 1978–1979, Gardner alludes to this earlier piece when she speaks of her old complaint that typological analysis lessened 'the force and actuality' of the Gospels (cf 'Poetry', 118): by this she meant not that it diminished their 'historicity' but that it 'ignored their presentation of a world that reflects the world of human experience' (*Defence*, 133). See 6E (p. 81, note 35) below and her criticisms of Kermode.

4.   Farrer must have in mind here K.L. Schmidt, 'Die Stellung', 1923, and M. Dibelius, *From Tradition to Gospel*, 1934. Jasper sees Gardner as separating poetry and theology, 'maintaining an absolute distinction between the historical Jesus and our own time'. Farrer, he says, 'sustains a delicate polarity between the two' (though he would prefer 'Scripture' to 'theology') and Jasper sees him here in 'the readerly tradition of Coleridge' ('Literary', 25). For Jasper's fuller treatment of the Farrer-Gardner debate, see *Coleridge*, 145–153.

history-like narrative is very much a part of Kermode's work, which we shall consider in Part III.[5]

What Gardner does offer, however, is an aesthetic criterion, and she judges that Farrer's riddling symbolism misses the point, the matter of Mark's narrative. Here she is more persuasive. It is indeed with a sense of anticlimax that we read Farrer's words in the *Glass* about the 'great images' in Mark – *is* the 'substance of the truth' to be found in the 'bloody sacrifice of the Lamb', or in the agony of Jesus to which such images point? (*Glass*, 146) – and as we listen for some hint of the raw power of the story of the Gospel among the intricate observations of the *Study*. So what sort of a writing does Farrer think Mark's Gospel is? What is his Mark trying to do? These are questions of *genre*, and they will occupy much of our time in later parts of this enquiry.

Gardner is again puzzling in her remarks about what texts mean. She chides Farrer for obscurity, and for one who has ploughed through the *Study* it is not hard to be in sympathy with her. Her antidote seems to be to be to reverse the practice of 'finding significance in what the work suggests rather than in what it says' ('Poetry', 126): that is, to attend to what we might call the 'plain meaning' of the text, though she does not use the phrase herself. What are we to make, then, a few sentences later, of this?

> I am not happy with the assumption that there is a royal road by which we can get at 'meaning', and I am particularly suspicious when the critic buttresses his claim that he has found the 'meaning' with the statement that this was the meaning the work must have had for men of its own age, since we know how men of this age thought. ('Poetry', 126)

This sounds like a contemporary argument for a view of texts as incurably open and plurivocal, a position if anything more congenial to Farrer's stance than to Gardner's. And what has she done in her attack on Farrer's typological approach (in which she objects that, for New Testament writers, this is always a limited and explicit strategy) but to say that *she* knows that people of Mark's day thought in a way somewhat different from that advanced by Farrer? Moreover, when she pleads that we hang on to the picture of a writer as 'a man speaking to men', that sounds like a very good description – for what could be more direct? – of the sort of 'royal road' to meaning she then decries ('Poetry', 125f).

If we consider Gardner's specific criticisms, it does seem from the psychological confusion of the Joseph parallels that one can only make a case either for saying that Mark is largely unaware of what is happening (as she suspects), or for saying that Mark is doing something less sophisticated than Farrer suggests. Her point about the simultaneous chasing of two hares, the author's barely conscious mental processes and

5.   See 13C (pp. 177–180) below.

the author's conscious intentions, is astute ('Poetry', 120). In the *Study*, Farrer wriggles at times over how far he wants to see Mark as deliberately drawing all these parallels, though he seems to claim conscious literary modelling whenever he can, retreating to semi-conscious processes only when he feels his case to be weaker.[6] In the case of Mark's ending, to be persuasive Farrer needs to show more elegance, more precision and economy than Mark's text (with if anything a derangement of the Joseph plot, and a synonym where we look for the same word) is able to yield. He urges above all that we must see Mark as an author and not a compiler. But if this is so, should we not then see Mark writing a narrative which shows just these characteristics?

It is nevertheless hard to deny that Farrer is on to something. As we have already said, if we can say anything about the author, can we not say that patriarchal and tribal typology would never be far from Mark's mind when writing a story in which the twelve disciples of Jesus are so prominent? And where in the Jewish Scriptures do twelve tribal personifications appear more vividly than in the Joseph stories? Farrer's position in this and other cases of alleged typology becomes more plausible as he moves away from a strong interpretation of 'conscious literary modelling', and we need not fully agree with Gardner that the unearthing of mental patterns from a finished text is 'like weaving ropes of sand', or that the admittedly conjectural conclusions will be of no real concern ('Poetry', 120).

We could make a case on Farrer's behalf in this way. Let us picture the author of Mark as a person whose mind is soaked in the Septuagint, perhaps some of the Jewish Pseudepigrapha, and the rhetorical conventions of the day. Such a person needs to write a text which would be persuasive to similar minds when read (or heard aloud), and will surely do it by the deployment of familiar 'landmarks', words, symbols, phrases. It would be hard for such an author not to write in a way that constantly showed verbal reminiscence of the Septuagint, and natural for such an author to move in a mental world of type and antitype. Is that not, after all, how human minds work, by repeatedly saying, 'Everything is like something: what is this like?' In his rebuttal of Gardner, Farrer himself says as much: 'we go on cheerfully treating everything in heaven and on earth as a parable of everything else' ('Surface', 55). In such a case as Mark's, the resemblances between the story of Jesus and the Joseph narratives will naturally lead the writer to portray the one – with a word here, a point of description there – in the familiar terms of the other. That portrayal will emerge from Mark's mental 'compost', or as Gardner puts it, 'the way his mind works' ('Poetry', 120). Mark might

---

6.   See p. 56 above, and Farrer's programmatic statement that he has found a scheme in the Gospel of which Mark is 'in some measure conscious' (*Study*, v). For the weaker claim see e.g. *Study*, 100f.

well be conscious of it, but that consciousness will often not reach the point of diligent intention. Indeed, even if his level of consciousness is sometimes higher, such a crude constraint as the difficulty of looking things up in scriptural books written on unwieldy scrolls (let us assume he has free access to them) may limit the possibilities of precision. The result will be a text showing the profusion of correspondences Farrer detects but also the incoherences which Gardner throws back at him. We can make an anachronistic but useful comparison with the hymnody of Charles Wesley, a sure case of a Christian poetical mind soaked in the Scriptures (as well as in the Book of Common Prayer). In Wesley's hymns there are dense packs of allusion to every part of these writings; phrase, word and image crowd together, but there is often a lack of literary or temporal sequence, and the threads of allusion will become tangled if you try to follow them back. When, however, Wesley uses a biblical passage as a literary model (as in his hymn 'Wrestling Jacob')[7] the lines of connection are very clear and the sequence of the original preserved.

All this is highly speculative, and we must take to heart Gardner's warnings about trying to discover such things without access to drafts and working papers (her 'ropes of sand' description resembles Farrer's verdict on form criticism!). Nevertheless, some speculation about Mark's mental stock-in-trade is permissible, since no-one can write extended narrative *de novo* and be intelligible. Gardner is right to find Farrer neglectful of history, of reducing Mark to a 'disembodied imagination', of speaking too easily of how a first-century mind would have thought, and using this as a charter to prospect for hidden meanings ('Poetry', 122): he does little to delineate an original setting, beyond the calling-up of the image of a 'Bible-reading Jew' (*Study*, 46). Gardner herself, however, does not offer even this much to support her alternative. It seems that historical rigour is only necessary for the breakers of consensus.

Here we see how the argument over meaning and intention very quickly develops a strongly historical character, as the original setting of writer and audience becomes the arbiter. We shall return to this in Part III.[8] On the specific question of the allegorical mentality in the New Testament world, Farrer defends himself by arguing that allegory is more, not less likely to be implicit in other places if it is explicit in some ('Surface', 60–63). We cannot make further progress in this discussion, however, without considering the work of students of Mark who try to locate the Gospel in its first-century setting in a way considerably more thoroughgoing than either Farrer or Gardner contemplate. This too must await Part III.[9]

---

7.   Donald Davie (ed.), *The New Oxford Book of Christian Verse* (Oxford: Oxford University Press, 1989), 167.
8.   See Chapters 10 and 11 (pp. 113–148) below.
9.   See esp. 10B and 11B (pp. 117–122, 132–138) below.

What is the point of tracing the lines of this fairly distant academic dispute? It is that we see here, in the mid to late 1950s, the signs of a debate which will resurface nearly twenty years later in study of the Gospels, and seems set to remain lively for a while yet. Both Farrer and Gardner agree that there is such a thing as Mark's authorial intention, yet their disagreement over what it is – the conveying of plain sense or traffic in esoteric meanings – throws up the very things which will undermine its identification. Gardner, in defence of the plain sense of texts, says more than she realises (if we try to get inside *her* mind!) in blocking the 'royal road' to meaning. Farrer cannot say that a text is there to bear any interpretation it may be made to bear,[10] yet Gardner is right to see in him the signs of an acceptance of what we call multivalency, the propensity of a text to say certain things and at the same time suggest others ('Poetry', 126).

We can see clear lines to later debates, like those in Stephen Moore's *Literary Criticism and the Gospels: The Theoretical Challenge*, a combative survey of developments in literary theory since structuralist analysis.[11] Moore speaks of authorial intention as the pre-textual 'something' to which the form of the text (and interpretations of it) might be answerable; reasonable perhaps, except that authors do not hold the fully formed content in their minds before they express it: 'How do I know what I mean until I see what I say?' (*Challenge*, 64f). Farrer would agree, as he sees Mark's Gospel 'growing under the pen' (*Study*, 10), but the door is now ajar: if aspects of the text are outside the author's prior plan, then it is a short step to identify significances outside the author's conscious intention, and even outside the author's control (*Challenge*, 38, 64f, 162). Who, or what, is to be the arbiter of the 'plain sense' of a narrative which different readers read differently? Moore describes a 'theological unconscious' underlying the yen of even secular critics for the univocal Meaning of a text (*Challenge*, 36).[12] This 'essentialist' position he dismisses as 'naive Platonism', and recommends instead the pragmatism of such as Stanley Fish, whom he describes as arguing that meaning is not an extract from the text but a construct of the reader, and that the limits of interpretation are set not by a text, let alone by its author, but by the rules of the 'interpretive community' to which the

---

10.   Farrer explicitly rejects this in his posthumously published 'The Mind of St Mark' ('Mind', 15).

11.   Moore concentrates on *narrative criticism*, a holistic approach to a text which uses categories of narrative theory such as plot and character; on *reader-response criticism*, a spectrum of approaches which tend to focus more on the 'implied' reader, or on actual readers and the factors influencing their readings; and on *poststructuralism*, a varied range of relativising strategies, often with a 'deconstructive' character (*Challenge*, 180f. See 7D, pp. 91–93, below).

12.   Moore is indebted to Barthes' 'Author-God' ('Death', 147).

reader belongs (*Challenge*, 113–15).[13] Against Moore we may set George Steiner, who, in his *Real Presences*, accepts the pluralism but reads it very differently:

> There is, there can be no end to interpretative disagreement and revision. But where it is seriously engaged in, the process of differing is one which cumulatively circumscribes and clarifies the disputed ground. (*Presences*, 214)

And while Moore further probes the theological unconscious to inveigh against the 'three hypostases [of] ... transcendentalized textual context ... transcendentalized *Sitz im Leben* ... and transcendentalized authorial intention' (*Challenge*, 172),[14] Steiner is happy to stand on holy ground:

> Can there be a secular poetics in the strict sense? Can there be an understanding of what engenders 'texts' and which makes their reception possible, which is not underwritten by a postulate of transcendence? (*Presences*, 223)

Steiner's mission is nothing less than to call the bluff (as he might see it) of literary criticism and all aesthetics, and to challenge the practitioners to deny that theirs is religious study, *opus metaphysicum*, 'dialogue with God' (*Presences*, 224f). As such his is quite a different exercise from Moore's or Farrer's, though pertinent to Moore in confronting the rumour of God in criticism and creativity, and to Farrer in affirming it. Steiner poses cogent questions to Moore's pragmatism and the *aim* of his work, and in the face of Steiner's application of the principle *datur, non intellegitur* to all artistic creation (*Presences*, 223), Farrer's distinction between 'prophet' and mere 'maker' (*Glass*, 126f) seems timid and parochial. Where Farrer converges with Steiner is in making his theology anything but unconscious.[15] In maintaining that there is always a deep unity beneath the different readings that are possible, he grounds it in the providence of God: 'Here is more than we are able to expound – who is sufficient for these things? Who can be the expositor of them, unless he

---

13.   Stanley Fish, *Class*. But note Brett, 'Future', who argues that Fish, while indeed saying that 'interpretation creates intention' (*Class*, 163), does not prohibit authorial intention as a legitimate readerly goal, but simply warns that it is hard to find ('Future', 15). Moore defines pragmatism as 'anti-essentialism applied to notions like "truth", "knowledge" ... and similar objects of philosophical theorising' (*Challenge*, 182, quoting Rorty, *Consequences*, 162). Some call Fish and Rorty 'neopragmatist' (*Challenge*, 115).

14.   Moore can nevertheless be a transcendentalist himself, when he questions Dawsey's argument for an unreliable narrator in Luke's Gospel: 'He presents us with a narrative technique and a matching audience response almost two millennia out of time' (*Challenge*, 33, referring to James M. Dawsey, *The Lukan Voice*, Macon: Mercer University Press, 1986).

15.   Steiner's creed is somewhat wrapped up, partly because of his prose style, but partly because, unlike Farrer, he *is* conscious of addressing a sceptical audience (*Presences*, 228). While, for reasons of my own belief, I find Steiner's project attractive, in pursuing the historical dimension of reading texts in Part III, I suggest that some progress can be made towards resolving questions of meaning without launching immediately upon mystical paths.

is himself inspired by God?' (*Matthew*, 11). His treatment of the riddling
narrative of Mark reveals in that 'more' something which others – less
in awe of the God he sees behind the author? – will seize and take in
directions that would alarm him, with his acute sense of Mark as a book
of Scripture.[16] Certainly Farrer is an exception to his own rule that 'in
matters of literary or scholarly fashion, theology is always a quarter of a
century behind the times' ('Surface', 57).

B. Farrer's Critics after Gardner

After Gardner's assault on Austin Farrer, it is hard to find a sustained
engagement with his New Testament work, especially in its literary
aspect.[17] What we find among the greater number of New Testament
scholars is either neglect or, at best, more or less reverent dismissal. We
shall briefly note some examples of the latter.

Vincent Taylor

The second edition of Taylor's commentary on Mark (1st edn 1952) notes
that Farrer 'calls attention to the presence of prefigurings, or typology, in
the Gospel tradition, but exaggerates the extent and importance of this
element', and argues that his number typology is a 'very restricted form'
of New Testament typology, which is, he says, mainly to do with persons
(Commentary, 68f). Farrer offers plenty of that too, of course, but Taylor
does not see fit to mention it; nor does he advance further arguments to
support his rebuttal.

Dennis Nineham

Nineham's 1963 commentary on Mark notes Farrer's remarks on
Papias, and says of his and Carrington's attempts to show the internal
arrangement of Mark that 'it cannot be said that any of the suggested
conclusions has met with really widespread acceptance' (Commentary,
29).[18] In a later book, *The Use and Abuse of the Bible*, Nineham refers
to Farrer occasionally. His one reference of direct concern here is about
what he sees as the great obscurity of Farrer's conception of image and
symbol. He allows the possibility that this may have been what a biblical

---

16.   See Part IV.
17.   But see T.A. Roberts, *History*, esp. 126–143, on its historical implications and
H.D. Lewis, *Experience*, esp. Chapter 7, on theological and philosophical aspects.
18.   The Index cites one other reference to Farrer, on p. 341, though none appears on
that page in the text.

book was designed to convey, but firmly believes it is inaccessible to more than a tiny fraction – as Farrer said of Bultmann's elitism, 'say one man in five thousand' – of the Bible's modern readers (*Use*, 250f, quoting Farrer, 'Appreciation', 214).

Ralph P. Martin

Martin's *Mark: Evangelist and Theologian* (1972) gives Farrer more space. Martin classes Farrer's exegesis as 'patternism', in which 'even the simplest gospel story becomes invested with cryptic significance and esoteric meaning', and he judges it to be an infirmity:

> The fact that this method of biblical criticism is so self-consciously subjective and inferential is its greatest weakness. Nor does the elaborateness of Farrer's reconstruction of the Markan enterprise argue in its favour. Rather its over-subtlety is an added liability. (*Evangelist*, 88)

Martin is impressed by Gardner's critique of Farrer and endorses her in his final verdict:

> The methods employed in this interpretation of Mark's Gospel tell us more of the interpreter's mind than the evangelist's; and the conclusion cannot be evaded that the patterns are read out of the Gospel simply because they have first been read into the text by the erudite scholar. And since it was Farrer's interest to bring us 'into touch with St Mark, a living Christian mind, a mind of great power' ... his endeavour must be judged a failure and his ambition unachieved. (*Evangelist*, 88f)

John Robinson

Robinson, introducing in 1984 a typological piece of his own ('Hosea and the Virgin Birth', 1948, a significant date for those to whom such symbolism appeals!), tells his readers how this type of exegesis was fashionable in the 1940s and 1950s and credits Farrer with successfully fostering it in England, or at least in Oxford. Robinson himself confesses to having become embarrassed about the method:

> Now Austin Farrer was an original and a genius, though this did not to me make his exegesis of Mark along these lines any more credible. Of course, there was obviously truth underlying the method ... But I subsequently became disenchanted with [it] ... not only because of the improbable extremes to which it could be pushed, but by discovering how easy it was to work. ('Hosea', 1f)

Though he publishes the original article after subsequent reflection 'that there may have been deeper workings of truth here than I recognised', his reconsideration does not extend to any rehabilitation of Farrer ('Hosea', 1f).

Anthony Harvey

We have already met Harvey's remarks on Farrer and Goulder, written in 1989. Farrer is for him a 'distinguished, if idiosyncratic, exponent' of the practice of seeing 'hidden meanings' and 'hitherto unnoticed literary patterns' in the Gospels. He notes Goulder's sense (perhaps justified, says Harvey) of not receiving a fair hearing for his theories. In the end he offers him little succour and (as we have seen) poses what is for Harvey the unanswerable question: 'But scholarly resistance to such suggestions is not motivated entirely by prejudice. The question posed again and again by the work of Farrer and Goulder is, How can we ever know whether they are right?' ('Rabbis', 246).[19]

C. Warmer Receptions

Michael Goulder

Farrer's pupil dedicates his *Midrash and Lection in Matthew* (1974) to the memory of his 'tutor and mentor', and acknowledges the 'seminal ideas' of Farrer that taught him 'to look at Matthew [as well as Mark, we presume] as an author' (*Midrash*, xivf). In *The Evangelists' Calendar* (1978) he makes use of typological material in the *Study* (*Calendar*, 193, 252, 257, cf *Study*, 251–264, 79–81, 308–316). Overall, he believes that a lectionary function for the Gospels gives a better 'fit' than the sort of 'literary theory' which Farrer advanced (*Midrash*, xiii). This function was a possibility Farrer himself had entertained (*Study*, 33).

John Drury

Drury's *Tradition and Design in Luke's Gospel* (1976) has a largely implicit generosity to Farrer's ideas. He identifies in himself an instinct which partly mirrors Farrer's in the *Glass*, when he speaks of having felt 'two vague but pressing concerns':

> The first was with the gospels as literature and the sense that the evangelists ought to be appreciated by the same disciplines as are used in non-theological literary studies ... The second was with history ... The gospels were studied with painstaking scholarship but in relative isolation and with little more than the occasional glance at similar and contemporary literature. (*Tradition*, xif)

We shall examine this sense of isolation in Gospel study in Part III. Drury's book shares Farrer's conviction about the priority of text-

19.   See Chapter 5 (pp. 54–59) above.

centred criticism (he is happy to call it redaction criticism) over the more conjectural activity of form criticism, though with an important caveat:

> The reader, like the critic he reads, has the text before him and can check ... The material is not the hypothetical teaching of Jesus or even the less hypothetical teaching of the Church. It is forms, themes, and vocabulary which are directly observable and can be studied as directly as another literary critic studies Shakespeare's or Milton's. But ... [h]ow can the reader be sure the meaning the critic sees is the meaning the writer intended? ... A mind as ingeniously poetic as Austin Farrer's could well be taking off on its own. Some kind of historical check is needed. (*Tradition*, 42f)

Nevertheless he recommends '[a]n understanding of the writer and his book' as the most accessible place to begin (*Tradition*, 43).

In an edition of *Theology* the following year, Drury reviewed the posthumous Farrer collection *Interpretation and Belief*. A brief but penetrating appreciation describes Farrer's biblical work as 'radical redaction criticism ahead of its time' (Review, 135). Drury praises Farrer for presenting us with the 'understandable (if dauntingly complex) human imaginative processes of the NT writers', and of his exposure of form criticism as a practice that 'does not work', while his criticism is of Farrer's failure to follow up (in public) the implications of all this for Christian believing (Review, 136).[20] Nevertheless, Drury is among the very friendliest of biblical scholars to take up Farrer's work.

D. *Farrer and The New Testament Guild*

In his survey of Farrer's impact upon biblical studies ('Austin Farrer's Biblical Scholarship'), Leslie Houlden sees the academic establishment's neglect of Farrer as springing 'out of mystification rather than vindictiveness' ('Scholarship', 201). Farrer certainly did not over-exert himself to situate his work in the scenery of contemporary biblical studies (Houlden notes that only six scholars get into the Index of the *Study*, and one of them is Origen! 'Scholarship', 201), so the two sides were not best equipped to converse, but what was it that mystified? Farrer's borrowings from literary criticism perhaps led some on to the thin ice of their competence, and a conventional Gospel critic, faced with the complexities of Farrer's Mark, would have been tempted to swat him aside for obscurantism rather than do battle with him, verse by verse. Can this, however, be all?

It would have been hard for a Vincent Taylor to engage seriously with Farrer without questioning and defending the fundamental presuppositions of all his own work, thanks to Farrer's wrong-footing move in bypassing form criticism at a time when most of his colleagues continued to build dutifully on its 'results'. One aspect of Farrer's eccentricity here seems

---

20. We return to this aspect of Drury's critique in Part IV.

to be a flimsy historical sense, hinted at by Drury and issuing in the 'disembodied imagination' Gardner so dislikes ('Poetry', 122), but another is his more firmly-founded determination not to assume that a text is an agglomeration simply because it has been treated thus hitherto. It is only with the dawn of mature redaction criticism, in which (as in Drury's book) a Gospel writer is seen as less an editor and more a genuine author, that other critics are ready to hear the preaching of the Gospel as a literary whole.

If these conjectures are sound about scholarly mystification with Austin Farrer, it is not surprising that a much more appreciative reader of his work is a critic who, in terms of conventional biblical-critical baggage, travels light.

E. Frank Kermode

In *The Genesis of Secrecy*, his wide-ranging Norton Lectures for 1977–1978, Kermode is exercised by the persistence of interpreters in the face of the obscurity of narrative. Why do Joyce scholars interminably try to answer Bloom's question in *Ulysses*, 'Where the deuce did he pop out of?' about the mysterious man in the mackintosh? He might simply be put there by Joyce, mischievously as a red herring, or unexcitingly to 'mime the fortuities of real life' (*Genesis*, 54), yet other more recondite identities (a character from the *Odyssey*, Joyce's brother, Joyce himself) seem more compelling.

The man in the mackintosh reminds Kermode of the young man in the shirt at the corner of Mark's canvas as Jesus is arrested (14.51f). Where, he asks, did *he* pop up from? Kermode considers the possibility that his presence is simply non-significant, the product of the blind copying of a source, or a later interpolation, inserted for reasons now obscure. But why (for Kermode is still unsatisfied) does he wear his garment *epi gumnou*, not the usual term for 'about his body'? Kermode rehearses the solutions proposed (all of them reminiscent of those offered for Joyce's figure): that he represents the author, that he is a bystander, added to give *l'effet du réel* (a common device in *fiction*), or that he is the development of a scriptural text, perhaps Joseph shedding his cloak in modest flight, or Amos' warrior, brave but fleeing nevertheless in the day of God's wrath (*Genesis*, 56, Gen. 39.12, Amos 2.16). He considers Morton Smith's thesis, which hinges on a letter of Clement which purports to quote from a secret Gospel of Mark: here in a text inserted before 10.35 of our Mark, a young man (*neaniskos*), wearing a *sindon epi gumnou*, visits Jesus by night and becomes a disciple.[21] Kermode's point is to show the persistent refusal to interpret the young man simply.

---

21.   Morton Smith, *Clement*. J.D. Crossan advances a similar thesis, arguing that our Mark is expurgated (*Four*, 91–121, esp. 119f).

At this point he adduces Farrer's interpretation of this Markan conundrum as the most elegant non-simple solution that he has met. He describes Farrer's linking of this scene and that at the empty tomb, his sense of a strong link to Old Testament passages such as those in Genesis and Amos, controlled by what Kermode calls the 'myth of fulfilment in the time of the end' (*Genesis*, 60f), and he strongly approves of Farrer's suggestion that the fleeing young man represents the flight of all the disciples, even Flight itself (*Genesis*, 62).[22] Kermode's treatment of Farrer is part of a larger project, that of demonstrating the determination of us readers – 'pleromatists' he calls us (*Genesis*, 72) – to show a text to be closed, ended, fulfilled.[23] It is a determination, he argues, which can withstand and even colonise apparent flaws in the text. A classic example is Farrer and his case for 16.8 as the proper ending of Mark, recruiting as he does one puzzle in the text, that of the fleeing figure in Gethsemane, to gloss another. Farrer, says Kermode,

> let his imagination play over the apparently flawed surface of Mark's narrative until ... fractures of the surface became parts of an elaborate design ... Farrer may persuade us that even if he is wrong in detail there is an ending here at the empty tomb, and it is for us to make sense of it. (*Genesis*, 62, 70)

Whence this determination to find closure in a text? Part of it, Kermode is sure, stems from a professional self-respect that jibs at a verdict of incoherence on a canonical text (sacred or secular), but he feels it runs deeper: 'Why...does it require a more strenuous effort to believe that a narrative lacks coherence than to believe that somehow, if only we could find out, it doesn't?' (*Genesis*, 53). He wonders whether its roots lie in our first experience of language, which can only function by achieving closure in well-formed utterances (*Genesis*, 64f).

Kermode has a high opinion of Mark as a storyteller, producing the sort of honing we look for in well-formed narrative, producing it indeed with a sophistication which undermines the Gospel of Mark as a text giving access to historical event, despite the investment of Christian faith in its evidential value.[24] He finds instances of this in Mark's frequent 'intercalations', insertions of one story into the middle of another, and the failure of most commentators to see this for the narrative sophistication it is. He has the death of John the Baptist (6.14–29), inserted between the

22. Unfortunately, Kermode does not tell us where he thinks Farrer says this. The closest Farrer comes in the *Study* is to suggest that the snatching of the garment is a sign of the speed of their flight, but says nothing about the motific significance of its owner (*Study*, 141). In the *Glass*, he speaks of the young man's loss of the σινδών (sindōn) as a 'dramatic symbol', not of Flight but of 'caught asleep on duty' like a dozing Temple guard (*Glass*, 144). He does speak of 'Flight' as 'the last word in Gethsemane' (*Glass*, 142), but not of the fleeing figure as a motif.

23. See further his *The Sense of an Ending*, esp. Chap I, 63f.

24. We consider Kermode's claims about Mark and historical event in Part III. See 13C (pp. 177–180) below.

departure of the twelve on a mission and their return, as an example.[25] Kermode criticises Taylor, Nineham and even Drury for their failure here, when they see the insertion as no more than a gap-filler during the disciples' absence – 'When, in sober fact, time passed, time must pass in the story' – though Kee fares a little better (*Genesis*, 130).[26] All this

> gives one an insight into the remarkable naiveté of professional exegetes when confronted with problems of narrative; behind it, perhaps, is a lingering obsession with historicity, a wish to go on thinking of a gospel narrative as a map of truth ... It is hard to avoid the conclusion that the commentators are swayed, perhaps unconsciously, by a desire to save their text from its own complexity. (*Genesis*, 130)

Though Kermode does not mention him here, Farrer's treatment is of the sort that should appeal. Kermode sees behind the Baptist episode the story of Esther, Farrer the story of Ahab and Jezebel, and both make much of the prefigurative function of this, the passion narrative of the Baptist (*Genesis*, 128–31, cf *Study*, 157). Much less congenial would be Farrer's treatment of Kermode's other example, the insertion of the healing of the haemorrhage within the Jairus story (5.25–34). Though Farrer, like Kermode, develops the numerical symbolism ('twelve', 5.25, 42), his treatment in the *Study* makes nothing of the narrative effect of the insertion, and in *Matthew* he sees it purely as a temporal filler, much as Kermode's culprits handle the Baptist interlude (*Study*, 85, cf *Genesis*, 132f; *Matthew*, 30, 86f).[27] Now Farrer certainly has difficulties over what Kermode calls 'historicity', but no-one could accuse him of saving Mark from its own complexity. Something else may be at work here besides historicist funk, perhaps a failure to sense in Mark 'the genre of the utterance' (Kermode's phrase, *Genesis*, 70): if Farrer is attuned to seek things other than *narrative* characteristics, then he is less likely to discern narrative effects. We consider questions of genre in the next chapter, and in Part III.[28]

Kermode is sorry that Farrer changed his opinions about Mark, then 'more or less gave them up', though he does not say where he finds Farrer doing this. He does cite, and dismisses, Farrer's retreat on the ending of Mark (*Genesis*, 67, cf *Matthew*, 144–59), but the 'retractations' in *Matthew* are hardly fundamental.[29] He is accurate, however, in identifying the threat discerned by the 'establishment', the 'institution', in Farrerian exegesis for the evidential value of the Gospel for the historian (*Genesis*,

25.　He speaks of 'the Salome story', following Josephus rather than Mark in naming Herod's daughter (*Genesis*, 128).

26.　Taylor, Commentary, 307; Nineham, Commentary, 172; Drury, *Tradition*, 95; Kee, *Community*, 55 (*Genesis*, 130, notes 8 and 9).

27.　See also 7E (pp. 94–96) below.

28.　See 7E and 11B (pp. 94–96, 132–138) below.

29.　Gardner's verdict, that Farrer subsequently modified but did not reject his views, is correct here (*Defence*, 136f, note 18).

63).[30] There is a telling reference to Taylor who, in discussing Mk 16.8, quotes W.L. Knox: the imputation of authorial subtlety here implies 'a degree of originality which would invalidate the whole method of form-criticism' (*Genesis*, 68).[31] It is easy to follow Kermode here in seeing an institution protecting itself and its investments, preferring 'to dissolve the text into its elements rather than to observe the fertility of their interrelations' (*Genesis*, 63), by foreclosing even on the asking of certain questions about the text. Knox' words are reminiscent of Lord Denning's when he stopped a civil action by prisoners over their treatment in police custody: the case should not proceed, he said, because of the 'appalling vista' of all it would imply for policing and justice *if the claims were true*.[32] In our case, it is the prospect of 'narrative graces' of the sort Farrer advanced, and the danger they pose 'if one is looking more for an historical record than for a narrative of such elaborateness that it is hard not to think of it as fiction' (*Genesis*, 63).[33]

Kermode comes to Mark with different interests from Farrer's but defends him doughtily in his pursuit of recondite allusions, for Farrer understands how all is governed by principles of fulfilment, eschatological fulfilment of Old Testament promise, and fulfilment promised within the text (*Genesis*, 60). Nor is he at all moved by the argument which holds it incredible that Mark has been misread, perhaps almost from the

---

30.   Gardner, in her counterblast to *Genesis*, can only be partly correct in assuming that Kermode's 'institution' must have been the Church of England (Taylor, for instance, was a Methodist, Martin is a Baptist), and wrong to say that such 'feeble' institutions have no means of 'rejecting' Farrer's views. This whole enquiry is predicated on the success of neglect and reverent dismissal in relegating Farrer to the margins of biblical scholarship; it *is* 'almost as if he had never been' (Houlden, 'Scholarship', 201). That neglect, however, has been practised by the wider academic-ecclesiastical complex.

It is another question whether Farrer (as Kermode, *Genesis* 63, might imply) was much affected by questions of approval, for Farrer's own neglect of contemporary scholarship in his writings suggests some disdain for the academic establishment. Moreover, he tended to be highly esteemed in Anglican circles: see e.g. Eric Mascall's Foreword to *Interpretation* (xiiif), Basil Mitchell's tribute 'Austin Marsden Farrer' in *Celebration* (13–16) and, much more recently, Jeffrey John's confession that 'one of my exegetical heroes is Austin Farrer' ('Sense', 52). John is no hero-*worshipper*, however, and we must admit that, even for his Anglican admirers, Farrer the philosophical theologian and Farrer the preacher tend to win more medals than Farrer the exegete.

Jasper says that the effect of Farrer on the literary reading of the Bible has been 'enormous', particularly through Kermode's work ('Literary', 25). If it has, it has been largely unacknowledged.

31.   Kermode finds Knox' words in Taylor (Commentary, 609).

32.   Denning was the Master of the Rolls, 1962–1982. The so-called Birmingham Six had been convicted (wrongly, as it turned out) of the 1974 Birmingham pub bombings (Judgement: *McIlkenny v Chief Constable of the West Midlands* [1980] Q.B. 283).

33.   Kermode leaves the impression that he thinks this still to be the state of affairs in biblical studies, though by the time of his lectures (1977–1978) mature redaction criticism was well established. For instance: by 1978, Weeden's *Mark – Traditions in Conflict* had been in print for seven years.

very beginning, until the text is opened by a particular pair of hands in Oxford:[34] all interpretation, however sober, implies the inadequacy of every previous interpretation (*Genesis*, 17). He sees Farrer's difficulties as a Christian with questions of history, notes the oddity of his pieties to a secular reader and yet finds Farrer's thinking readily convertible into his own currency. Kermode claims Farrer as a comrade, 'for his notions of order were literary ... he makes bold to write about Mark as another man might write about Spenser' (*Genesis*, 72). Above all, he sees Farrer as bearing the classic mark of the interpreter: 'like the rest he sensed that despite, or even because of, the puzzles, the discontinuities, the amazements of Mark ... his text can be read as somehow hanging together' (*Genesis*, 72). Sensing in Farrer a fellow outsider in the realm of Gospel interpretation, Kermode makes a good attempt at profitable conversation. At one point, however, he slightly misjudges his man. He says that Farrer, in his pursuit of patterns in Mark,

> detected delicate senses, many of them ironical. And since he was not an adherent of the latest school of hermeneutics, he believed that Mark must have intended these senses, and that he must have had an audience capable of perceiving them. (*Genesis*, 61f)

Kermode's verdict on audience is fair, even though it rests on Farrer's scanty references to the 'Bible-reading Jew' and what was 'current in ... [Mark's] world' (*Study*, 46, 79). On authorial intention, however, Farrer's position is more complex. We have seen how he sometimes seeks to think Mark's thoughts, yet sometimes argues that the author was not fully conscious of what is legitimately to be seen in the text (e.g. *Study*, 27, 100f, 177, 361). Kermode's wider point, that we are all instinctive pleromatists, seekers after fulfilment and closure in narrative (*Genesis*, 72), is well made, and Farrer is a very good example. As we listen to him, inviting us to think his thoughts and so embrace his solution – 'There is surely some symbolic motif here, if only we could hit upon it' (*Glass*, 143) – we hear the very cajoling and wistfulness which Kermode describes: 'If there is one belief that unites us all ... it is this conviction that somehow, in some occult fashion, *if we could only detect it*, everything will be found to hang together' (*Genesis*, 72, emphasis added).

   To explain this belief Kermode offers (as we saw) our primal experience of language, but this does not satisfy him (*Genesis*, 64). What else might explain it? A conviction about discovering an author's intention is one possibility, but Kermode is both ambivalent and ambiguous on this; he does not say how far *he* subscribes to 'the latest school of hermeneutics'. So what foundation can there be for the lingering belief (always disappointed, *Genesis*, 144f) that there is an essence of meaning in the text? This is, at the end of his lectures, an unresolved question

---

34.   As advanced e.g. by Harvey ('Rabbis', 246f).

for Kermode; but not so for Farrer. He is a believer and a theologian, who assumes as he works on Mark's Gospel a fully fledged doctrine of inspiration, itself an outworking of his conception of God's action in the world. For him, if there is an overplus of significance in Mark, and a subtlety of coherence, more than the conscious mind of the author could contain, then that is because the text is the product of double agency, the fruit of 'inspired imagination' (*Study*, 100).[35]

If Farrer, in studying Mark's Gospel, has 'thought his thoughts after him' (*Study*, 142), he has by the logic of his own position done more. Though never quite rash enough to say so, Farrer, like Einstein, has thought God's thoughts after him too.

F. Conclusion

In this chapter we have traced the generally cool reception which greeted Farrer's work on Mark. Helen Gardner, the scholar of English literature, is uneasy with the obscure and obscuring complexity of his labours, with his stated aim of laying bare the processes of thought of the evangelist, with the sort of literary reminiscences he proposes, with Farrer's treatment of the evangelist (as she sees it) as little more than a talking head, and with what she adjudges his failure, for all Farrer's own imaginative powers, to do justice to the heart of the Gospel. On the other hand, she shares with Farrer a concern (maintained over decades) for authorial intention as a constraint upon interpretation. This immediately raises questions about genre – 'What does this text seem to be designed *for*?' – about setting and about audience, but only historical enquiry can rescue the discussion of these questions from mere assertion. Without this 'historical check' the debate will simply provide evidence against authorial intention as an accessible possibility.

The intellectual distance between Farrer and other New Testament scholars, seen most notably in his untimely suspicion of form criticism,

---

35.   Gardner in her own Norton Lectures (*In Defence of the Imagination*), berates Kermode for affirming that texts have meaning, but then saying that they are potentially infinite in number, except as they are curtailed by 'institutional control' (*Defence*, 131, 133). She offers, as an alternative to both Kermode and Farrer, the viability of the insistence, from Augustine onwards, upon the 'main sense' of a text or the 'principal intention' of its author (*Defence*, 115).

Hauge supports Gardner, and accuses Farrer and Kermode of the 'sin' of remaking the text in their own image ('Sin'). This, however, leads him to the implausible conclusion that Gardner is a champion of fluidity and openness in texts, while Farrer, guilty like Kermode of 'freezing' the text (Kermode's word, *Genesis*, 71) into crystalline patterns, becomes a proto-structuralist ('Sin', 126f). Jasper makes a similar claim, more approvingly, for Farrer (*Coleridge*, 149). Structuralist analysis seeks to reduce any given text to patterns and codes common to *all* texts. Farrer seeks structure of course, but a structure of *particularity*. Brown agrees with Hauge's 'general thrust' ('Role', 91, note 23).

explains the scant attention they pay him. We have seen by contrast how accessible Farrer's ideas are to someone less concerned with the historical preoccupation out of which classical Gospel criticism arose. Kermode is undecided about authorial intention, and puzzled by a perennial though endlessly disappointed desire to discover non-negotiable coherence and meaning in a text, a desire which he cannot entirely explain away. Farrer's thoroughly theological reading of Mark enables him to embrace the desire without the perplexity.

Chapter 7

MARK'S LITERARY CRITICS: RHOADS, DEWEY AND MICHIE

Does St Mark tell a story which, as a story, makes sense?
A Study in St Mark, 186

In the discussion of *The Genesis of Secrecy*, we found in Frank Kermode someone engaged in conversation with Austin Farrer as part of an enquiry with a rather wider field of view. In this chapter we move firmly into that wider field.

In 1982 David Rhoads and Donald Michie published what was to be the first edition of *Mark as Story*. It proved to be in every sense a literary event. Subtitled *An Introduction to the Narrative of a Gospel*, it opened up new horizons for Markan criticism, to the extent that, in Jack Kingsbury's view, 'History will show that more than any other single work, this book has pointed the way to a literary (narrative-critical) study of Mark's Gospel' (*Conflict*, 143).[1] Stephen Moore concurs (*Challenge*, 41–43).

The authors (naturally) make no mention of Austin Farrer, yet they take up some of the themes that Farrer plays in his work on Mark: an attention to the text and its character before looking (if one looks at all) for what may lie behind it, and an appreciation of the author of Mark as much more than a passive compiler.[2] Joanna Dewey joined them to

1.   The question about Mark which heads this chapter, though irresistible as an overture to *Mark as Story*, is actually posed by Farrer as part of his enquiry into the *historical* value of Mark. There is some force in Kermode's charge of professional exegetes' 'naiveté' before narrative, as we shall see in Part III (*Genesis* 130, see 6E above and 13C, pp. 76–81, 177–180, below).

2.   The choice of this single book for comparison with Farrer stems from its acknowledged influence upon literary approaches to Mark. Other books might fruitfully be held beside Farrer. J.G. Williams' *Gospel Against Parable* (1985) espouses the same methodological priority of wholes over parts, and brings insights into the symbiosis of literary and historical readings (see 9A, pp. 104–108, below). Like Farrer, Williams is a firm intentionalist, and open about his credal presuppositions. A good comparison by contrast would be with Ernest Best's *Mark: The Gospel as Story* (1984). Published after *Mark as Story*, it is (despite the promise of its title) a rather atavistic piece, proceeding uncritically from the assumptions of form criticism.

produce the much-revised second edition in 1999. Since our study of Rhoads, Dewey and Michie will be longer than those of Gardner and Kermode, we shall describe their work fully (with reference to the second edition unless indicated otherwise) before evaluating it in comparison with Farrer's. From this comparison we shall see points at which one might correct the other; and again we shall identify matters of concern to the wider debate within Gospel criticism.

A. Mark as Story: *A Summary*

The authors set *Mark as Story* within the category of narrative criticism, and so from the outset speak of the text of Mark in terms originally derived from 'secular' literary criticism; their concern is the Gospel's 'story world', with its conflict, suspense and irony (and even, in the first edition, its 'hero', *Story*, 1st edn, 1). Their analytical tools are therefore derived from those originally devised for use with modern novels and short stories (as the first edition acknowledges, *Story*, 1st edn, 2). Without saying as much, in both editions they take a particular stand in the debate about authorial intention, and talk not only of the text but of the writer, or author (e.g. *Story*, 1–3, 61).

In the *Introduction* to the first edition, Rhoads and Michie had had to contend for laying before us 'the story as a whole … [for] the final text is a literary creation with an autonomous integrity' (*Story*, 1st edn, 2f).

> The author of the gospel has not simply collected traditions, organized them, made connections between them, and added summaries, but has also told a story – a dramatic story – with characters whose lives we follow to the various places they travel and through the events in which they are absorbed. (*Story*, 1st edn, 3)

That battle now won, the second edition can confine itself to finding in Mark a 'narrative … of remarkably whole cloth': a consistent narrative voice, a coherent plot (anticipated events actually happen, predictions are fulfilled), characters behaving consistently from one scene to the next (*Story*, 3).

Rhoads, Dewey and Michie bid us lose ourselves in the world of this rounded story, viewing it apart from the historical events to which it might refer and from the other Gospels in our New Testament. They do not shut off all recourse to knowledge of the first-century world, but wish to limit it to 'helpful background information' so that, as far possible, we seek clarity 'within the story itself' (*Story*, 4f). To 'unpack' the narrative they point to five 'key features' of narrative for analysis: narrator, setting, plot and character are the basic features, and the fifth, rhetoric, 'refers to the various ways an author may use the combined features of narrative to persuade readers to enter and embrace the world presented by the narrative … what a narrative *does* to change its readers' (*Story*, 7). They often refer to the 'reader' or 'readers'. At the end of their study they make clear that the reader they almost always have in mind is an 'imaginary' one, who responds 'correctly' to the various rhetorical devices employed in the text: that is, an 'ideal' or 'implied' reader (*Story*, 137f).

In their first chapter Rhoads, Dewey and Michie offer their own translation of the text, arranged not by chapter and verse (they use not a single such reference) but according to what they see as the movement of the story. Words which recur in the Greek text but which are often variously translated according to immediate context are rendered consistently, so as to express their function as motifs in the story as a whole; for instance, παραδίδωμι (paradidōmi), variously translated as 'arrest', 'hand over' and 'betray' in other English versions, is here rendered 'hand over' throughout.

The second chapter of *Story* considers 'The Narrator'. The narrator 'represents the sum total of the author's choices in getting a story told' (*Story*, 39). Mark's is an *omniscient* voice outside the time and space of the narrative, that leads the reader to trust the protagonist Jesus; the narrator's *standards of judgement* constitute a *point of view* that can be summarised as 'thinking in God's terms', in contrast to the point of view of Jesus' opponents who 'think in human terms'; the narrator's *style*, we are told, is terse, with brief episodes and relatively little discourse, and a quick-moving dynamic, though the tempo slows markedly with the arrival in Jerusalem and the events there (*Story*, 46f). There then follow long sections on the narrator's *patterns of repetition* (to which we shall return[3]) and other literary features.

The third chapter considers the *settings* of the story, 'the "world" where events take place and characters act': the 'cosmic' setting of God's world out of kilter, the 'political-cultural' setting of Roman occupation, and the 'journey' that Jesus makes to Jerusalem (*Story*, 63–66). This last takes in Jewish and Gentile territory, public and private space, locales that recall Israel's past, and the final arrival in Jerusalem (*Story*, 66–71). The journey as whole is a metaphor for following Jesus himself (*Story*, 71f).

The fourth chapter turns to the *plot*, 'how [events] are arranged, how they are connected, and what they reveal' (*Story*, 73), the keys to which are Jesus' various *conflicts*, with demonic and natural forces, with the authorities, with his own disciples, and even with himself as he faces death (*Story*, 73–97).

The fifth chapter introduces us to *characters*, 'agents in a plot' but also 'autonomous figures' whom we can assess 'as we assess real people'. Jesus is the protagonist and his antagonists are the 'authorities', who can be considered as one character, as can the disciples. Other, minor characters, including the crowds, momentarily cross the pages of the text. Generally, the narrator 'shows' the character to the reader through what they say

---

3.   See 7E (pp. 94–96) below.

and do, rather than 'tell' the reader what the character is like (*Story*, 98f).
Jesus is a 'round' character because he has many traits and is surprising,
whereas the authorities constitute a 'flat' character, being less complex
and quite predictable. Though treatable as a group character, the disciples
are nevertheless 'round' (*Story*, 102). The rest of the chapter explored
Jesus' character (*Story*, 103–115), while the sixth chapter describes the
remainder (*Story*, 116–136).

The Conclusion considers the overall effect of the author's rhetoric on
the implied reader: 'the story of Mark seeks to create ideal readers who
will receive the rule of God and have the courage to follow Jesus whatever
the consequences' (*Story*, 137f). Rhoads, Dewey and Michie then consider
what might have been the actual first-century audience – or multiple
audiences – that the author of Mark had in mind. Mark's rhetoric, they
feel, makes most sense addressing followers under threat of persecution,
and they envisage a response close to that of the implied reader (*Story*,
143–46). Readers nowadays will lack the expectation of the imminent
establishment of the rule of God, but may still find their world reflected
in Mark's story world and, having experienced 'the astounding figure of
Jesus', may still be prompted to think anew about life's purpose (*Story*,
146).

Mark as Story ends with an Afterword on the ethics of reading, a
plea to read in 'dialogue' both with the text, by approaching it 'on its
own terms', and with other readers, especially those of different 'social
locations', and so be open to Mark's particular transformative power
(*Story*, 147–150).

B. Evaluation: Farrer and Mark as Story – Introductory

To turn back from *Mark as Story* to *A Study in St Mark* is to receive
an initial shock, because of the remoteness from Farrer of much of the
latter's terminology. Despite this linguistic divide – which is, as we shall
see, more than cosmetic – the emphasis of Rhoads, Dewey and Michie
upon the unity and coherence of the text is deeply sympathetic to Farrer's
view. Both essays proceed from a firm belief in the text of Mark as the
product of an authorial mind: *Story*'s 'artful Gospel' is, in the *Study*'s
rather different idiom, 'a genuine, and profoundly consistent, act of
thought' (*Story*, 62; *Study*, 7). Moreover, both share a sunny estimation
of the possibility of the diligent reader discovering the intentions of this
artful author of Mark. One point of contrast between them, which we
shall explore below, is the extent to which the authors wish to remain
solely within the text.

C. Evaluation: The Author

Rhoads, Dewey and Michie speculate briefly about the social setting of the author of Mark' – Did he write in Rome or Palestine? Was he Jew or Gentile? Was he educated, or a peasant? (*Story*, 2) – rather as Farrer does, though he is less tentative, and stresses the writer's familiarity with the Jewish Scriptures; he also offers asides, such as the suggestion that the author was a Christian preacher (we shall return to these in Part III).

Though *Story* follows contemporary orthodoxy in distinguishing the real from the implied reader (*Story*, 137f, see pp. 91–93 below), it does not make the corresponding distinction between the real and implied author. Moore defines the implied author as '"a core of norms and choices" immanent in a work, that "we infer as an ideal, literary, created version of the real [author]"' (*Challenge*, 180),[4] which finds an echo when Rhoads, Dewey and Michie say that the *narrator* 'represents the sum total, of the author's choices' (*Story*, 39). It seems that they have silently fused the implied author with the narrator.[5] What, then, is the relation of narrator to (real) author? The narrator, they are clear, 'is not the author but ... is a rhetorical device the author uses'; yet they suggest that 'it is helpful to think of the narrator as a figure with strategies and beliefs who addresses readers' (*Story*, 39). What is gained, though, when we are told that the narrator, this rhetorical device, 'wants' the reader to see Jesus in a certain way and, further, 'could have chosen' to portray the end of Jesus' life triumphantly (*Story*, 114, 112)? It feels here as if they wish be talking about the *real* author. Perhaps the articles of current literary theory inhibit them from doing so.

These formal distinctions are of course foreign to Farrer. He speaks everywhere of 'St Mark' or 'the evangelist', both as author (e.g. 'what he has written in these last three paragraphs should be freshest in St Mark's mind' *Study*, 69) and as narrator (e.g. 'The evangelist says that the priests saw that the part of the vinedressers was being fitted upon themselves' *Study*, 238f). Whatever the theoretical pitfalls, his lines are cleaner.

Similarly, while Farrer would not look for what *Story* calls the *narrator's* ideological point of view (*Story*, 45), it is precisely the *author's* interpretation of the story (or, as Farrer would say, the history) of Jesus which Farrer is trying to contemplate. He tells us that the author has, in the best sense, an axe to grind: 'it is no use our blaming the Evangelist for being a Christian' (*Matthew*, 24). Some of the distinctions that Rhoads, Dewey and Michie do make in this area readily collapse into one another:

4.   Quoting Wayne Booth, *The Rhetoric of Fiction*, 2nd edn, Chicago: Chicago University Press, 1983, 74f.
5.   If this is because they posit a narrator outside the story who is omniscient and reliable (that is, with a point of view that agrees entirely with the author's), they are not alone in this. Smith declares that 'there is essentially no difference between implied author and narrator in the Gospel of Mark, and there is no problem with treating them as one' (*Lion*, 23, note 28).

'standards of judgment' and 'point of view' are hard to distinguish even formally in their description (*Story*, 44f), while the narrator's point of view/standards of judgement, already deputising for the author's, entirely reproduce those of Jesus. These elisions should not disturb us in themselves, but the effect of this kind of analysis is to create an impression of over-elaboration, the result of using literary-critical equipment honed on literature of rather different sorts ('modern novels and short stories', *Story*, 1st edn, 2) from that of Mark's Gospel. Farrer's treatment (in this respect at least!) appears lean by comparison.

We find similar over-elaboration in the discussion of character. Rhoads, Dewey and Michie tell us that a character is more than a mere plot mechanism, though they imply that so-called 'flat' characters, like the authorities, are little more than that (*Story*, 102f). The disciples, however, they see as 'rounded', because they exhibit conflicting traits (*Story*, 123). For all that, however, *Story* can deal with them in a group quite as easily as they can the 'flat' authorities, and only Peter (styled – with a rather 1950s feel – as 'Rock' in the second edition) emerges into anything like individuality. Jesus alone among the characters in Mark comes out of their analysis as fully rounded, and their discussion of character often repeats what they have already offered us as a function of the plot. For instance, the spluttering progress of the disciples from their call in Galilee, through fleeting and inadequate discernment at Caesarea Philippi, to their collapse into utter failure at the passion: all is well grasped in the discussion of Jesus' conflict with the disciples as a motor of the plot (*Story*, 90–96), and when it is rehearsed in the discussion of the disciples as characters, we learn little that is new (*Story*, 122–129).

This is not to suggest that character is an illegitimate term to apply to Mark, but that it brings the baggage of relatively modern literature, and so the risk of leading the critic to exaggerate the modernity of an ancient text, to make it dance to an anachronistic tune. Does the Gospel of Mark need to come up to scratch under all headings in order to qualify as genuine literature? Rhoads, Dewey and Michie do acknowledge that, whereas characters in modern novels are 'dynamic', most of Mark's 'show little change or development', but then claim that they can be 'surprising', as befits 'a story that assumes that people will be able to turn around and ... undergo a reorientation in life' (*Story*, 100f). Such change as there is, however, only ever arises as a function of the unfolding action. When do we find any of the *depth* of portrayal of the disciples (their strongest candidates) that might warrant our seeing them as 'autonomous figures' whom we can assess 'as we assess real people'? Mark's characters are indeed better described as 'agents in a plot' (*Story*, 98). Elizabeth Struthers Malbon, responding to the first edition of *Story*, saw the Markan characters existing not 'for their own sake' but 'for the sake of the communication between audience and author' ('Major' 59, 84); and it is still hard to dissent from that.

Farrer is aware of much that *Story* identifies in the characters of Mark, as in the case of the disciples. He makes very similar points about their slowness to learn, the war in their hearts between loyalty to Jesus and self-seeking, yet his observation of character always arises out of his discussion of literary patterning. We see this in his many references to the slowness of the disciples (e.g. *Study*, 104), and his fine treatment of the request of James and John for places of prominence, which he relates to the Transfiguration and to the 'willing sacrifice' of the disciples (*Study*, 117, 120). Again, it all proceeds from his description of the writer choosing and framing material. This is not just a matter of interpretative economy but of method.

In his critique of the first edition of *Story*, Moore traced the methodological debt of Rhoads and Michie (as they then were) to Seymour Chatman's *Story and Discourse*, from whom, he said, they inherited a formal error. Chatman advances what Moore calls a 'two-storey model' of a text, the first being its content – 'story' – and the second its expression – 'discourse' (*Challenge*, 41–43). Rhoads and Michie use instead the terms 'story' and 'rhetoric': to 'story' (the content, or 'what' category) they allocate plot, character and setting; to 'rhetoric' (which describes 'how' the story is told) they allocate the narrator, point of view, standards of judgement, style, narrative patterns and other rhetorical devices (*Story*, 1st edn, 4f). But if a text is a notation, a 'telling' (as Moore calls it), is not the 'story' all *in* the telling? The whole of *Story* then becomes an enquiry into the *rhetoric* of the Gospel, and the effect of the authors' (false) distinction is to reify such 'story' elements as plot, character and setting; that is, to treat them as though they had some privileged existence apart from the 'selection, framing, arranging, filtering, slanting', all the 'rhetorical' devices through which we encounter them (*Challenge*, 42–45; the list is Moore's, *Challenge*, 45). On this reckoning, Farrer's analysis is more thoroughly 'rhetorical' than that of the first edition of *Story* and, in the matters discussed so far, finds a better fit for Mark's text.

In their Preface to the second edition, Rhoads, Dewey and Michie generously acknowledge Moore's critique and signal an evolution of their method from the 'bifurcation' of story and rhetoric (*Story*, 1). They now advance a method which they intend should keep form and content together, analysing the five key features of narrative: narrator, setting, plot and character are the first four, and the fifth is rhetoric, 'which refers to the various ways an author may use the combined features of narrative to persuade readers to enter and embrace the world presented by the narrative' (*Story*, 6f). This is indeed a better model, though the narrator, as the voice through which we encounter setting, plot and character, is closer to rhetoric than to the other three: it is the instrument of the author's rhetorical activity on *all* the material, because it is 'the sum total of the author's choices' (*Story*, 39). As their study unfolds, however, we seldom encounter the language of authorial choice. The *narrator*, as we have seen, has some quasi-authorial moments, but the significance of *settings* is either simply described – 'The final scene points back to Galilee, back to the beginning of the story' (*Story*, 69) – or analysed in impersonal statements. Thus we hear: 'the settings are related to the actions and events of the story' (*Story*, 63); rather than 'the author relates the settings ...'; and 'the journey of Jesus ... provides a frame for the events' (*Story*, 66), rather than 'the author frames the events by setting them within Jesus' journey'. In the discussion of *plot*, 'how [events] are arranged' (*Story*, 73), we do discover that 'sometimes events are connected rhetorically, such as those episodes that occur in a concentric pattern'; but in a *story*, are not *all* events connected rhetorically, even those with 'implied causal connection' (*Story*, 75)? At the start of their analysis of *character*, Rhoads, Dewey and Michie tell us that Mark '*creates* characters that are consistent' (*Story*, 99, emphasis added) but this has to serve as a rubric for the many pages that follow, which are largely descriptive, apart from occasional statements that the narrator 'depicts' or 'portrays', say, Jesus in a certain way (e.g. *Story*, 107, 111, 109) and one other unambiguous reference to the author: 'Mark has *produced* flat, entirely negative figures' in the person of the authorities (*Story*, 113, emphasis added). 'Mark' appears often of course, but – here as elsewhere – can usually can be construed at least as plausibly as referring to the work as to the writer.

By the time we reach the Conclusion of *Story* and its section on *rhetoric*, there has built up a sense of the givenness, the sheer 'thereness' of much of Mark's narrative (though less so than with the first edition). Could it not all have been very different if Mark the author had made different choices? These last few pages move towards an answer, mainly in matters of plot, but it is all rather implicit, and leaves an impression that the author to whose story Rhoads, Dewey and Michie introduce us is writing under some constraint. That he is has been a commonplace of traditio-historical criticism: 'character', 'plot' and 'setting' are indeed 'given' to the author, either because of the constraint of being faithful to the events they refer to, or because they constitute authoritative material which the author does not feel at liberty to change. The authors of *Story* do not explore these matters, except to say that 'Mark is a version of historical events'; and, even then, though 'Jesus, Herod and the high priests were real people', we are to treat them as 'characters portrayed in a story' (*Story*, 5). They do not speculate upon what might be the limits of those portrayals.

Farrer acknowledges these constraints, but is happy to say of Mark that 'whatever his materials or sources, he dominated them' (*Study*, vi). (With the constraints of history Farrer will have greater difficulty, as we shall see.) He uses the word 'plot' himself in likening the writer's position when about to write the Gospel to that of a playwright; he does not distance himself from the fictive connotations of the term, but he brackets it with 'pattern', and when he moves on to describe the Gospel itself he prefers the latter term (*Study*, 33f). This pattern he traces through the cyclical forms he finds in the Gospels and through the practice of prefiguration, which draws the story forward both on the local and on the general level. Character and setting (he does not use the terms as such) find their place within the patterning, and Farrer is consistent in seeing that patterning as the fruit of the very sorts of selection and presentation which Moore lists. For Farrer, the text is supremely the creation of a mind. His study of Mark is 'an essay in literary analysis', concerned with 'the sentences St Mark writes and the mental processes they express' (*Study*, vii), and he writes the shaping presence of that mind into page after page of his study. As such it is more purely 'literary' criticism, more explicitly concerned with the internal 'story world' as the creation of an author, than is *Mark as Story*.

D. Evaluation: The Reader

One objection to this verdict might adduce Farrer's treatment of the subtle question of the reader. The whole of the *Study* is an exercise in enquiring how a reader should approach Mark, because for Farrer the text is a place for the meeting of minds – the author's with Farrer's and, by extension, with ours. Farrer's Mark knows what he wants to say, and even when he says more than he knows, he does so in an extension of his conscious intention. Thus, by thinking his thoughts after him, we too can know what he has to say, for it is there in the text. While it would be wrong to expect from Farrer the fastidiousness we find in current discussion of implied readers, he betrays no great awareness that there might be a problem here, a gap between the reader implied in the text and the reader who now approaches Mark. He casts the meeting of minds in the text of Mark in a rather ahistorical light, only occasionally stressing the distance that lies between Mark's audiences of the first and the twentieth centuries; as when he says of the symbolism of Mark that '[w]e reconstruct ... with pain, but that is because we are men of a different generation' (*Study*, 79). Sometimes, however, he lifts more of the veil on the original audience: 'Many people', and he includes himself in their number, 'suspect that St Mark wrote his book with a view to church-reading' (possibly under the influence of synagogue lectionaries) and 'common edification'; then of course we have the 'Bible-reading Jew' who would grasp Farrer's theories with ease (*Study*, 33, 173). Simply think yourself, he seems to say, into the shoes of an ancient Jew who knows the Old Testament (*Study*, 173), and the task of understanding Mark aright will be strenuous but quite manageable.

Rhoads, Dewey and Michie say much more about the reader, though most of it is about the implied or 'ideal' reader, that is 'a mirror image of the narrator ... the reader that the author creates ... an imaginary reader with all the ideal responses *implied* by the narrative itself' (*Story*, 137, original emphasis). The implied reader is a kind of hologram projected by the text, and so is firmly within the story world. If, however, the implied reader is a creation of the (real) author, this takes us beyond the story world to where the author stands, and the implied reader must correspond to that author's perception of an actual person, group or groups the author wishes to address. So, as they tell us, 'when the author of Mark wrote, he had actual first-century people in mind' (*Story*, 143). But who were they? What did they bring to their encounter with Mark's story? Do not we all make sense of a book by knowing and remembering more than that book supplies?

Both editions of *Mark as Story* offer suggestive answers to the first question: 'a Roman soldier, a Syrian peasant, a Jewish nationalist, a moderate Pharisee' were the original suggestions; the second edition added, among others, 'people with ailments ... women ... upper class Judeans' (*Story*, 1st edn, 140; *Story*, 143). The first edition is weak, however, over the question of what they might bring to their reading (or, more likely, hearing) of Mark, and therefore what modern readers need to be briefed about if they are not to miss much of this story.

In their anxiety for Mark to be heard as a self-sufficient story and not be added to, Rhoads and Michie are immensely austere about allowing extrinsic pieces on to the interpretative board so that Mark might be 'better' understood (*Story*, 1st edn, 4). Like Farrer, they note the significance of numbers in Mark, especially the number three (*Story*, 1st edn, 54f) but they mention none of the numerical symbolism (or indeed the rest of the typology) which for Farrer inescapably ties the text of Mark back to the Old Testament, and which requires the reader to supply detailed knowledge from outside the story world for the story itself to make full sense. The correspondences they detect are within the text, and are of a sort that would disclose themselves upon a careful reading by an untutored reader, an internal typology: 'a' corresponds to 'b', where 'a' and 'b' appear in the text as 'naturally' similar (e.g. the tenants in the vineyard, and the Temple authorities unable to bring forth the 'fruit' of faith (*Story*, 1st edn, 119–22), or as 'natural' opposites (e.g. Peter's denial and Jesus' confession, *Story*, 1st edn, 51). At times Rhoads and Michie cannot resist including extrinsic data, however, as when they describe the healing of the cripple and the healing of the withered hand as both involving 'serious legal penalties' (*Story*, 1st edn, 52, the text of Mark mentions none), and when they explore the motific function of settings important in Israel's past, like the river Jordan or mountains (*Story*, 1st edn, 65–67). Why do they mention river and mountain but say nothing, for instance, about the symbolic number of disciples?

The implied reader and, by extension, the real audience/s envisaged in the first edition of *Story* emerge as implausibly lop-sided, needing to know certain things which the text does not supply, but not others. If we seek a first-century reader, Farrer, for all his apparent naiveté in the matter of the reader, produces a better picture in his Bible-reading Jew. So, when Farrer advances his schema of progressively condensed healing miracles, he offers it as a self-contained system within the story world, suggesting itself (as he claims) to the diligent reader. He also offers it as a sequence requiring extrinsic knowledge (e.g. of Psalm 115) for its fullness to be perceived. His putative original audience would, in this case, be adequate to this second task, though perhaps not to the first.

The second edition of *Story* wisely opens the windows of the story world a little, acknowledging that in Mark's narrative '[t]here are ... unintentional gaps for twentieth-century readers that result from our lack of knowledge that Mark and his first-century audience possessed' and then tackling some of them. For instance: 'The whole story is painted with strokes from the Judean writings'; characterisation in Mark 'might be influenced by the narratives of the Hebrew Bible'; and an understanding of Jesus' words at the Last Supper requires a grasp of ancient understandings of 'covenant' (*Story*, 4, 62, 100, 114). Farrer is of course still far readier to import extrinsic information, like Old Testament allusions.

There is a real dilemma here for literary critics. If they shun the extreme and ultimately unsustainable rigour of looking simply at the text in itself,[6] they have two choices. One leads to *laissez-faire* reader-response criticism, which lets readers make of a text whatever they will. The other seeks the intention of the author, as Rhoads and Michie – with and without Dewey – do. Speaking of this intentionality, J.L. Houlden says: 'Behind texts are minds, and minds exist in humans, who live in society and do other things beside write texts – in a welter of activities which affect each other, each having its bearing on the rest' ('History', 5). Those for whom they write also do other things beside *receive* a particular text, and one of the things they do is to receive other texts, which belong to the shared world of author and audience. To exclude this consideration is arbitrary, and strengthens the case of those who would purge literary criticism of any hint of intentionality. To embrace it, however, entails taking the indeterminacies of real audiences into your calculations, and how far do you go? Rhoads, Dewey and Michie improve upon the excessively tight limits of the first edition of *Story*. Farrer goes vastly further than they do – or should, given *their* audience, of people who need an *introduction* to reading Mark as story (*Story*, xi) – but does he search broadly enough? These questions lead us into a conversation with historical criticism. In Part III we shall consider some proposals to simplify the complexity of reader-centred criticism with which we have just brushed.

---

6. I have in mind here something like Culpepper's formula for textual analysis: 'what it is, and how it works' (*Anatomy*, 5).

E. Evaluation: Unity and Genre – What Sort of a Whole is Mark?

So far, Farrer has come off pretty well in this comparison with *Story*. There are, however, important aspects of reading Mark that Farrer's study does not comprehend, and which emerge vigorously in the later book. Rhoads, Dewey and Michie write a short work and do not pretend to the detail of Farrer's study; indeed, there is something about the 'feel' of the Gospel in their hands (for instance, the setting-aside of chapter-and-verse classification) which suggests that they would not want to work in such exhaustive detail anyway. Theirs is like a small-scale relief map of the text; they boldly show up salient and recurrent features of the terrain so that we can feel the roll of the countryside, but they are content to leave the minor contours unplotted. Farrer, in contrast, gives us more of a vast Ordnance Survey map (with full use of the grid references of chapter and verse) which strives to leave no hillock unmeasured, no copse unmarked. And as we follow Farrer in his exhaustive orienteering, it sometimes seems that he cannot see the narrative wood for the schematic and typological trees. Part of Farrer's complexity stems from his determination to see the whole of Mark cohering, both in sweep and detail, within a total theory of composition. This presents him at many points with a choice between the abandonment of coherence and more acrobatic exegesis; and he prefers the latter.

Rhoads, Dewey and Michie state that the Gospel of Mark is a literary unity, but it is not an exhaustive statement. Certainly they allow that Mark has 'gaps': some are intentional (to create suspense), some exist only for us modern readers, and some stem from 'unexpressed assumptions, inconsistencies, lack of resolution', but these last are found in every narrative (*Story*, 3f). Their Mark has features that are (if we revive the map-making metaphor) in a *literary* sense unplotted. Being a longish narrative and not, say, a sonnet, it is naturally open in texture, as they suggest in a fine observation: 'it is important to observe that narratives in general are a lot like matter: They feel solid to the touch, but they are really composed of empty space' (*Story*, 3). This raises the question of the genre of Mark, which we shall pursue at the end of this section.[7] For now, let us note some of the aspects of Mark which the more loosely textured analysis of *Story* is able to encompass much more successfully than is the *Study*.

We take as our first example that well-established aspect of Markan rhetoric, what *Story* calls the 'sandwiched episodes' of material (Kermode's 'intercalation'). The authors see the effects of these passages in the creation of tension, and in the illumination which each of the related stories throws on the other. They give several instances, including these: the scribes' accusation that Jesus is possessed, set amid his family's

---

7.   See 7F and 11B (pp. 97–99, 132–138) below.

concern for his sanity; Jesus' sending of his disciples – travelling light and with no rations – and their inability to eat because of pressure of work, surrounding the story of Herod's banquet; Peter's denial embedded in Jesus' confession before the High Priest; and the inadequate fig tree straddling the inadequate Temple authorities (*Story*, 52). Farrer of course discusses these passages and notes the alternation of material, but does not describe it as a Markan narrative technique in its own right (see e.g. his discussion of the fig tree, *Study*, 161–63). This is remarkable, since it as an aspect of Mark that might rear up before a reader approaching the text in a 'docile state of mind ... willing to examine the pattern that is there' (*Study*, 6).[8]

Another Markan feature which *Study* identifies is the propensity for 'concentric episodes'. One case is found in Mk 2.1–3.6:

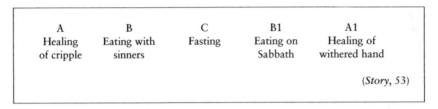

A	B	C	B1	A1
Healing of cripple	Eating with sinners	Fasting	Eating on Sabbath	Healing of withered hand

(*Story*, 53)

Figure 7.1: Concentric Episodes

The identification of parallels is clear and plausible. A and A1 are both set indoors, involve bodily healing and have as their 'cast' Jesus, the authorities and the person healed; both include a delay for accusations and show Jesus' rebuttal in the form of a rhetorical question. B and B1 both involve eating and uncleanness, have as their 'cast' Jesus, disciples and authorities, and comprise an act, an objection and an explanation by Jesus, the last in the form of a proverb, followed by a statement of his purpose and authority. C is a non-conflictual story in an indeterminate setting, and illuminates the themes of the material surrounding it, notably the question of authority. This analysis is of a sort which would be quite congenial to Farrer with its 'architectural' character. Farrer picks up some of the parallels, but cannot approach the elegance of Rhoads, Dewey and Michie, because – both in the *Study* and in *Matthew* – he has split these passages between two of his cycles (*Study*, 67–78, *Matthew*, 19–35).

The most illuminating comparison, however, we find in an intercalation which Farrer makes much of, the very familiar episode of the haemorrhaging woman and Jairus' daughter. Farrer spots allusive correspondences (the 'twelve' motif and reference to each as 'daughter'), details which *Story* does not mention and which invite attention of the sort Farrer lavishes

8.   See, for instance, Hooker's many references to 'sandwiching' (Commentary, Index, 412).

on the text; but nowhere among nearly thirty references to this passage in the *Study*[9] does he say what is to Rhoads, Dewey and Michie (and to us?) the obvious thing, that the delay of the healing of Jairus' daughter by the healing of the woman creates suspense and prompts comparison between the two – for instance between the faith of the father and of the woman – within the story world (*Story*, 51). Farrer is of course aware of the singularity of this composite passage, but he can only find an explanation within the recondite categories of his shrinking series of healings; and we saw that there was awkwardness even then.

In *Matthew* he comes a little closer to *Story*. In a footnote to one of his largely arithmetical discussions of the patterning of healings, Farrer asks how the healing of Jairus' daughter can both reflect and surpass the earlier healing of another prostrated female, Peter's mother-in-law, for that is what Farrer's scheme requires of it. It does this, he says, by starting as a straightforward story of restoration to health, and changing, thanks to an interval (filled by the healing of the haemorrhaging woman), from a healing to a raising, since the girl has died in the interim (*Matthew*, 30). He returns to this discussion rather later in the book, and now speaks overtly of the effect of this passage on the reader of Mark: the inserted healing is 'a narrative filling … which helps the reader to appreciate the passage of time' (he compares it with the later digression on the death of John the Baptist), providing 'a lapse of dramatic time, a scene before the drop curtain while the stage-set is being changed'; in this dramatic lapse the girl dies, and what began as 'a cure of the bedridden' becomes 'a raising of the dead' (*Matthew*, 86f). Farrer is here aware of the rhetorical character of the passage, but only in the rather cerebral senses of its function in indicating the lapse of narrative time (a kind of narrative rubric, the sort of thing that would be covered in a play-script by a stage direction) and in developing earlier themes; and his slight rendering of the inserted story as a front-of-stage filler certainly underestimates the power of that episode in its own right, let alone within the whole. So, despite attending to the passage in a manner more akin to that we find in *Story*, Farrer still emerges with a very different picture of the experience of reading this section of Mark. The effect on the reader envisaged by *Story* is that of tension created and resolved; Farrer's reader seems more given to the mental enjoyment of pattern and allusion. How is it that one so attuned to the literary possibilities of a Gospel can make so little of some of its more obvious literary devices, and come to such bloodless estimations of their effects?

9.   See *Study*, Index, 376.

F. Conclusion

Mark as Story approaches Mark as 'literature', and treats the Gospel in the manner of prose fiction, yet Farrer's rather different treatment approaches Mark as 'literature' too. Parson Thwackum, the rather aggressive cleric in Henry Fielding's *Tom Jones*, says that when he mentions 'religion', he means the Christian religion; and not only the Christian religion, but the Protestant religion; and not only the Protestant religion, but the Church of England. When Farrer speaks (less polemically) of the 'literary' character of Mark's Gospel, what does he mean by literature?

> St Mark's book is neither a treatise nor a poem, but is more like a poem than a treatise. Now a poem of any extent has a rhythm, not in the sound only, but also in the sense. Themes and symbols recur, not monotonously, but not chaotically either ... There may be several overlapping systems of symbolic or thematic rhythm in any one poem. (*Study*, 30)

Despite the difficulty of finding *the* system, Farrer maintains that it is sensible to seek a basic design and find in it a pointer to the genre of Mark's work: 'For he started with something already in mind, surely; he set out to write some sort of a work rather than another' (*Study*, 30). He draws a comparison with the work of a playwright, who, before writing, has to have some idea of plot, and, before that, a conception of the characters and *dénouement*. Farrer offers external and internal criteria for settling the question of genre, and gives as an example of the former the plays of Shakespeare, for we know quite a lot about the sources upon which Elizabethan dramatists drew, and about what their public expected of them. If we turn to Mark, he now says, the position for our external criterion is less happy, for we know much less about the sort of literary model Mark would consider himself to be following. Farrer mentions possible models in the sacred histories of Elijah and the Books of Kings, but does not find in the Old Testament any candidate for a literary design to which Mark is indebted, though the Septuagint provides a model for Mark's phrasing; the (to Mark) contemporary Jewish Pseudepigrapha fare no better.[10]

Despite this nod towards drama, when Farrer says 'literary' he chiefly means 'poetic'. This should not surprise us, for in his Preface to the *Glass* we read that one of the three poles around which the lectures revolve is his 'sense of poetry', and in Lecture VII he likens Paul's or John's minds working on revealed images to the poetic mind and its inspiration (*Glass*, ix, 113–16). Farrer sees poetry resting on the invariable facts of human language and imagination, from which comes our tendency to play with the musicality of words and the creations of the imagination.

---

10.   Brown, 'Human', 91, notes the same. The ancient biographies, the βίοι (bioi) receive similar neglect: see 11B (pp. 132–138) below.

But what does Farrer mean by 'poetry'? He accepts that the word covers
a vast range of literary phenomena, but is himself drawn in a particular
direction. In considering the abrupt ending of Mark, he momentarily
invokes the works of Eliot, which often hinge on subtle literary allusions,
but for Farrer poetry *par excellence* is found in England in the period from
Spenser to just after Keats. From that 'happy post-Renaissance period' he
forms his 'instinctive opinion of poetry' (*Glass*, 118, 138). When he says
'poetry', that is the poetry he means.[11] If that period influences Farrer's
conception of poetry as much as he suggests, it explains a great deal.
He speaks of the great poets of those times evoking symbols which they
held to have universal significance; 'The phrase which is just right has
infinite overtones: or it awakens echoes in all the hidden caves of our
minds'; the words of a poem 'are intended to arouse all possible echoes'
(*Glass*, 115, 119f). The transfer of this frame of mind to the reading
of the Book of Revelation (which Farrer attempts in the rest of Lecture
VII) is not too difficult, for there the forest of images readily allows of
description in these terms (a readiness Farrer will exploit in *A Rebirth of
Images*). Farrer is confident, however, of transferring it to Mark as well;
he states his intention in this lecture and does it with some panache when
considering the end of the Gospel in Lecture VIII. Its application to Mark
does, however, limit Farrer's critical vision.

To return to the Jairus episode in the *Study*, here Farrer shows us what
senses honed on the allusiveness of, say, Shakespeare's imagery will seek,
and what a memory soaked in the Old Testament will then supply. The
double reference to 'twelve' is striking, and it immediately evokes – by
correspondence – the Twelve Patriarchs; once in that patriarchal world,
the mind readily links – this time by contrast – the two sons of Joseph ('the
most Christ-like of the Patriarchs', *Study*, 335) and the two 'daughters'
of Jesus; and why is the story of the woman embedded in the story of the
girl, so that Jesus first agrees to heal the girl, but actually heals the woman
first? Surely in order to follow the model of Joseph's sons: Manasseh was
the elder, but Ephraim came before him in the roll of tribes (*Study*, esp.
80f 144f, 328, 330).

Now if we allow, as Farrer does, the many levels of significance which
may subsist in a text, it is hard for us to say that we cannot allow his reading
of this episode, however contrived or bizarre it seems to decidedly post-
Renaissance, indeed post-Enlightenment, sensibilities. We can observe,
however, that here we see a mind attuned to the workings of a certain
sort of poetry approaching what is primarily a *narrative*. Narrative has
its own rhythm and texture, its peculiar ways of maintaining its tensile
strength; it is these which *Mark as Story* lifts out, and which Farrer, for
all his extraordinary instinct that a Gospel is primarily a literary entity,
is not well equipped to identify. This is because for him literature is more

---

11.   See also his subsequent reference to 'early modern poets' ('Surface', 56).

a setting for the jewel of a word or an image than a channel for the flow of a story. It is interesting to speculate how his reading of Mark might have changed if he had spent as much time with prose authors from his favourite epoch. Kermode salutes Farrer as 'he makes bold to write about Mark as another man might write about Spenser' (*Genesis*, 72). How might it have been if he had written of Mark as one might write of Sterne, or indeed Thwackum's Fielding? Or how would it have been, in the case of Hamlet (for he alludes to it, *Glass*, 118f), if he had been as much struck by the structure of the play as by the poetry of its hero's speeches?[12]

12.   For an approach with definite resemblances to Farrer's which retains a sense of Mark as narrative, see Drury's 'Mark'. Drury assigns Mark to the genre of 'folktale', and uses semiotics-inspired headings like 'Structures and Codes', but takes a Farrerian line on Mark's typological relationship with the Old Testament and on prefiguration within Mark itself, where both use the 'seed' metaphor for the unfolding of the text to the reader or hearer ('Mark' 406f cf *Study*, 54). Drury's Markan 'code' of baptism resembles Farrer's water-and-cleansing symbolism ('Mark', 409 cf *Study*, 45, 50, 87), both make much of the triangular correspondences between Jesus, John the Baptist and Elijah ('Mark', 411 cf *Study*, 59f), and Drury makes identical use of Psalm 115 ('Mark', 406 cf *Study*, 48). When he tackles the miraculous feedings and the loaf-in-the-boat scene (Mk 6.35–44, 8.1–10, 14–21), Drury's exegesis is based on typological resemblance between Jesus and David (1 Sam. 21), and numerical juggling of loaves and baskets. It conforms substantially to Farrer's much longer account ('Mark', 415f cf *Study*, 290–304, revised in *Matthew*, 57–80). Drury's suggestions for further reading direct us to Lightfoot, but not to Farrer ('Mark', 417).

Chapter 8

MARK AS LITERATURE: CONCLUSIONS

Farrer's literary instincts about Mark, and his conviction about its total coherence, adumbrated in *The Glass of Vision*, lead in *A Study in St Mark* to an eventually oppressive elaboration of structure and allusion. From the time of its writing and until recently, it has been hard to situate the *Study* within the wider landscape of Gospel studies. This has contributed to a neglect which has denied students of Mark some fine insights which Farrer offers, particularly from the smaller patterns he describes in Mark. Criticism among Farrer's contemporaries now seems to reveal its own ambiguities, while Farrer's critique of form criticism has grown in cogency. His avant-garde literary instincts find echoes among present-day interpreters of Mark within the 'literary paradigm'. Indeed, when compared, their precursor can sometimes stand up to them remarkably well. We can summarise the salient features of these comparisons thus.

Genre

Farrer's treatment of Mark as 'more like a poem than anything else' is largely an error. *Mark as Story* fares better, with a looser frame of reference derived from prose fiction, but its interpretative tools, developed for nineteenth and twentieth-century fiction, can be at risk of foisting on Mark an unhelpful modernity. If genre is not after all a timeless thing, there must be a *historical* aspect to competent genre criticism. The question of genre is critically important, as it all but determines the characteristics the reader will then seek in the text.

The Author

Farrer repeatedly affirms his allegiance to the intention of the author, but Gardner, a fellow intentionalist, criticises him for a disembodied picture of the evangelist. Their disagreement shows up the great assumptions Farrer makes about the author of Mark, but also the perils of any attempt to discover an author's intention. Moore stresses these, and sees the only route from the death of the author as leading to (neo-)pragmatist reader-response criticism. Rhoads, Dewey and Michie also have a place for the author but, despite their fiction-derived tool box, they are in this respect less thorough than Farrer at treating Mark as 'story', because of his abiding emphasis of the creative influence of the author on *every* aspect of the text.

The Reader

Several times Farrer refers to the original audience of Mark, and to their remoteness from a modern audience. Though his definition of them is vague, his approach is better than Rhoads and Michie's first attempt. They mean to confine themselves to the reader implied by the story, yet cannot avoid importing data from outside the story world to make it intelligible to that reader. Their collaboration with Dewey produces a fuller, more nuanced picture, and raises the question of what constitutes an audience definition that is adequate for establishing a credible authorial intention.

Priorities in Interpretation

Farrer's *a priori* belief in the wholeness of Mark leads him to reverse the traditional order and delay form-critical study until the complete text has been adequately treated. (In practice, he delays it for good.) Drury follows him in this more rational approach (in that the book as a whole is all that we have),[1] and Kermode approves of him even as he himself is seized by the possibilities of delusion in making a text 'hang together'.

Presuppositions

Farrer is always candid about the Christian faith which prompts him to read Mark. It gives him a fundamental belief in the wholeness of the Gospel (a belief severely examined by Kermode) as an authoritative act of religious communication. It can obtrude upon his exegesis, in terms both of vocabulary and, more seriously, of judgement.[2] Given the impossibility of complete objectivity, however, Farrer's candour is a virtue, in that it eases his own readers' task in defining the purpose of Farrer's reading and

1. As does Williams (*Parable*, 25).
2. See Part IV.

in taking account of his ideological stance. Too seldom do interpreters make these things clear.[3] Kermode's affection for him shows how his ideas can be readily heard by secular critics, for all that they lack 'circumcised ears' (*Genesis*, 3).

Historical Implications

What has been the status of my assessment of Farrer as 'convincing', or 'implausible'? We here address the problem of what Moore calls 'transcendentalized textual content' (*Challenge*, 172), a standard of judgement for every reading of a text which is itself independent of any reading. Moore denies that there is such a thing, and so places the whole weight of meaning and content in the constructive activity of the reader. This is indeed one solution. For the exponent of a freewheeling brand of reader-response criticism, the difficulties discussed in these pages will evaporate in the sun of thoroughgoing subjectivism. For other readers, who are not happy to make their personal response the judge and jury of all interpretation (subject only to institutional constraint), the problems remain. I suggest above that some may admit of a historical resolution. In Part III I shall suggest that some problems of meaning and content become less vexatious when they are removed from the sphere of Platonic forms and placed at earthy moments in history. Despite all that has been said, I believe that this was never far from Farrer's intention.

3.   For exceptions, see *Story*, 175, note 6, and Watson, *Text*: note his persuasive argument that *no* discipline can be seen as autonomous, having no social base outside the academy, and owing no debts except to the quest for truth (*Text*, 8).

PART III

MARK AS HISTORY

The principal importance of St Mark's Gospel lies in its historical content.
Study, 182

In Part II we considered the implications of Farrer's work on Mark for an understanding of that Gospel as literature. Farrer was very far from seeing Mark as literature in any fictive sense, and although in the *Study* he has much more to say about literary design than about history, the latter is never far away. We found that such literary considerations as those of genre and reader (let alone that of author) could not be adequately broached within a narrowly 'literary' frame, but drew us in the direction of 'history'. But what is 'history' for Farrer, or for us? And in what sense can the Gospel of Mark be history? Before we can ask such questions sensibly, we have to define the way or ways in which we can apply the category 'historical' to a text. This will be our first task. Having done this, we shall discover that history and text have a multi-storeyed relation to each other, and we shall examine those traces we can find of each stratum in Farrer's work on Mark. As before, we shall open up the wider implications in conversation with more recent contributions, notably Mary Beavis' *Mark's Audience* and Richard Burridge's *What are the Gospels?*.

Chapter 9

READING MARK HISTORICALLY

We desire to view the Marcan history as a history.

A Study in St Mark, 186

In his contribution to a set of New Testament essays set firmly in a historical-critical mould ('What Might Martyrdom Mean?'), Nicholas Lash is unhappy with 'the mistaken belief that texts "have meaning" in somewhat the same way that material objects "have mass"', preferring to see texts as 'notations' requiring the performance of reading ('Martyrdom', 192).[1] So instead of asking baldly whether or not – or to what degree – Mark is 'history', we should rather ask what it might mean to read Mark historically. I shall describe five levels at which we can ask this question. There are connections and overlaps, but we can still usefully distinguish between them, as (to change the metaphor) a musician distinguishes between keys in musical notation. As we read Mark, we become conscious of the level, the 'key' in which we are performing, by keeping certain questions in mind.

A. Levels of History

Level 1: the historicality of the reader

In his poem 'Burnt Norton', Eliot broods on the connection of present and past time, and on the memory as a place of echoes. He addresses his reader directly: 'My words echo/ Thus, in your mind.'[2]

1.   On 'notation', Lash quotes Raymond Williams, 'Base and Superstructure in Marxist Cultural Theory', *New Left Review*, 82, 1973, 14. On 'performance', see further Frances Young, *Art*, esp. Ch. 7, and Hirsch, *Validity*, 13f.
2.   T.S. Eliot, 'Burnt Norton' ('Four Quartets'), *Collected Poems, 1909–1962* (London: Faber & Faber, 1974; 189, ll. 1–15).

Any reading of a text is a historical reading, for reading is done by people, who are creatures of time. Thus my reading of Mark, your reading of these words of mine, are performances of a text in a mind in which there are various desires and dislikes, hopes and regrets, various cultural and political affiliations; and in which there are already echoes of things heard and seen, done and said, recollections of other texts read, memories perhaps of earlier readings of the text now before the eyes, or reports of others' readings of it. All these colour the sense the reader perceives in reading the words on the page, and all of these are born of the reader's inhabiting a particular place and time; they are the fruit of the reader's own embeddedness in history. This is the first and inescapable sense of historicality. In his *Gospel Against Parable*, J.G. Williams (who calls it not historicality but 'historicity') believes it bridges the gap between historical and literary criticism of the Gospels:

> We are obliged to acknowledge *historicity*, our own and that of the works and writers we study. Historicity is our innate condition as caring beings who are constantly seeking ourselves in the past (thus we know satisfaction, regret and guilt) and in the future (thus we know hope and anxiety). This historicity takes many forms; sometimes it is expressed in works that we call historiography, and another important expression is in works of 'literature'. But literature, too, represents historicity, even if it does not directly represent a history that occurs outside of the work. *The most important link between historical and literary criticism, the referent that both orientations are concerned to know and elucidate, is historicity as it takes specific forms* ... To be a historical being is to be human; to understand this historical being is not to look to 'history' in a narrow sense. (*Parable*, 13, original emphasis)[3]

'What makes me read Mark as I do?' The asking of that question makes me aware of my own historicality as a reader.

Level 2: the historicality of other readers

If, as I read and interpret Mark, I bring to the text my own history and in turn make my reading of Mark part of what will become my history, I may then ask how the reading of Mark has been part of other people's histories as well (its 'reception history'). This is a second sense in which I might read this Gospel historically. It may, for instance, be my interest to ask how Mark was received by certain people of some earlier time. In the case of other biblical documents like the writings of Paul, we can see easily how salutary such an exercise might be. In the Reformation period, Martin Luther offered a reading of Paul the influence of which spread far beyond his own locality and indeed beyond his own epoch. Contingent

---

3.   This awareness of historical embeddedness is the motor of the so-called new historicism, which is beginning to appear in biblical interpretation. See the discussion in Carroll, 'Poststructural', 52–57.

circumstances made 'salvation by faith' an overriding principle – and a productive one – for Luther in his appropriation of Paul; but has not a failure to attend fully to the historical locality of Luther's interpretation led many subsequent interpreters (Bultmann for instance, and others in the Lutheran tradition) to tend to read Paul as if he were Luther?[4] Each audience receives a text in its own place and time, but sometimes the echo of a particular audience's response carries to other places and later times.

This second level of historicality is important for any readers whose aim is to get somewhere near the author's intention in writing a text (see Level 3 below): those who have not been completely disheartened by warnings against the intentional fallacy will do well to pay attention, among the numberless other readers of Mark, to the author's primary target, the first audience to receive the text, and all the concerns and habits of thought which shape its setting in history.[5] To summarise: if I read Mark while asking how this text has been received by anyone (including Mark's first audience) other than myself, this constitutes a second sense in which I might read Mark historically.

Level 3: the historicality of the author

Why did Mark write Mark's Gospel? Seeking the author's intention is itself a third way of reading a text historically, for any author is embedded in history. In the case of Mark, lacking evidence for identifying the author of the Gospel with a figure we know of independently, we can know nothing of the author – beyond the most general observations about first-century milieu – apart from what we read in the text of Mark. The figure thus delineated we have met before, in the person of the literary critic's 'implied' author; we may, however (indeed Williams, *Parable*, 13, says we *should*), still view this literarily constructed person in a historical frame. As I look at what is present in the text and what is absent from it, I find myself speaking of the 'choices' which produced these presences and these absences, and inferring the concerns and objectives which might have prompted such choices. It is a task a little similar to that of an

---

4.   On Luther, Lutherans and biblical interpretation see Nineham, *Use* (esp. 36, 114f, 264); and Werner Jeanrond's critique of Fuchs, Ebeling and the New Hermeneutic ('Hermeneutics', 91f). On these matters in Pauline studies, see E.P. Sanders, *Paul* (esp. 492), and John Ziesler, 'Justification'.

In the case of Mark, there is little to report about readings of that Gospel until the recent past. Matthew (long accepted as the earliest Gospel) and John would be more fertile ground.

5.   This exercise takes on an extra subtlety if we posit an original setting in which the Gospel is read out. The 'reader-out' then becomes the primary and the hearers the secondary original audience. Furthermore, the reader-out might well be the author!

astronomer, trying to work out the nature of an asteroid from the shape and size of the crater it has left.

The quest of the historical author seems to be accepted even by one so sceptical of the accessibility of real authors as Moore. Let us recall his description of the implied author as '"a core of norms and choices" immanent in a work, that "we infer as an ideal, literary, created version of the real [author]"' (*Challenge*, 180).[6] Despite his qualifications – 'ideal' and 'created' – it must follow that there is no point in talking of 'choices' without inferring an agent capable of choosing; that is, a real author. Even then, we must preserve a formal distinction between the historical figure who is the author and the authorial mask that the author puts on in the act of writing the text. In the case of Mark, we can only know the mask. However confident a reader feels that the mask closely resembles the face behind it, the distinction is a necessary reminder that there is much more to the life of an author than what is revealed or betrayed in the text. It is on this third level that we should place both redaction- and composition-critical studies of Gospels.

Level 4: the historicality of the materials

No author, embedded as we all are in history, writes *de novo*. We may next ask, therefore: what are the proximate origins of the story and the characters of the text? How did the author come by them? Of what other texts is this text the transformation? In the case of Mark, we shall have to consider the quotation of prophets and psalms, verbal echoes of other Christian writings the author could have known, or resemblances of stance between them.[7] These questions, customarily associated with source and form criticism, constitute a fourth way of reading historically, seeking the pre-history of the text, the routes by which material was created, shaped, preserved and transmitted until it came into the hands of the author.

Level 5: the historicality of the referents

The word 'created' brings us to a fifth sense of historical reading. The text of Mark that I read is in some irreducible sense created by the author,[8]

6.　See p. 87 above.

7.　E.g. the composite citation of prophecy in Mk 1.1–3; possible Pauline allusions: 'the cup that I drink' (Mk 10.38 cf 1 Cor. 10.16), baptism and death (Mk 10.38 cf Rom. 6.3), 'Abba Father' (Mk 14.36 cf Rom. 8.15, Gal. 4.6).

8.　Though textual criticism argues caution even here; see Parker, 'Scripture', who argues cogently for the manuscript tradition as evidence of 'a continuing interplay between the scripture – the text copied – and the tradition – the person engaged in the process of copying in and for the Church' ('Scripture', 17).

yet the text may come to appear, as we apply the questions just described, as a *re*-creation of things received. Furthermore, a narrative, referential, 'history-like' writing such as Mark, may then lead us to ask: is this text a (re-)creation which is itself a representation of historical events, happenings either directly witnessed or mediated by the representations of others? To read Mark historically in this sense is to regard the Gospel as a window on to those events. There are windows of many sorts. I may conclude that Mark is most like a stained-glass window, or like a flawed, frosted, cracked or dirty window, a window not transparent but translucent, or a window that is all but opaque; but nevertheless I seek to regard it as a window of a sort, which gives some access to deeds done and suffered, words said and heard, which are beyond the internal, 'story' world of the text, beyond the immediate worlds both of its audiences and of the author seeking to address them, and beyond the literary and oral antecedents of the text.

B. Farrer and Levels of History

There is, then, a fivefold sense to the phrase 'a historical reading of Mark', and this may appear to make Austin Farrer's approach to matters of history quite ingenuous. He too, however, is somewhat aware of different levels of history. Among his opening remarks in the *Study* we read:

> To interpret Mark historically may mean either of two things. It may mean that with good will and intelligence we can read him as history, that is, as actually exhibiting ... continuity and development ... Or it may mean that he supplies the sort of discontinuous evidence from which our historical wisdom can reconstruct an historical continuity not set forth by Mark. (*Study*, 3)

Farrer here aims at a fifth-level reading of Mark by way of the third, authorial level, while observing that he may then be forced to work at the fourth level as well, examining the author's materials in the hope that they can be read at the fifth level. Much later on in the *Study*, we return to Mark as history.

> When he [the Christian historian] distinguishes between what Christ said in Galilee and the interpretation of that saying which Christ taught St Mark through the Holy Ghost, the distinction he draws is not one of truth but one of time. He is not dividing fiction from fact but the later from the earlier. To him as an historian St Mark's making the inspired interpretation is as much a fact as Christ's giving the original oracle; to him as a Christian the inspired comment is as true as the divine text. (*Study*, 370)

This passage bristles with difficulties, about the identity of this 'Christian historian', and the currency there can be in public discourse for such privileged agents as 'Holy Ghost' and 'inspired' writers, but for now we note simply how Farrer is happy not to confine historical enquiry to the examination of the events allegedly giving rise to the writing which purports to represent them. Here too he shows some awareness of the historian's task as a many-layered activity.

So what are the implications for Farrer's reading of Mark of the five layers we have described? How aware is he of them as he pursues his detailed exegesis? We shall take each in turn. In some cases Farrer gives us full and explicit treatment of the matter we are considering, in other cases what he offers is implicit or meagre, and this unevenness will inevitably be reflected in the length and scope of the different sections which follow.[9]

C. *The Historicality of Farrer's Reading of Mark*

Some of what we considered in Part II could be described as material for a 'history' of Austin Farrer as reader, an enquiry into the historical embeddedness of his own reading of Mark. We sought one or two glimpses of Farrer in his intellectual and cultural milieu; we speculated on the possible echoes in his mind which emerge from his writing; and we examined ways in which they might have influenced his reading. Most notable was the suggestion that it is Farrer's assumption that Mark should be read as a sort of poetry, coupled with Farrer's own tastes in poetry – Spenser, perhaps Shakespeare and Keats, possibly Eliot – which so colour his interpretation. (There is a hint here of the Luther-and-Paul phenomenon we touched on above.[10]) We also noted that his belonging

---

9.   There is a potentially bewildering methodological question here, which must be clarified. Farrer's *Study* and his other writings are themselves texts, and so is this book. Any reading of this book therefore invites the same questions about levels of history, as the reader is reading a text about the reading of certain other texts (Farrer's books and papers) which are themselves about the reading of a text (the Gospel of Mark). Well might George Steiner deplore the 'parasitic discourse' of books about books (*Presences*, 47f)! The reader of this text will decide at what levels to read. I must make clear the levels at which I am working in reading Farrer.

While providing, as I write, evidence of the historicality of my own reading of Farrer (Level 1), I also advert to other readers of Farrer (Level 2) in pursuit of a third-level reading, seeking to describe and evaluate the aims, achievements, deficiencies and setting of the author. In reading a given text of Farrer's, I consider (at Level 4) the influence of his earlier writings upon it, and evidence of other materials which might shape it. The pointed lack of footnote and citation in Farrer's writings may make the prospects for identifying those 'other materials' little better than those for the quest of Mark's Christian sources, though Farrer's literary asides (as when he tells us his favourite poets) give us something to go on. I read Farrer at Level 5 insofar as I weigh up the plausibility of the account he gives of the 'event' he tries to describe, that of Mark composing his Gospel.

10.   See 9A (pp. 105f) above.

to the household of faith as an Anglican Christian is another pole influencing the magnetic field in which Farrer the reader moves.[11] The quotation above about the 'Christian historian' is further evidence of this. So it was that we noted, for instance, that his reading of the ordered entry of Gentiles into the circle of Jesus betrays Farrer's own experience of church order.[12]

On the strength of his writing in the *Study*, how aware is Farrer of his own – and his readers' – historical rootedness? There is one clear moment of recognition, when he acknowledges that his proposals about symbolism in Mark might seem excessively tortuous. The difficulty, he says, is that the evangelist was using 'certain symbolical conventions' which are not readily exportable to the twentieth (and now the twenty-first) century. Mark 'could use them without any painful labour of building them up, because they were current in his world. We reconstruct them with pain, but that is because we are men of a different generation' (*Study*, 79). Otherwise, Farrer seems largely oblivious. Latterly, this preoccupation has become prominent within that bundle of attitudes and perceptions which go by the name of 'post-modern'. Thus, Stephen Moore sees post-modern poetics as embracing 'a criticism which would include in its own discourse an implicit (or explicit) reflection upon itself' (*Challenge*, 181).[13] Awareness of one's own historical relativity is not an easy thing to maintain – like trying to jump off your own shadow, as Farrer says in another context (*Saving*, 11) – but it was hardly a revolutionary thought even in his day.[14] If Farrer was oblivious or refused to entertain it, this would have fitted well with his wider sense of the privileged position of those belonging to the inspired, Spirit-led community of faith, yet his is still an unusually interesting case to consider from this perspective. This is not because he stands out for his limited self-awareness among British scholars of this period, as we see if we recall our earlier mention of Knox and Taylor, and their verdict on the possibility of Mark deliberately ending at 16.8: incredible, they say, for such originality would overturn the whole method of form criticism.[15] What presuppositions underlie this *auto-da-fé*? We might suspect a desire to get back to the historical Jesus which makes them hold tight to 'nurse', despite form-critical scepticism

11.   And he was a 'convert' at that (not the ideal word to describe moving from one Christian denomination to another). For Farrer's path from the Baptist Church to the Church of England, see Curtis, *Hawk*, esp. 20–24.

12.   See Chapter 5 above, and *Study*, 298.

13.   He quotes Linda Hutcheon, *A Poetics of Postmodernism: History, Theory, Fiction* (New York: Routledge, 1988), 13.

14.   See e.g. Troeltsch (p. 14, note 8 above); also Isaiah Berlin on Vico (1668–1744): 'there is no immutable structure of experience' (*Current*, 107f); and Collingwood's saying (in 1940) that each civilisation has its own 'constellation of absolute presuppositions' (quoted by Nineham, 'Cultural', 156).

15.   See 6E (pp. 78f) above. Taylor, *Commentary*, 609.

about reaching that wellspring of Gospel tradition, for fear of something worse, the alarming vision of a genuine creative author. We can speculate, but no more, for Taylor's pages show less inclination than Farrer's to plumb these introspective waters.

Farrer's case is quite different, and not only because he is not in thrall to the form critics. He has his own prejudices and presuppositions, yet he parades them, brazenly mixing creed and argument, faith and reason, and making manifest what others keep hidden. At several points in the *Study* he reminds his reader that 'we' are believers, reading Mark for the building up of faith, and that his own prejudices (though he does not call them that) about the wholeness of the text of Mark and the fecundity of its author stem from a prior confession that the evangelist is inspired by God. The opening words of two paragraphs very early in the *Study* leave Farrer's readers in no doubt about what sort of hands they are in: 'Now we are Christians too ... We assume that St Mark is subject to the two controls of fact and inspiration' (*Study*, 8).[16]

Farrer, to be sure, does not betray any sense that his *a priori* commitments may skew his judgement, though later (*Matthew*, 2) he will tell himself off for having taken refuge in mystery when the exegetical going got tough. To that extent we are dealing here more with naive candour than with proto-post-modern self-reflexivity! In one passage, however, he comes very close to describing the suspicion of ideological commitment which is the source in our time of the call for this rigorous self-reflection. Farrer has just offered, using the material in Mark 13, an account of Jesus' own perception of his fate, and that of his followers. He continues:

> What I have just written about Christ's prophecy is more like a confession of faith than a page of historical criticism. No harm, perhaps. If I were reading an historical argument like the one I am writing, and found the author however justifiably skirting round a point of faith, I should be continually asking myself, 'But what does the man believe?' So I have made my profession. (*Study*, 362)

Returning to Moore's description, we can already say that Farrer allows himself with remarkable readiness to be exposed to the scrutiny of an ideologically sensitive reader, even perhaps that he sometimes comes close, though implicitly, to the self-reflection which she commends. We can now add that, at one point at least, the self-reflection becomes explicit.

To be fully aware of the historicality of your reading of a text is to appreciate that your perceptions, however impressive, do not fully transcend the limits of a particular place and time, and to realise

---

16.   For other references by Farrer to his implied reader as another Christian, see e.g. *Study*, 2, 366, 367f; and to inspiration, see e.g. 9, 25, 53, 100f, 179, 361, 367. See also 'Bible', 9–13 (esp. 9).

that, were you at another place or in another time, things might look different. Farrer manages some of this, perhaps manages a surprising amount of it for his day, but the dominant impression he makes is still that of someone believing that his standpoint transcends the bounds of historicality, enjoying an excessive confidence that he and Mark are in the same tradition, and evincing a theological obstinacy which insists, 'you need to be a Christian to understand this', with no real sense of the truth that only a stranger might see. Nevertheless, Austin Farrer gives his readers a quite remarkable amount of scope for doing their own work on identifying what have been called the legitimating 'metanarratives' which inform and underpin his enquiry.[17] When in a more overtly apologetic mode, Farrer can confess the temptation 'to slip away into a museum of medieval or scriptural images, and to work out a pious pattern unrelated to the way we think about anything else' (*Saving*, 5). In his writing on Mark, however, we suspect that Farrer would protest that he was making explicit his metanarrative – if he could bring himself to use such a word – not so much for scrutiny's as for devotion's sake.[18]

17. See Lyotard, *Postmodern*, xxiv.
18. See also the Postscript to Chapter 12 below, and Part IV.

Chapter 10

MARK'S ORIGINAL AUDIENCE

Was [Mark's Gospel] ... not from the first in use for the purpose for which it was
surely designed – for Church reading and common edification?

A Study in St Mark, 173

In this chapter we examine the attention Farrer pays to the character of
the first audience to receive Mark's Gospel. We compare his work with a
monograph devoted to this subject, Mary Beavis' *Mark's Audience*.

A. Farrer and the Markan Audience

Reading the *Study* may sometimes feel like being a spectator at a piece
of psychic surgery. In this controversial form of alternative medicine, the
practitioner simply rubs or touches the skin of the patient, and claims that
this is effecting changes within the body, which no-one else (not even the
body's owner) can discern, but which will bring a cure. So it sometimes
seems when Farrer speaks so confidently and intimately of 'the mind of
Mark', whether in the earlier book or in his more chastened *Matthew*.
The unease of a modern reader of Farrer may derive partly from those
difficulties of essentialism we have already discussed. But if we are
unsatisfied with saying that Farrer's programme is simply uncongenial to
our own reading preferences, we are trying to set limits to what may be
said about Mark. Even if we cannot say what Mark is, we claim to have
a sense of what it is *not*. Where might such limits come from? When it is
an ancient text we consider, a large part of the answer lies in an appeal
to the original audience.

From audience to author

If it is the mind of Mark that we seek, we still do well to see a first-
century audience standing between us and that author, because the

original audience stands between the author-seeking reader and the worst excesses of self-projection. The act of trying to stand among them is fraught with misunderstanding and doomed to failure, for it is indeed true that we cannot jump off our own shadow, vacate our own historicality and occupy someone else's. The very attempt, however, acts as a brake upon those more serious misunderstandings which come when we conceive of a text as the product of an author in isolation, a timeless mind writing almost as it seems for us alone. Such a 'mind' can easily be no more than a blank canvas on which we can paint whatever colours we are pleased to find in the palette of the text as we read it. To ask about the original audience is immediately to anchor the authorial mind in a particular place and time, and so to set limits to what that mind may be assumed to have thought and believed it possible to communicate. Authors usually write with an audience in mind or, more elementarily still, with an expectation that what they write will prove generally intelligible, though this is no guarantee that they will succeed. (Some write purely to express themselves to themselves, as in a diary; but would a first-century Christian do that?) It is therefore a useful control upon conjecture about an ancient author to ask: 'How much of my "insight" might conceivably have been grasped by an audience of that time?' The purpose of this section is to examine Farrer's attitude to the reading of Mark with an eye to the original audience (that is, at the second of our five levels). Apart from a brief and exceedingly general survey of other scholars' treatment of Mark, and his despatching of the testimony of Papias (*Study*, 10–21), Farrer pays no attention to any other audience of Mark's, unless we count Farrer's own readers as such an audience. Nor, of course, is it the original audience that is really in his sights, but the intentions and the barely conscious mental processes of the author who addresses them. How, then, does he conceive of the authorial mind in relation to the original audience?

Farrer's enquiry into Mark seldom stops to question his 'insight', and when he does – as when he mentions ancient 'symbolic conventions' (*Study*, 79) – it is with the immediate presumption that Mark's first-century audience would find Farrer's elaborations more congenial than will the latter's twentieth-century one. It may be so, but we need more than Farrer's word for it. In Part II we noted occasions in the *Study* when Farrer does give space to this question of audience.[1] To these we can add: a reference to the Gospel's provenance, 'Say he was writing in Rome ...'; a claim ('who doubts it?') that Mark was a preacher before he was a writer; and Farrer's view that preaching was 'a Jewish art in an advanced state of development' (*Study*, 186, 367). These are really just hints about audience (in the last two the reference is only implicit), but there is also

---

1.   *Study*, 46, 79, 83 and 173 (the quotation at the start of this chapter); see 7D (pp. 91–93) above.

a longer passage (*Study*, 360–365) which comes in the discussion of the Gospel's date of composition. Farrer looks at the Markan apocalypse of Chapter 13, and sees Mark taking Jesus' prophecy (Jesus having taken Daniel's prophecy to himself), and re-expressing 'for the benefit of his contemporaries' what Farrer takes to be (in v. 14) a prophecy implicitly concerning the fate of the Temple: 'It is unlikely that Mark will do so without betraying the point of view, the place in history, from which he and his friends look at the course of events which Christ had prophesied' (*Study*, 360). Applying historical-critical method in a quite orthodox way, Farrer anchors the discussion with the externally verifiable date of the fall of Jerusalem and the consequent destruction of the Temple. He then asks whether the text implies a 'place in history' for Mark and his audience before or after this event. But can we be sure that the rather allusive 'abomination' of v. 14 refers to the desecration of the Temple? Farrer says we can be sure enough, because of the opening context of the prophetic discourse (Jesus' oracle about the Temple in 13.2) and the disciples' question in v. 4, 'When will these things be?' – that is, when will the Temple's demise and all related events take place? – to which the discourse provides Jesus' answer. The succeeding verses should therefore bear in some way on the Temple. But why is there no specific mention of it?

> If St Mark can trust his readers to see where the fall of the temple fits into this complex of events he has every reason for not mentioning it explicitly, since he has already recorded Christ's oracle about it. But if the exhortation, 'Let him that readeth understand' (XIII, 14), does not evoke the response it demands, if the reader does not see where the fall of the Temple comes in, then Christ will not be seen to have answered that part of his disciples' question which bears on the fall of the Temple. (*Study*, 363)

Farrer here combines attention to internal evidence, 'interpreting St Mark by St Mark' (*Study*, 364), with an appeal to the principle of intelligibility: is it reasonable to think that the audience would infer 'Temple' from the mention of Daniel's 'abomination of desolation' (Mk 13.14 cf Dan. 9.27, *Study*, 363f)? The question still remains, however: if the Temple is what is implied, at what place in history does Mark imply it? Before its destruction, or after? Again the putative original audience is the key witness:

> The answer is 'Before'. XIII, 5–13 contains a comparatively long and detailed exhortation about the conduct of Christians during a disappointing period of serious but desultory persecution before the events connected with 'the end' begin. It would be strange indeed if St Mark should so much expand the mere prelude to the apocalyptic drama, unless that was where he and his contemporaries were, anxiously looking for the curtain to go up. After briefly rehearsing the last things in XIII, 14–27, he returns in 28ff to an exhortation addressed to men who are looking for signs of the end ... Would St Mark have retained the words 'Pray that it may not happen in winter' if the matter were past praying for when he wrote? ... [I]t is

> obvious that St Mark is not an evangelist who makes an attempt to report all the
> words of Christ he has heard. (*Study*, 365)

Farrer's strategy is to try to place himself among Mark's first audience
and ask: If I were hearing all this after the destruction of the Temple,
would some of it sound odd? Would it sound less odd if I heard it
before the destruction? Which perspective would make the material
more intelligible? If the choice is between an earlier date and a bemused
audience, he bids us choose the earlier date.

So much for dating. Farrer's purpose of course is 'to understand how
St Mark wrote, not to determine when he wrote' (*Study*, 358), and when
he defends his case for the 'how' of Mark's Gospel, different criteria
apply for him. Apart from the most general invocation of first-century
'Jewishness' to allay the suspicions of sceptical moderns, there is none of
the public accountability of an audience which he brings to his argument
about chronology. We are left to trust the genius of Farrer himself. His
position is well stated in one of the appendix-like chapters at the end of
the *Study*, entitled 'Tribal Symbolism' (Chapter XV). This is one of the
three chapters Farrer describes as extensions of his thesis (*Study*, vi) and
it shows the same luxuriance of pattern and allusion as we find in the
main body of the book. We may, then, take it as a fitting sample of the
whole, not least for the way in which Farrer defends his ground. On a
page headed 'Meaning of the symbolism' Farrer rests his case:

> the men of the New Testament age ... searched for the New Testament in the Old,
> and it was there that they found it ... It is only by a serious grasp of this principle
> that it is possible to think intelligently about the subject-matter of this present
> chapter. Otherwise we must remain completely at the mercy of a whole sheaf of false
> questions. This, for example: 'But are you telling me that St Mark was attempting to
> convey all this tangle of Old Testament allusion and allegorical subtlety? If so, he was
> surely very unlucky, and not a little unreasonable. For he has certainly failed to make
> himself understood.' The right way to answer this question is, that what St Mark was
> attempting to convey was what he did convey, the portrait of Christ. How much of
> the Old Testament allusion he wished his first readers or hearers to understand is a
> point on which it is both unnecessary and impossible to dogmatize. But his primary
> purpose in allegorizing the Old Testament was not to make us follow his allegories,
> but to find Christ for himself, so that he could show him to us. (*Study*, 346f)

Farrer might of course be correct. But once you say that an aspect
of an author's method is a thing essentially for the author's own
benefit, something that readers might not even have been *supposed* to
understand, then unless your observations are quite disarming in their
elegance and clarity, compelling an amazed 'Of course!' which banishes
all reservations, then you are very likely doomed to be unpersuasive, for
you are offering a thesis quite incapable of demonstration.

We must emphasise that in these failings Farrer is to an extent a child
of his time, for the lack of sustained interest in shaping an authentic

context for Christian origins in first-century Judaism is one of the most marked contrasts with the current milieu in New Testament studies. When Farrer says that he does not 'pretend to know any more about first-century history than everyone picks up' (*Study*, 358) we may sense an Oxonian pose of learning lightly worn, but also a hint of the secondary, almost incidental, importance which he and others of his generation seem to have accorded such matters. Indeed, with his ten pages in the *Study* on the Testaments of the Twelve Patriarchs (*Study*, 348–357) he manages more than some.[2] But it is this lack, combined with highly speculative propositions, which makes Farrer's position vulnerable.

Ironically, there was a little help at hand. If there were few with the breadth of vision to see the value of defining the wider context or audience, there was one strain of scholarship which could have given a pointer. Form criticism in this period was not over-concerned with first-century Judaism, but it did spend time asking what the *church* might use the traditions about Jesus *for*. Such an enquiry entails asking what the recipients of a unit of tradition would find intelligible. Among all the unexamined assumptions which Farrer exposed so well, the form critics did have an incipient notion of audience definition, though their investment in agglomerate texts rather than whole compositions will have made it hard for Farrer to see or value it. Just as Farrer berated the form critics for shouldering the evangelist aside to grab his materials (*Study*, 7), so we might see in his own approach a tendency to shoulder Mark's audience aside to lay hands (as he hoped) on the evangelist's mind. But let us not forget that if Farrer's is sometimes a rather ahistorical conception of the authorial mind, he still does better than the early Rhoads and Michie, who, for all their thoroughly story-centred methods, cannot escape working with a historical conception of the audience, yet fail to describe it.[3]

B. *Mary Beavis*: Mark's Audience

Beavis' aims to describe the literary and social setting of that crux in Mark's Gospel in which Jesus says that he tells parables so that the outsiders, οἱ ἔξω (hoi exō), 'may look and not see, hear and not understand' (Mk 4.11f). Rejecting the significant though minority view that this passage is an 'alien element' in the Gospel, she sees it as a moment which concentrates the central Markan themes of perception and comprehension (and the lack of them), and introduces the important Markan emphasis on Jesus' private teaching. These verses, she concludes, have a 'rhetorical and propagandistic function with respect

2. See e.g. Taylor, *Commentary*.
3. See 7D (pp. 91–93) above: their collaboration with Dewey brings better things.

to the original audience', by inviting the hearers to join that group who are insiders, who are party to 'the mystery of the Kingdom of God' (*Audience*, 175).

Describing the audience

Beavis devotes much of her book to delineating an audience within a first-century society under the influence of Graeco-Roman patterns of reading, education and rhetoric. In her enquiry literary and social-historical questions overlap, as she asks a series of questions about the text's reception. What sort of literature would such people understand, or be drawn to? How, then, would they have 'heard' Mark? Why, if the author was from the same cultural milieu, did he write this Gospel as he did (here we dip into the level of historical reading which most interests Farrer)? What was the Gospel's function? Her general conclusion is that a plausible place can be found for the Gospel of Mark as a piece of writing that would be intelligible and acceptable in a Graeco-Roman context; her more specific conclusion is that its plot and characters make it most resemble a five-act Hellenistic play, which might in principle be performed publicly. Its function she can best describe as a text designed for missionary preaching, written by 'an early Christian missionary/ teacher' (*Audience*, 66). Beavis sets this against the widespread view that the Gospels were written for Christian audiences only. In describing a setting for the audience, Beavis is very soon led to lengthy description of the characteristics of the author. Her point of departure in studying Mark is that of mature redaction criticism, as she emphasises the creativity of the writer and the unity of the composition. She also works from the perspective of reader-response criticism, tempered by her thorough attention to the social context of the original audience. She is aware of the danger of conjuring up an ahistorical 'reader ... unaffected by factors of place, time and culture', who is in danger of becoming a cipher, no more than a projection of the modern reader's own preferences (*Audience*, 10, 16).[4] Beavis' aim is rather 'to identify the means by which the author of the Gospel sought to convey meaning to his audience'; or, more specifically, to ask: 'what attitude toward Mediterranean society did the evangelist want to convey to his audience?' (*Audience*, 10f, 14).

---

4.   In this respect she criticises the reader-response study of Mark by R.M. Fowler, *Loaves and Fishes: The Function of the Feeding Stories in the Gospel of Mark*, SBDLS, 54, (Missoula: Scholars, 1981).

Influences on Mark and the Markan audience

Adopting Stanley Fish's phrase, Beavis proceeds to locate Mark's 'interpretive community'[5] (or 'historical reader', or 'authorial audience' *Audience*, 17) within a literary and social milieu dominated by the norms of Graeco-Roman rhetoric. A string of citations from Greek and Latin rhetoricians establishes her view that reading in this world was primarily reading aloud (ἀνάγνωσις (anagnōsis), cf Mk 13.14), that the 'reader' was often a performer (and so the go-between of the text and the audience), that the aim of such performance was to persuade and to affect behaviour, and that it therefore had a great affinity with oratory. Mark's Gospel is, on her estimation, a text that would originally have been read (out) in a pervasively rhetorical culture (*Audience*, 18f).[6]

The ability of the author of Mark to read and write Greek, says Beavis, is evidence of education at least to the primary stage of Graeco-Roman schooling, that provided by the γραμματιστής (grammatistēs)/ *primus magister*. One aspect of this was the use of the χρεία (chreia, though Beavis uses the Latin form, *chria*) a pithy, instructive anecdote (not dissimilar in form from the 'pronouncement story' identified by form criticism in the Synoptic tradition). Students would work on these, memorising, amplifying, refuting and so on. Beavis gives as another emphasis of Graeco-Roman primary education, at least in its more senior stages, the study of the structure (*dispositio*) of classic texts, though she offers only a modern authority to substantiate it (*Audience*, 24).[7] The heart of Beavis' case, however, rests on the firmer foundation of her argument about the pervasive influence of the *chria*, and its formal similarity to what biblical-critical parlance calls the *pericopé*. This leads her to see the *chria* form affecting Mark's compositional technique. He does not so much inherit *pericopae* as oral units in the tradition, as *compose* a Gospel made up of so-called *pericopae*, under the influence of the *chria* form. She quotes V.K. Robbins:

> [The Synoptic writers] had learned to compose Greek in a setting that had incorporated preliminary exercises of rhetorical education as they are discussed and illustrated in Theon's *Progymnasmata*. Both as they wrote their gospels, and as they read other people's collections or complete narratives, they saw the material in terms of the discrete units they had been taught to see and write in the educational setting where they had learned to compose Greek. Also, in accordance with their level of

---

5.   She interprets Fish's term very softly indeed. The community she envisages is one to which an author conveys – through the stable substance of a text – some preconceived meaning, not one which *constitutes* the properties, the 'meaning', of a necessarily insubstantial text (cf *Class*, 171f).

6.   Joanna Dewey, 'Gospel', develops the implications of this.

7.   S.F. Bonner, *Education in Ancient Rome from the Elder Cato to the Younger Pliny* (London: Methuen, 1977, 244f).

rhetorical training, they expanded or condensed these literary units – incorporating, excluding and rewriting – by means of procedures they understood to be persuasive rhetorically. (*Audience*, 29)[8]

Beavis observes that a number of luminaries in Gospel studies, including Dibelius, noticed the similarity between the *chria* and the Synoptic *pericopé*, but she argues that they were anxious both to emphasise the difference, even the uniqueness, of the Gospel material, and – having defined them as the products of oral folk literature – to minimise their writtenness. On neither count would a scholastic literary model commend itself (*Audience*, 27f).

Beavis sees a second influence upon Mark in Hellenistic theatre. She notes the work of Bilezikian and Standaert, both of whom (independently) have seen in Mark pronounced similarities of shape to that of the five-phase Graeco-Roman tragedy.[9] Bilezikian discerns in the unbending desire of the hero Jesus to do God's will the ἁμαρτία (hamartia), the 'tragic flaw' envisaged by Aristotle in his Poetics, and in God's raising of Jesus the act of an (invisible) *deus ex machina*. Standaert argues for the influence of the five *partes orationis*,[10] and tells how first-century audiences expected that even historians would write with an eye to tragic plotting and rhetorical convention. But would Mark or his audience know anything of theatre? Beavis thinks they would, even if they were Palestinian: theatres were prevalent throughout the Empire, Herod the Great was a theatre-builder, and there is evidence of theatre-going in the *Corpus Papyrorum Judaicorum* (*Audience*, 31–35).[11]

Beavis' third candidate is what is loosely described as the Greek Novel, a prose genre of a lowbrow character, exhibiting features she thinks reminiscent of Mark: an 'artlessness' of style (for instance in the repeating of nouns instead of the use of pronouns), mistaken identities (cf 'Who do people say I am?' Mk 8.27), rich detail mixed with rapid summary, sea voyages and so on; though she concedes that the subject matter of an erotic adventure story is markedly different from that of a Gospel. Beavis makes a small but interesting comparison between Mark and the early-first-century writer Chariton in the citing of revered texts:

8.   V.K. Robbins, 'Pronouncement Stories and Jesus' Blessing of the Children: A Rhetorical Approach', *Semeia*, 29 (1983), 43–74, 49.

9.   G.G. Bilezikian, *The Liberated Gospel: A Comparison of the Gospel of Mark and Greek Tragedy* (Grand Rapids: Baker, 1977); B.H.M.G.M Standaert, *L'Evangile selon Marc: Composition et genre littéraire* (Brugge: Sint-Andriesabdij, 1978).

10.   Standaert's five *partes*, or τὰ μέρη τοῦ λογοῦ (ta merē tou logou), are: *exordium*/προοίμιον (prōoimion, Mk 1.1–13), *narratio*/διήγησις (diēgesis, Mk 1.14–6.13), *confirmatio*/πίστις (pistis), κατασκευή (kataskeuē, Mk 6.14–10.52), *refutatio*/ἀνασκευή (anaskeuē), λύσις (lusis, Mk 11.1–15.47), *peroratio*/ἐπίλογος (epilogos, Mk 16.1–8) (*Marc*, 263–272, *Audience*, 33).

11.   V.A. Tcherikover and A. Fuks (eds), *Corpus Papyrorum Judaicorum* (Cambridge, MA: Harvard University Press, 1957).

Haven't you ever heard where Homer himself tells us ...? (Chariton 2.3.7)
Have you never read what David did ...? (Mark 2.25)
[H]ave you not read in the book of Moses ...? (Mark 12.26) (*Audience*, 35–37)

As a final secular influence on Mark, Beavis offers the Graeco-Roman biographical literature, the βίοι (bioi)/*memorabilia*.[12] Again, she says, the comparison with the Gospels is not new, but she holds that further progress was halted by the ascent of form criticism.[13] This comparison leads Beavis into some complexity. She has argued up to now that Mark's Gospel shows the influence of rhetoric, but exhibits in its prose the 'cultural tone' of the lowbrow romancer. Most of the biographers she cites, however, like Xenophon the son of Gryllus (fourth century BC), Philodemus (born c. 110 BC), Plutarch and the Jewish Philo (both writing in the first century AD), are firmly in the higher echelons of literary culture. Furthermore, her examples straddle some seven hundred years of history, from Xenophon to Porphyry, who was probably writing in the mid to late third century AD. She argues nevertheless that the wide variety of subject and purpose among our extant biographies justifies us in regarding Mark as a Christian biography of a teacher and wonder-worker, though on a lower cultural level than other examples we have of this genre (*Audience*, 37–39).

Beavis has one more strain of influence to identify, however. Was Mark, she asks, a Jewish scribe? She sees a disjunction between the awkwardness of Mark's prose and the rather more sophisticated job the Gospel makes of interpreting and arranging the material. This suggests to her that the author, while enjoying only an elementary 'classical' education, also received a fair amount of Jewish tutelage, perhaps as the disciple of a rabbi. Evidence of this, she says, is the presence in the Gospel of legal and apocalyptic/esoteric material, both of which were concerns, she says, of Hellenistic Jewish scribes. Overall, Beavis devotes very little time to this source of influence on the writing of Mark, and not much either to the one literary influence which the text acknowledges, the Jewish Scriptures (*Audience*, 39–42)

What, she then asks, would a 'moderately educated and sympathetic' first-century audience make of Mark, and how might it have been put to use? In considering the use of the Gospel, Beavis acknowledges the circularity of the quest whereby, with our lack of external evidence for the use of the text, we infer function from content in order to say what sort of material the text contains. Nevertheless, she can confidently despatch the calendrical and lectionary theories of Goulder and others (*Audience*, 46),[14] and opt instead for a picture of Mark's Gospel in use as a Christian

---

12. See 11B (pp. 132–138) below, when we consider Richard Burridge's *What Are the Gospels?*

13. Beavis makes a number of observations about the shadow cast on Synoptic studies by form criticism. See 12B (pp. 151–154) below.

14. See M. Goulder, *Calendar*, and e.g. P. Carrington, *Primitive*.

teaching aid. Her case rests on external and internal support. The external is the prominence given to teaching and to the office of teacher in the New Testament and early patristic literature (*Audience*, 50–54), and on Papias' account of Mark as the interpreter of Peter's teaching, or διδασκαλία (didaskalia; here she makes her one direct encounter with Farrer, rebutting his rejection of Papias, *Audience*, 64f). Internal support is supplied by the amount of didactic vocabulary – διδαχή (didachē), διδάσκαλος (didaskalos), ῥαββί (rabbi) – and didactic material (e.g. biblical exegesis, doctrinal disputes) in the text of Mark; and a further discussion sees resemblances between the portrayal of Jesus in Mark and the characteristics of teachers described elsewhere in the New Testament, such as itinerancy and dependence on others for support (*Audience*, 58–63).[15]

C. Evaluation: Farrer and Beavis

It is a pity that Beavis lacks original evidence for the place of structural analysis in rhetorical education, because she draws from it the important contention that the emphasis of redaction critics on the literary structure of Mark is well-placed indeed. Beavis' case is weakened, however, by the lack of the sort of original citation which she offers in the case of the *chria*. The bearing of this on Farrer's elaborate account of Markan structure we need not stress: the more evidence we find for the writer of Mark being more than a naive compiler, and for the audience's sophistication (in this case, the possibility of the study of literary structure as a standard educational topic), the less implausible Farrer's schemes become.

Beyond his asides in the *Study* about Mark being read to Christians and probably in worship (*Study*, 33, 140, 173, 246), Farrer himself does not pay much attention to matters of original context. In a late piece of writing on Mark we do, however, see him using a similar argument to that of Beavis, though he finds Mark's literary exemplars in rabbinic tradition of Mishnah and Talmud, and in Jewish Scripture, rather than in Graeco-Roman education:

> We know ... in what sort of units oral tradition about famous rabbis and their sayings was preserved. Suppose, then, we allow that scholarly [form-critical] doctrine about the pre-Marcan state of Gospel tradition is roughly correct. What we still cannot allow is any justification for ruling out St Mark's having freely composed paragraphs conforming to the criteria for pre-Marcan oral tradition. Why should he not? He was (it is reasonable to propose) a preacher and oral narrator before he was a writer. What other style would he know, when he took the pen, than that which had directed his tongue? If he adopted literary models, they were presumably scriptural. And what tract of Scripture was best adapted to his purpose? Which, in fact, most visibly influences his narrative writing? What but the histories of Elijah

15.   For teachers in the NT, see e.g. 1 Cor. 12.28f.

and Elisha? And in what do these histories consist but a pile of anecdotes, suitable for oral narration? ... If for St Mark to become literary was for him to write like the author or authors of the Elijah and Elisha cycles it gave him little reason to depart from the style of oral narrative or of traditional anecdote, whether he was closely reproducing current anecdotes or not. ('Mind', 18)

He is studied in confining Mark's exemplars to scriptural ones, no doubt because he conceives Mark himself as knowingly writing a text which is itself specially inspired (*Study*, 53); Scripture in the making, we might say.

Beavis' study is much more firmly grounded contextually, but this does not stop her engaging in some extended analysis of internal structure and motif; nor should it, if what she says about *dispositio* can be maintained. She sees the elements of Mk 4.11f (allusion to Isaiah 6.9f, hardness of heart, private teaching, insiders/outsiders, the Kingdom of God, seeing-and-hearing, and so on) amply reflected in the rest of the Gospel. She proceeds to explore echoes and structural recurrences in various sections of the Gospel, chiefly Peter's confession at Caesarea Philippi, and Jesus' confession in the trial before the Sanhedrin (Mk 8.27–33; 14.53–65). Both, she says, show repeated questioning, a saying about the Son of Man and a condemnation (first of Peter by Jesus, then of Jesus by the High Priest). This leads Beavis down a rather Farreresque path, for the harder you look, the more everything seems to be connected to everything else. The two trial narratives have, in their false witnesses, echoes of the 'some say ... others say ...' of Peter's answer to Jesus at Caesarea Philippi, and – in Peter's denial – ironic echoes of his confession to Jesus; Peter's path to enlightenment there has in turn some resemblance to the progressive healing of the blind man of Bethsaida (Mk 8.22–26, 27–30, *Audience*, 114–124).

Farrer is attuned to all Beavis' resemblances.[16] He also follows her in the parallels she sees between the blind man and the deaf-mute of 7.31–37 (e.g. *Study*, 104–107, 121 for Caesarea Philippi and Bethsaida, 151 and 284 for Peter's confession and the trial before the High Priest). Beavis patiently sets out her material and is cautious in her conclusion: 'Our observation that the healings of the deaf-mute and the blind man are structurally similar to the three confessions may help to illumine the "symbolism" of these passages' (*Audience*, 124). Farrer, on the other hand, is characteristically majestic:

> St Mark is using a triad of sensitive and communicative powers, ears, tongue and eyes, the special instruments of the mind ... Before the healing act [the disciples] have neither perception nor understanding, their hearts are hardened, their eyes without vision, and their ears without hearing. Christ opens the villager's eyes, and St Peter confesses Christ. The villager and the apostle are, then, symbolically equivalent: the physical healing of the one stands for the spiritual enlightenment of the other. (*Study*, 105)

16. As are others. Beavis cites several authorities, including Farrer's favourite, Lightfoot (*Audience*, 121).

And, again, of Peter: 'He had confessed [Christ] at Caesarea Philippi and denounced the doctrine of the cross in the same breath. Under the shadow of the cross at Jerusalem he had not confessed but denied Christ, and wept for his infirmity' (*Study*, 151).

How convincing are Beavis and Farrer as they try to locate these readings of Mark in the historical context of its original audience? In discussing Mark 8, Farrer has one of his moments of apparent (but pretended?) doubt: '[t]he complexity of such a process [of authorial imagination] is endless, but the description of it does not look plausible' (*Study*, 101). When discussing things like this, matters of structure and rhythm, he does not plead, as he does with questions of typology, that much of it would seem relatively digestible and uncontrived to a first-century audience (see e.g. *Study*, 79, but cf 346f), but takes refuge, as we have already seen, in the workings of inspiration, and his claim to be describing not 'what St Mark *saw himself* to be doing' (emphasis added), but simply 'the phenomena in the text' (*Study*, 101). Beavis, by contrast, comes readily to the contextual point: 'Would Mark's first reader/audience have picked up the ironies inherent in the parallelism among these pericopes (ironies which most modern readers have missed!), or were the evangelist's literary efforts wasted?' (*Audience*, 120).

Or (we must add) did the evangelist ever intend them? Are they only 'there' in Beavis' *reading* of Mark? Both she and Farrer sense some unease with the obscurity of their interpretations, though neither openly addresses the question of whether these things are in any case 'there' to be seen. But unlike Farrer, Beavis points to one restraint upon her interpretation, for she elects to be judged at the bar of history.

> Our purpose is to show that ... the structural similarities among these passages, and their implications for the interpretation of the Gospel, would have been recognized by a Graeco-Roman reader because of the way in which he/she was taught to read. (*Audience*, 114f)

Graeco-Roman education, she says, was dominated in its early stages by teaching to equip students to read aloud. If Mark was written to be read and heard, then there would be many people on hand equipped to perform it. A properly prepared, expressive public reading of a text like Mark, she says, would emphasise structural features and repeated motifs, so as to give shape to the performance. The lector might give some introductory explanation, and might take questions from the audience after (or perhaps even during) the performance (*Audience*, 124).

Beavis identifies (as do Farrer and others) a tension between public and private teaching in Mark, and the grouping of teaching material into blocks. These lead her to suggest a chiastic structure for the Gospel as whole, with narrative punctuated by teaching scenes:

1'		3'		5'		3'		1'
	2'		4'		4'		2'	
Narrative		Narrative		Narrative		Narrative		Narrative
	Teaching		Teaching		Teaching		Teaching	
[1.1–3.35]		[4.35–6.56]		[7.24–9.29]		[10.46–12.44]		[14.1–16.8]
	[4.1–34]		[7.1–23]		[9.30–10.45]		[13.1–37]	

Audience, 127

Figure 10.1: Narrative Punctuated by Teaching Scenes

This is a pattern quite different in detail from that proposed by Farrer, and simpler, though we might say it belongs to the same broad category of analysis. Many others have proposed quite different arrangements for Mark, however, as Beavis admits. What then makes hers authoritative? It is at this point that she reintroduces the influence of tragedy. The five-fold structure would be readily recognised by a Graeco-Roman reader, since it is very close to the structure of a five-act Hellenistic tragedy, the teaching scenes taking the place of the choruses. By Mark's day, she says, this arrangement was well established (*Audience,* 124f, 127f).

As with her earlier observations about *dispositio*, Beavis is light on her use of original sources. Her references to substantiate her claims about training for public recital are from modern works, except for her remarks about audience questions, which she derives from Plutarch's *On Listening to Lectures*, 42–48 (esp. 39, 43), and about the five-act Hellenistic play, for which she draws on Horace's *Ars Poetica*, 189 (*Audience,* 124f, 128). Again, when she returns to Mark 4, she is reluctant to exclude any influence: the gathering of parables in this section resembles the sayings collections found in Graeco-Roman biographies (e.g. Plutarch's *Cato the Elder*), yet the crucial verses 11f look like an oracle in a Hellenistic play, foretelling the development of the narrative (*Audience,* 154, 166).

D. Conclusion

Beavis presents rather a patchwork piece. She envisages an author receiving a scribal training, though with a liberal sprinkling of Graeco-Roman education, who thus produces a Gospel with a mixture of rhetoric and Jewish legal debate, which is like Greek drama in one place though unmistakably apocalyptic in another, and which portrays a prophetic-charismatic Jesus who would be a model for the Markan community of preachers. Similarly motley is the combination of popular linguistic style with a degree of rhetorical sophistication, though in this she sees Mark resembling Greek romance or popular biography. Her Mark is a teaching text for the διδάσκαλος (didaskalos) of the community, though with its accessibility to a wide first-century audience it could well have been directed at potential converts as well as to the already committed. Indeed, the references to the 'suffering' of social alienation in Mark 13 would be more applicable to those weighing up Christian faith against the concomitant rejection by peers and family, than to those who had already crossed this particular Rubicon. She sees among her contributions to Markan studies the demonstration that the Gospel is constructed for performance, resembling the five-act Hellenistic play (though she would like to have more information on the sort of plays performed in Mark's time and place), and that this parabolic, multivalent text was not written for a Christian audience only (*Audience*, 167–176).

The final impression of Beavis' Mark is of an even more hybrid beast than she explicitly allows. βίος-like (bios) in its subject and in the form of some of its passages, in structure much more like a drama, though with an admixture of Hellenistic romance, suffused with the tones of rhetoric, but with a liberal dose of rabbinic disputation, what sort of a writing *is* Mark? Ironically, the web of resemblances to surrounding and disparate literary forms could be an argument for what she considers the untenable view that the Gospel is indeed a new genre (*Audience*, 38). Even if we allow for the impact of rhetoric on most forms of writing, what does this crowd of literary exemplars add up to, beyond the modest conclusion that the writer of Mark breathed a general literary atmosphere of the first century, and not just a sectarian fug?[17] Although her study is at once about the writer of Mark as well as that writer's public, Beavis is wise to focus in her title on Mark's *audience*, for it is here that her work is at its most telling. If the impression she gives of the genre of Mark remains blurred, she shows how much weightier a particular assertion about Mark becomes, if you can show how the first-century public might have recognised this sort of thing from somewhere else. To say that Mark is (or that Mark wrote) a sort of Hellenistic tragedy may not get us very far (especially if it means interpreting the absence of the risen Jesus as a *deus ex machina*). To say that the Markan public might well have grasped this or that nuance of plot or structure because of their acquaintance with Hellenistic tragedy is a more modest claim, but a serviceable and a defensible one. It sets limits to what can be said about the possible intention of the author, and it cannot be so readily dismissed, as so many have dismissed Farrer's proposals, as the creation of an over-active academic mind.

Beavis' soundings in first-century culture bring results which are not altogether hostile to Farrer's reading of Mark. People who had enjoyed

---

17.   Burridge's distinction between genre and mode would help Beavis here. See *Biography*, 41f/40f and p. 133 below.

only the briefest brush with Demetrius or Longinus might see a more familiar face in Farrer's Mark than in Dibelius'.[18] It remains to ask why Farrer attended so little to this area of support.[19]

18.　Demetrius, *On Style*, Longinus, *On the Sublime* (*Audience*, 19).
19.　See 11C (pp. 138–146) below.

Chapter 11

MARK'S WORK

Mark ... may have thought himself to be writing a 'so-and-so' ... but our difficulty is that we do not know what sort of a 'so-and-so' he would feel himself to be writing.
A Study in St Mark, 30

This third level of historical reading seeks access to the author, which is Austin Farrer's overt objective (*Study*, 9, *Matthew*, 2, 'Mind', 14). Part II sought to discuss Farrer's accounts of Mark at work. We need now to note now that Farrer in doing this is participating in a historical activity, reading Mark historically and then writing a history of the Gospel's composition, an account of the process by which it tumbled out of the author's head (he would have us believe) during a certain period of '[d]ays or weeks' in the mid-first century (*Study*, 367). And, of course, Part II was itself the fruit of a historical reading of *Farrer*, as an author in his own right. In this chapter we shall concentrate on what we identified as a critical aspect of any reading which seeks the authorial intention, the question of genre. The question is only helpful if it is posed in terms of the possibilities which obtain at the time of the work's writing, and we shall pursue it in conversation with a thorough attempt to place Mark (with the other Gospels) in a first-century generic setting, Richard Burridge's *What are the Gospels? A Comparison with Graeco-Roman Biography*. First, however, we ask what are our historical evidences for an author, ancient or modern.

A. Evidences for an Author

We know a lot about the author Austin Farrer. We can compare one book of his with another, his earlier writings with his later, his learned writings with his sermons. Some will exhibit the studied impersonality of the narrative voice, others will offer valuable 'first-person' remarks, though such remarks are never entirely transparent. We also have 'unofficial' writings of his, private letters or unpublished academic material. We can date his books, and other events in his life, quite precisely, and we can consider his 'audience' in some detail, what they write and indeed say about him, for we are still in the age of eyewitness testimony. Indeed, we can have in our hands a thorough attempt to bring all these threads together in a full-dress biography, Philip Curtis' *A Hawk Among Sparrows*. These are the advantages of investigating a recent life lived in an accessible culture. If, then, we read the *Study* in a quest for the historical author – why did Farrer write this book at all, to what end? – we have a complex but feasible task. While attending to the text of the book and its reflection of the authorial mask, we also adduce other information: reflections of other masks Farrer wore, like those of the preacher, the private correspondent or the philosopher, the earlier and later versions of his biblical scholar's mask, and to these we add the opinions of others about these different masks and the face behind them. All this makes us dare hope that we may in the end have some reasonable certainties about that face, about the rounded life of the historical figure who was the author of our book, despite all that must be said about the impossibility of getting at historical figures 'as they really were'.

How meagre are our resources, however, when we (and Farrer) turn to 'the historical Mark'. The author of our Gospel lived so long ago, and cannot even be named with certainty, or positively identified with any independently known historical figure; nor do we know of any other document which is the writing of this person. There is nothing with which to begin the sketch of a rounded life, for although the author of Mark no doubt did much besides write that book, we cannot know what it was, beyond tentative inferences from what we know of the times. Virtually all we have is the text, the impersonal narrative, of the Gospel, and the reflection it gives of the authorial mask. The fruits of our biographical efforts are therefore bound to be small. We may say, given the social mores of the period, that the author was almost certainly male; from certain signals in the text (such as use of Jewish Scripture), that he was probably a Jewish Christian; and from the text itself, that he was a literate Greek-speaker and therefore at least basically educated, probably a member of the lower middle classes.[1] But where was he living, and when, apart from 'some time after the death of Jesus'? What were his aims in writing the Gospel? What audience did he have in mind? Apart from the precarious business of arguing from the generalities of a distant social milieu to the particularity of one person, answers have to be inferred from gleaning the text itself. Even then, our reading of Mark will give us only the *implied* author, but since we are nearly two millennia from such contrivances as the unreliable narrator, we may conclude that there will be continuity between the narrative voice and

---

1.   Beavis elaborates; see esp. *Audience*, 20–31. See also Kee, *Community*, esp. 77–105.

the implied author, and that a clear reflection in the text of the authorial mask will give a reasonable likeness of the face behind it. The clarity of the reflection is the nub; for some critics it is a mirage.

A text is a notation, needing appropriation by an addressee, so if we wish to read the text to discern its author, we will help ourselves if as we read we ask questions about the original audience the author addressed. In one sense, audience-focused reading is logically prior to an author-focused reading, and this priority is critical when we read an ancient text: we ourselves are audiences, on 'this side' of the text, so it is sensible first to approach the audience closest to the author and thus shorten the leap to the author on the 'other side'. In practice, however, questions about audience lead at once to questions about author – the distance between them is literally paper-thin – and so the greatest overlapping between the different layers of historical reading occurs just here. Thus in the last chapter we saw Beavis seeking to delineate Mark's audience but inevitably spending a great deal of time on Mark himself: his background, education and cultural awareness. With Burridge we shall see a shift in the direction of the historical author, but in defining a genre for Mark's work he says his proposal must be judged by how a first-century audience would have regarded the Gospel.

Farrer and the historical Mark

Below, we discuss Farrer's consideration of genre in its historical aspect. First, we must re-emphasise that Farrer's neglect of an original audience and a social context for the Gospel leads him to have a picture of the author that is much more disembodied than it need be. For all that he asserts that the author was a preacher (*Study*, 24f, 367), Farrer's Mark emerges as a mind and little more, 'a brain on a stalk', as Farrer once said in describing himself (*Hawk*, 127); in fact, he appears as a rather Farrer-like figure. When Farrer goes on to claim that the processes he has uncovered may have lain unrecognised, not just by Mark's audience but by Mark himself, and when he invokes divine agency to make up the debt of plausibility, his 'historical author' becomes historically intractable (*Study*, 100f, 347). *Matthew* and 'Mind' add nothing to the picture of Mark the author in the *Study*, though in the later of the two he firmly repeats his intention:

> We must first settle the question, what an author as a matter of historical fact intended to say. For a written book is simply the expression of a writer's mind; to understand the text is to understand the author: not the author outside the book, but the author as author of the book ... What did the author set himself to do? ('Mind', 14)

Again we sense the cerebral narrowness. At one point in the *Study*, however, Farrer considers some external evidence about Mark which we do possess from near his own period, the words of Papias. Farrer quotes in full the passage from Eusebius: Papias, a stupid person in Eusebius' opinion, though speaking on the authority of (?John) 'the Elder', said of Mark that he was Peter's 'interpreter', and that he wrote down Peter's recollections of Jesus' words and deeds 'accurately, but not in order'; Matthew then 'concatenated ... the divine teaching (*logia*) in Jewish speech' (*Study*, 15, Farrer's translation). Farrer believes Matthew to have been written in Greek, and so rejects Papias' story as an 'invention' to explain why Matthew, traditionally an apostolic Gospel, did not 'enjoy prevailing authority' as soon as it appeared: Papias saves Matthew's reputation by saying it was not translated into Greek until after Mark had appeared (*Study*, 21f). Farrer takes from Papias corroboration of the view that Mark's was the first Greek Gospel to gain authority; and once Aramaic Matthew is rejected, Mark then becomes simply the earliest Gospel (*Study*, 21f). He also finds in Papias support for Mark's association with Peter; Farrer alludes here to references to 'Mark' in the New Testament that 'make ... the suggestion to our minds' (Acts 12.12, 25; 1 Peter 5.12). He sets it beside the evidence of Papias, and suggests that the Papias hypothesis might indeed have been deduced from these very verses, which it fits rather too neatly (*Study*, 20). He does not, however, commit himself on whether we should take them to refer to the evangelist, though he is tempted (*Study*, 187).[2] Beavis is kinder to Papias: his testimony she regards as no worse than 'equivocal' and she actually bends slightly in his favour. She regards Farrer's objection that the Papias tradition accords too well with the New Testament as 'rather perverse' (*Audience*, 63).

Beavis presents herself with some difficulties here, for Papias' description of Mark's Gospel sounds a little less sophisticated than the book she believes it to be, and on the strength of his rejection of an Aramaic Matthew (whose use of and dependence on the Septuagint would then be hard to explain) we should side with Farrer. Farrer's potential difficulty here, of course, is the same as Beavis': the picture of Markan sophistication he will paint is at odds with Papias' Mark, a dutiful recorder of Peter's reminiscences. But now, having demonstrated that 'Papias' words do not place any obstacle in the way of a free attempt to investigate the process and order of St Mark's writing', he can set Mark's mind as free as his own (*Study*, 21).

Apart from such material, the historical stratum occupied by the author of Mark is composed of no more than the text of Mark itself. Its slenderness may tend to deter one reader (like Moore)[3] from saying anything, while giving another (like Farrer) *carte blanche*.

---

2.   See also his St Mark's Day sermon, preached surely before 1960, the publication date of *Said or Sung*: 'perhaps the Mark of the gospel was the John Mark of Acts, after all' ('S. Mark', 98f).

3.   See Moore, *Challenge*, e.g. 172.

B. *Richard Burridge:* What are the Gospels?

The cornerstone of Burridge's work is that we must discern the genre of a text before we can hope to make sense of it.[4] He attributes the lack of success among Gospel scholars in placing the Gospels generically to an inadequate theory of genre and to inadequate acquaintance with the first-century literary milieu, especially in its Graeco-Roman aspect (*Biography*, 4f/2nd edn, 24). He devotes a significant part of his book to the primarily *literary* question of genre theory, and if we are to make sense of Burridge's text, we must do likewise, though in mitigation for conducting such a discussion in the 'history' part of our enquiry we note that Burridge's aim is to place the Gospels in a genre that would be recognised by a *first-century* audience, hence his stated preference, when describing Graeco-Roman Lives of the famous, for the term βίος (bios) – or, in the plural βίοι (bioi) – over 'biography/ies', with the latter's anachronistic connotations in modern usage (*Biography*, 62f/59f).[5] Our apparent meander will, therefore, be worthwhile. At the end of this section I shall argue that Farrer's case suffers from a lack of the kind of theoretically informed and historically grounded work upon genre which Burridge exemplifies.

The question of genre

Burridge briefly traces the history of attempts to identify the genre of the Gospels (*Biography*, 3–25/3–24). He then surveys the history of genre theory, and the way in which succeeding ages sought to clarify and classify the characteristics of both older and contemporary literature. He takes us from the prescriptivism of the classical period, where an ideal form was offered as the goal of a particular sort of writing but was often ignored in practice, through the influence of classicism upon medieval and Renaissance thinking, and on to the descriptivism of the nineteenth century, with its less programmatic but still rigid patterns of classification. Finally he introduces some recent developments which argue a more supple notion of genre (*Biography*, 26–32/25–31). On this last understanding, the genre of a text is constituted by a set of expectations which the text evokes in the reader; they form a kind of contract between author and reader. These expectations the reader builds into 'Corrigible Schemata' (*Biography*, 36/35)[6] which may be confirmed, refined or even invalidated as the reading unfolds; some texts indeed, it seems by the writer's deliberate plan, subvert the early expectations they

---

4.   Hirsch (*Validity*, 76, 222f) and Kee (*Community*, 1f) take a similar view.
5.   As we shall be using these terms pervasively from now on, they will not be transliterated.
6.   A phrase derived from Piaget via Hirsch (*Aims*, 32f). Hirsch informs much of Burridge's discussion of genre theory.

evoke (*Biography*, 32–38/31–36). Burridge's considered position is worth quoting in full, as it informs the rest of his study.

> Genres operate in the middle ground between the two extremes of classical prescriptivism and nineteenth-century descriptivism. They are conventions which assist the reader by providing a set of expectations to guide his or her understanding. Such expectations are corrected and further refined in the light of actual reading. Through genre we are enabled to understand even old or unfamiliar works, like the gospels. (*Biography*, 38/36)

He distinguishes between broad and intrinsic genre, the one initial and vague, the other more precise, being refined in the light of actual reading. Beyond these is 'the final understanding of the actual meaning as expressed precisely in the specifically chosen words' (*Biography*, 40/39). Burridge offers a scheme for coming to understand a text:

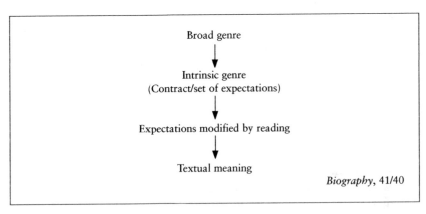

Figure 11.1: **Understanding a Text through Genre**

He warns that the process he charts is rarely 'simple' or 'linear', partly because genres are elastic: what holds them together is 'family resemblance' rather than uniformity; so there can be elements of several genres in one text, as well as a variety of books in one genre. Thus a text may move into tragic *mode* by exhibiting certain features of tragedy, but without giving rise to the set of expectations we associate with a text that in its entirety belongs to the *genre* of tragedy: mode is a matter of 'motifs and styles', genre of 'form and content'; similarly, Burridge finds it helpful to talk of *subgenre*, which denotes 'subject and material' (*Biography*, 41f/39f). Texts, he observes, often drop broad initial hints about their generic character, and these evoke the expectations which we then test and refine in the reading (*Biography*, 42f/41f).[7]

---

7. Burridge borrows the terms 'mode' and 'subgenre' from Alastair Fowler, *Kinds of Literature: An Introduction to the Theory of Genres and Modes* (Oxford: Oxford University Press, 1982), 111–118.

Burridge's elasticity of genre is also a matter of development in time as well as of diversity at any one time. Genre is 'history-bound' (*Biography*, 46/44): it cannot arise from nothing, but begins as an extension of an existing genre or a combination of existing genres, and only on passing a certain threshold of novelty does it become a genre in its own right. We must therefore pay attention to both literary and sociological setting to have a good appreciation of a genre's origins, and this requires comparison with other literature contemporary with the time of the work's *composition*, and investigation of the genres that were available *at that time* (*Biography*, 45–7/44f). Burridge holds that the lack of a robustly historical context can lead to all sorts of incongruities, like deciding that Mark cannot be biography because it is quite unlike a *modern* biography (*Biography*, 48f/46f). He describes genres as 'filters' through which both the act of writing and the act of reading must pass, and as his goal is to reconstruct the 'original meaning' of a Gospel-writer, a 'first-century Hellenized Jew', there is no escaping the need to identify the author's generic filter and (so far as this is possible) to draw his reading of the text through that same filter; for recognising the genre of the writing is an essential part of 'deciphering the conventions' through which the author transmits the sense of the text (*Biography*, 49–51/48f). Burridge pauses to note the 'death-of-the-author' objection, which would see here a case of the intentional fallacy. He does not so much rebut it as express another preference, when he sides with Hirsch's 'Defence of the Author' in the striking of a contract not between reader and text, but between reader and author.[8] This is, he says, a control on the subjectivity of the reader's response, exerted by attention to 'the author's purpose' in writing; the way to get at this purpose, in the absence of any extra-textual signals from the author, is to look at what 'the text reveals', and this is primarily done by the identification of its genre. In short, genre is 'a system of communication of meaning … [a] guide to help us re-construct the original meaning, to check our interpretation … and to assist in evaluating the worth of the text' (*Biography* 51f/51).

For Burridge this has the following implications: the Gospels (*pace* form criticism) cannot be described as *sui generis*, and must be compared – not just contrasted – with the literature of their day; in locating them in the first-century literary landscape, we must distinguish between mode and genre; the failure to do this has led to a riot of proposals about Gospel genre (*Biography*, 52–54/53f). Having set out his methodological stall, Burridge proceeds to apply his apparatus to Graeco-Roman biography, before turning to the Gospels and trying the βίος-genre for size.

---

8.   Hirsch, *Validity*, Chapter 1.

Graeco-Roman Biography

Surveying classical literature over a wide period, Burridge develops a picture of βίος as firmly 'within the whole web of literary relationships' of its day, a genre lying between history and encomium, enjoying a variety of manifestations, and often borrowing from its *genera proxima*, such as the novel, moral philosophy and polemic (*Biography*, 68/65). Scanning Greek literature from the fifth century BC onwards, and tracing the beginnings of Roman biography, he finds βίος-like elements first taking shape in the form of character sketches within historiography, and βίος proper emerging from rhetorical encomia. βίος then comes into its own with the writing of lives of philosophers, playwrights and poets by the Aristotelian school. Burridge cites as a notable and early (fourth-century BC) instance of βίος the *Life of Socrates* by Aristoxenus. He wrote it, as tradition has it, as a piece of polemic after he had been passed over as Aristotle's successor by Theophrastus.[9] This is the first example of the polemical or apologetic motive from which, in Burridge's view, many subsequent βίοι were to spring (*Biography*, 72f/69f). With the establishment of Roman biography in the late first century AD, Burridge finds a sustained interest in political lives, often written with the motive of enjoining the reader to emulate the *exempla maiorum* (e.g. Paetus' *Cato*; *Biography*, 75f/72). With the early Empire come Plutarch's *Parallel Lives*, a marriage in subject and form of the Greek and Roman biographical tradition, and Suetonius' *vitae* of the Caesars (*Biography*, 77f/75f).

Burridge examines each of ten examples according to a number of 'generic features' he has already established in his theoretical section on genre identification: opening features (e.g. title, prologue), subject (degree of dominance of the main character, allocation of space to different periods of the subject's life), external features (size or length, structure, sources, method of characterisation) and internal features (setting, topics, tone and mood, quality of characterisation; *Biography*, 109–127/105–123). He finds that they 'exhibit a similar range of generic features within a flexible pattern', the chief similarity being that each is 'an account of a person' (*Biography*, 152/148). In other respects there is diversity: space is not allocated evenly over the subject's life, or consistently between various βίοι; the tone is usually serious and respectful, but not always; the purposes behind his first five writings are varied; three are prose narratives, but one (Isocrates' *Evagoras*) is a speech and another (Satyrus' *Euripides*) a dialogue which quotes dramatic verse. He classes his samples as largely medium-length works (i.e. about 7,000 words), though

9.   *Not*, as Burridge states, Theopompus, who was a historian. See Diogenes Laertius 5.36–57, and 'Theophrastos' in A. Pauly, G. Wissowa and W. Kroll (eds), *Real-Encyclopädie d. Klassischen Altertumwissenschaft* (Stuttgart: 1893–1963). Burridge correctly identifies Theopompus as author of the *Philippica* (*Biography*, 73/70).

Nepos' *Atticus* is about 3,500 words and Philo's *Moses* 32,000, and in discussing the five later texts he extends 'medium length' to the range of '5,000 to 25,000 words' (*Biography*, 152f/148f, 177/172). All ten have a basic chronological structure, but contain topical inserts; all use a variety of oral and written sources, and portray the subject's character largely by oblique means, narrating significant deeds and words (*Biography*, 152f/148f). Finally, Lucian's racy *Demonax* demonstrates how a chiefly highbrow genre can yet be downwardly mobile (*Biography*, 181/176).

Βίοι *and the Synoptic Gospels*

Turning to the Synoptic Gospels,[10] Burridge traverses the same categories and finds the Gospels sitting comfortably within the variegated but recognisable habitat which he has identified as βίος. Among their 'opening features' they show an early-appended formulaic title (The Gospel κατά (kata) Matthew, etc.) which suggests conformity to a recognised – but unspecified – type; also, Matthew and Mark mention the subject, Jesus, in the first few words, while Luke does so very quickly after his formal prologue (*Biography*, 192–195/186–189). In Mark, Jesus is the subject of 24.4 per cent of the verbs, and another 20 per cent are delivered from his lips, while no other individual attains more than 1 per cent, and even so significant a group as the disciples manage only 12.2 per cent both jointly and severally; the other two Synoptic Gospels show similar results and they accord with what Burridge has found in Graeco-Roman βίοι (*Biography*, 195–197/189–191). This 'biographical tendency' in the Synoptics is not vitiated by their often-remarked lack of attention to Jesus' early life and their concentration upon his death, for these reflect a similar unevenness in acknowledged βίοι: for instance, Mark's treatment of events from the Last Supper to the Resurrection occupies some 19.1 per cent of the text, yet Plutarch uses 17.3 per cent of his *Cato Maior* on the end of Cato's life, and Tacitus 10 per cent on the end of Agricola's (*Biography*, 197–199/191–193).

As to their 'external features', all three are surely *prose narratives*. Burridge says that though they may exhibit parabolic or tragic aspects, it is no help to call them – as some have – 'parable' or 'tragedy' *tout court* (*Biography*, 199f/193f). They are *medium-length* pieces: Mark has 11,242 words, corresponding to Plutarch's average length of 10–11,000 words; Matthew (18,305) and Luke (19,428) are somewhat longer (*Biography*, 199f/194).[11] All three present what is fundamentally a *chronological* account, with a geographical progression from Galilee to Jerusalem, less structured than the βίοι of military figures like Agricola or Agesilaus,

10.   He defers discussion of John.
11.   Burridge cites the figure in R. Morgenthaler, *Statistik des neutestamentlichen Wortschatzes* (Zurich: Gotthelf, 1958), 164.

but more so than the *Demonax*, or Porphyry's *Pythagoras* (*Biography*, 200–202/194–196). Into this they all insert *topical* material (e.g. Mark's parables in Chapter 4, and the apocalypse in Chapter 13); they limit the *scale* of their operations to the life and times of Jesus, and build up their picture using a range of *literary forms* (or 'units') – stories, sayings, speeches – very similar to that found in βίος; in particular, the Synoptic pronouncement story, 'a brief narrative in which the climactic (and often final) element is a pronouncement which is presented as a particular person's response to something said or observed', finds frequent echoes in the pithy anecdotes of the *Demonax* and various of Plutarch's βίοι (*Biography*, 202–204/196–198).[12] For Burridge, redaction criticism's disclosure of the creative and selective use of written and oral *sources* in the Gospels indicates another shared feature (though only Luke follows Graeco-Roman convention and actually mentions sources, in its preface); another is their *method of characterisation*, which is oblique, employed through narration of deeds and words rather than through direct analysis (*Biography*, 204–206/198f).

The 'internal features' of *setting* (determined by the person of Jesus) and topics – ancestry, birth, childhood, great deeds, virtues, death and its consequences – reflect those of βίος (*Biography*, 206–209/200–202). Burridge acknowledges that Mark is marginal here, having no real treatment of the first three topics, and that all the Gospels are even more implicit in their portrayal of virtues than many βίοι; but the passing-over of early life and the oblique treatment of qualities are both found in acknowledged βίοι (*Biography*, 207–209/201f). The linguistic *style* of the Synoptics (especially Mark) is that not of Attic but of Koiné Greek, and in this they resemble Plutarch. Their reverential *atmosphere* is reminiscent of the more heavyweight βίοι such as the *Agricola* or the *Moses* (*Biography*, 209–211/203f). Burridge sees in the Jesus of the Gospels a *quality of characterisation* which exhibits a βίος-like tension between the stereotypical (e.g. Matthew's Jesus as in part a new Moses) and the 'real' (notably the pithy sayings and teasing stories; *Biography*, 211f/205). Burridge finds no convincing case for a particular social setting or occasion for any of the Synoptics, though their audience does seem to have been lower on the social scale than those of most surviving βίοι (*Biography*, 212–214/205–207). More compelling for him is the congruence between the *authorial intentions* which he finds behind the Synoptics and those of the authors of βίοι, above all in the *didactic* value of the material as an aid to teaching and preaching, and in its *apologetic* and *polemical* character. He finds this especially true of Mark, whom some see struggling to rebut false views of Jesus as a wonder-worker. Overall, Burridge sees in the Synoptic Gospels a mixture of features

12. Quoting R. Tannehill, 'Varieties of Synoptic Pronouncement Stories', *Semeia*, 20 (1981), 1.

readily recognisable as belonging to the genre of βίος (*Biography*, 214–217/208–210). A further chapter comes to the same conclusion about John: for all its differences from the Synoptics, it is much more like them than it is like any other extant literature from the period. Burridge concludes:

> This is surely a sufficient number of shared features for the genre of the synoptic gospels to be clear: while they may well form their own subgenre because of their shared content, **the synoptic gospels belong within the overall genre of** βίοι. (*Biography*, 218f/212, original emphasis)

C. Evaluation: Farrer and Burridge

When Burridge says that the goal of his genre analysis is to get at 'the meaning' of a text in its original context, we must question his ease in using the vocabulary of exactitude: 'final', 'actual', 'precisely' and 'specifically' (*Biography*, 40/39). There are two difficulties here, and the first is with the existence of 'the meaning'. Putting the stress on either word in that phrase, or on neither, serves only to shift the load of difficulty: what can be 'the meaning' of a long and varied text like Mark? We may guess what Kermode or Moore,[13] with their sense of the elusiveness of texts, would say to this, and one hardly needs to be a post-structuralist or neo-pragmatist devotee to be perplexed by Burridge's confidence.[14] Does he have in mind some distillation of the 'message' of Mark, like Farrer's own?

> God gives you everything.
> Give everything to God.
> You can't.
>
> ('St Mark', 98)

Or is he seeking a succinct statement of the *effect* the author hoped would be wrought upon the audience (we should in fairness remember that Burridge's stress is upon not the timeless but the original meaning)?[15] Can a complete narrative 'mean' any single thing? If we picture Farrer's tongue-in-cheek scene of the arrest of the author of Mark – 'Here what's all this? You'd better come along with me to the praetorium' (*Glass*, 137) – just as he is about to write verse 9 of Chapter 16, we can imagine the author's perplexity, during the interrogation which would follow,

---

13.   See 6A and 6E (pp. 62–72, 76–81) above.
14.   Burridge's mentor Hirsch can also be somewhat 'objectivised', as when he says that 'meaning' is constant while only 'significance' changes (*Validity*, 213).
15.   Cf Hirsch, who acknowledges no other permanent meaning than the author's meaning (*Validity*, 216).

when the official asks the traditional question put to the inconvenient writer under a totalitarian regime: 'This book of yours – what does it *mean*?' The *author* might manage a one-paragraph summary, but it is quite beyond the consensus of distant, modern readers. There appears to be a yen in Burridge for something too determinate, solid and tangible (something you can 'reconstruct'), even a desire for *propositions*, when such things are very hard to come by in and from a narrative, which is not written in a primarily *ideational* register.[16]

The second difficulty follows from the first. Even if we grant the formal possibility of the project of seeking meaning, Burridge also (and oddly, for one so insistent on the need for a historical sense) makes rather light of the task of 'reconstructing' original meaning from an *ancient* text, which is bound to be culturally alien to the current enquirer's world. The problem is compounded by the archaeological connotations of his term 'reconstruction'. To explain: we may, by the diligent use of archaeological methods, expose the foundations of an ancient site, and have a fair idea of where a fallen stone originally stood. We may have a good idea, a conceptual if not a physical 'reconstruction', of the layout and character of the buildings at, say, Qumran. Even before this point there are jobs of interpretation to be done, but the next stage, the investigation not just of the construction of the buildings or of their functions (refectory, wash-house and so on), but of the *significance* of their functions for the inmates (what the buildings *meant*?), is a thoroughly interpretative task. And it is a task for which the term 'reconstruction' is not the most helpful, for it is not a matter of tangibilities. We might say the same of the Gospel of Mark, once the establishment of a tolerable Greek text (an exercise itself not free of interpretation) has been achieved.[17] In seeking the text's meaning, Burridge is nevertheless right to posit a process (whether or not it ever arrives at his 'final' destination) 'of narrowing and closer focus', and he does admit that it is 'rarely a simple, linear process' (*Biography*, 41/39). He is also correct to observe that, while there is something unique about every text, each one will all but invariably resemble other texts closely enough for it to be helpful to see them, in all their diversity, as members of the same genre (*Biography*, 41–43/39–41). If we can move Burridge away from his repeated stress on 'meaning'[18] and more towards his 'expectations' about structure, tone and plot, his essential thesis about

16.   Stephen Moore makes this same point in his strictures about the over-conceptual reading of the Gospels by some redaction critics (*Challenge*, esp. 59).

17.   On the intangible text see Lash, 'Martyrdom', 192; he also produces a nice modern (if dated) parallel to our overall difficulty here: 'what was the "original meaning"... of Mr Whitelaw's speech, at the 1979 Conservative Party Conference, announcing the government's intention to set up detention centres to administer "short, sharp shocks" to juvenile offenders?' ('Martyrdom', 186). On interpretation in textual criticism see D.C. Parker, 'Scripture'.

18.   See e.g. *Biography*, 34/33, 41/39, 50–52/48–50.

the necessity of appreciating genre still holds good. It also sheds light on Farrer's work, as we shall see.

Burridge rapidly convinces that the idea of the Gospels' being *sui generis* is untenable, and his case is well made for an understanding of genre as a flexible set of expectations, producing family resemblance more than rigid conformity. Particularly helpful is his observation that a piece of writing in a particular genre can operate in various *modes*.[19] Burridge's approach means that any argument in favour of a particular work's belonging to a certain genre must be cumulative: it must patiently build up the features which gradually form a face that we, and even more the original audience, might recognise. Cumulative arguments can flatter themselves, however, and what on the surface seems an impressive accumulation of characteristics by Burridge actually includes some double counting. For instance, ancestry and birth appear first under the heading of chronological structure (one of the 'external features' *Biography*, 139/135) but appear again as topics or motifs (under 'internal features' *Biography*, 178/173), and the dominance of a single person as the literary subject is established once by their predominance as the grammatical subject of verbs (*Biography*, 134f/130f), and again by the (now-all-but-otiose) observation that the scope of the writing is limited to the subject's life and times: how could it not be, with the distribution of grammatical subjects already identified? What appear to be further items of evidence are actually different ways of saying the same thing.

There is a further problem when Burridge reaches a crucial stage of the argument and turns to the *purpose* of the Gospels. Again, he seems insufficiently aware of the genuine difficulties in saying what any book written by a long-dead and now-obscure author was *for* (though he does say that it is difficult to restrict any Gospel or βίος to one purpose, *Biography*, 216/210). Moreover, he makes the centrepiece of his case the apologetic and polemic purpose of the Gospels, aims which he has earlier demonstrated to be central to the composition of many βίοι, but offers as evidence only the retailing of modern authorities on the apologetic and polemic aims of Mark (*Biography*, 214–216/210).[20] It is surprising, after Burridge has exposed the weakness of current scholarship in saying wise things about the genre of the Gospels, that he writes as if the quoting of a contemporary scholar on the purpose of Mark settles the matter, as when he says that '[t]he titles of Weeden's works on Mark *demonstrate* … [Mark's] polemical purpose' (*Biography*, 216/210, emphasis added). They do not, and neither does Burridge, for he offers no evidence from the Gospels themselves. The fact that he can offer good original evidence

19. This distinction would have considerably sharpened the focus of Beavis' work on Mark: she detects a variety of resonances in Mark which are quite plausible as *modes* of writing, but she then plumps for a *genre* – Hellenistic drama – of which a prose narrative cannot be a full member.

20. Weeden, 'Heresy', 145–58; Weeden, *Mark*; Bilezikian, *Liberated*, 145.

for the apologetic function of, say, Xenophon's *Agesilaus* (*Biography*, 151f/147), but not for the Gospels, is disappointing. Farrer, too, is prematurely definite about the purpose of Mark, though no one could describe him as leaning on other scholars' shoulders.

Burridge is doubtless right that previous attempts to locate the genre of the Gospels within the scope of Graeco-Roman biography have foundered because of an inadequate theory of genre and a lack of familiarity with the biographical literature itself, but the family resemblance he describes between Gospel and βίος is a resemblance within a decidedly extended family. How much is gained by excluding, say, Xenophon's *Memorabilia* (partly on the grounds of length) when so much else is included (*Biography*, 153/149)? The question is not so much whether Burridge is right to class the Gospels as βίοι: although he has no evidence for βίος as an *ancient* generic term, by *his* description they *can* be seen as such. It is rather: 'Given that the Gospels are βίοι in Burridge's terms, what is the gain? Can we now interpret them better?' Genre's value as an interpretative tool is in proportion to its ability to exclude, until you approach the post-structuralist extreme of a genre for every text. Burridge himself realises that a narrower genre would be more useful, but less able to contain the Gospels (*Biography*, 255/247f). So he delineates a wide genre, a more comfortable home for the Gospels, but a less revealing one.

Austin Farrer sees the need for generic identification – surely Mark 'set out to write some sort of work rather than another' (*Study*, 30) – and for that identification to be fairly tight, for 'the cogency of its results is in proportion to the narrowness of the field taken' (*Study*, 352), but he himself makes assumptions about the genre of Mark which are not really scrutinised. Mark, he believes in *Rebirth*, is *sui generis*, though he tempers this in the *Study* with a more cautious 'on the face of it' (*Rebirth*, 306, cf *Study*, 31f). And what is the character of Farrer's unique *genus*? Burridge describes how a text gives off signals, especially at its beginning, which can help a reader to come to a hypothesis about its genre, but Farrer's great imagination is untrammelled by any such signs. It may be held that Mark begins by calling itself a 'Gospel' (whatever that might be),[21] but nowhere does it hint at itself being poetry, the category Farrer most often uses, not even by the sustained use of the 'rhythmical prose' which Farrer detects in Revelation (*Glass*, 117). Nevertheless, Farrer can still write that 'St Mark's book is neither a treatise nor a poem, but it is more like a poem than a treatise' (leaving Farrer's own audience wondering, not only about 'poem', but where he plucked 'treatise' from)

---

21.   Or the 'ἀρχὴ τοῦ εὐαγγελίου Ἰησοῦ' ('archē tou euangeliou Iesou') of Mk 1.1 may refer to the 'good news' of salvation, cf Rom. 1.1. Or, indeed, we may legitimately hear echoes of both (see further Collins, *Commentary*, 16).

and then go on to apply the idea of poetic rhythm (now denoting the 'rhythm' of sense and symbol) as his chief instrument of interpretation (*Study*, 30). Genre, we agree with Burridge, is basic to the understanding of a written communication, and we agree with Farrer that it would indeed be good to know what sort of a 'so-and-so' Mark felt himself to be writing (*Study*, 32). Farrer identifies the need to know the genre, but confuses what Burridge carefully distinguishes: Farrer describes in Mark what are very often *modal* features, but he considers them to be *generic*. Mark does contain 'poetic' elements, but it is not a poem, and to read it with poetically tinted spectacles (and a post-Renaissance pair at that) will distort and mislead. Farrer reads Mark, in Burridge's terms, through the wrong generic filter.

This debate would be merely a battle of personal reading preferences, but for its attention (however scanty in Farrer's case) to the first-century literary milieu, the original audience and the author's intention in addressing them. For although (*pace* Burridge) we cannot arrive, via genre theory or by any other route, at 'the final understanding of the actual meaning' (*Biography*, 40/39), we can come to some provisional conclusions and, more definitely, rule out certain others. Mark must be 'some sort of work rather than another', and though, like detectives, we may never discover the 'culprit', we can conclusively eliminate some suspects from our enquiries. We do this by careful examination of what was available, feasible, familiar and intelligible in the time when Mark was written. Here, while Burridge exhaustively unearths the features of βίος, Farrer concedes far too much to the difficulties of finding a setting in first-century literature.

In the *Study* Farrer nevertheless begins well. He draws the now familiar parallel with Elizabethan drama, and sets two criteria for studying the character of a Shakespeare play. First is the 'external criterion of historical probability', that is our knowledge of 'the playwright's task in his day', of Elizabethan theatrical settings and sources: 'From such considerations as these we can reach a fair idea of how the poet is likely to have gone about his task, and what sort of project or design he is likely to have set before his eyes' (*Study*, 30f). Second comes the 'internal criterion ... the schemes and rhythms discernible in the poem', by which the probabilities suggested according to the external criterion must be tested. To be sustained, they need to be shown from the internal character of the text to be 'basic and fertile' (*Study*, 31). When it comes to Mark, however, the assumed uniqueness of what seems 'on the face of it' to be 'a new sort of book' (*Study*, 31) and the obscurity to our time of the first-century milieu mean that the external criterion is difficult to apply. He is clear that Mark would have had literary models, and has a suspicion (as we know) that one might have been the 'sacred history' of the Elijah stories in the Books of Kings (*Study*, 32);[22] but this does not get him as far as one might

22 See also 'Mind', 18.

think, as he shows in a brief but cogent comparison with Bunyan. Mark's phrasing, says Farrer, owes much to the Septuagint; but then *Pilgrim's Progress*, a very 'biblical' book, is indebted to the King James Bible for phrase and allegory, but the debt does not extend to Bunyan's design; no, Bunyan's general pattern comes from 'a popular late medieval strain of allegorized pilgrimage story, crossed with a Calvinist account of the plan of salvation and the stages of spiritual progress' (*Study*, 32).

Farrer's instincts here are sound, as he employs something akin to Burridge's mode/genre distinction. It is not enough to discern traces or modalities of the Greek Bible; you must show what Mark does with them, and the best way to do that is to look at what can be found of the things people are reading or hearing in the world round about (here Farrer touches firmly on the methods of Burridge): '[p]erhaps he [Mark], like Bunyan, had his plan from what was being written in his own time, or shortly before it' (*Study*, 32). At this point we may say, risking a crude distinction, that Farrer has two possibilities for exemplars: contemporary (or near contemporary) literature from Jewish sources, and that from the wider Hellenistic writings. He rejects the first cursorily:

> Perhaps we ought to ransack the Jewish Pseudepigrapha for the missing indications. But nothing leaps to the eye as being what we want, and we must understand St Mark profoundly before we know what to look for. (*Study*, 32)

He then reverses his criteria:

> It would be a comfort, certainly, if we could discover after the event that our interpretation of St Mark attributed to him a sort of literary design not wholly strange to the world he knew. That would be to use the external criterion for subsequent confirmation. But it seems clear that we shall have to begin by trusting in the internal criterion. (*Study*, 32f)

The rest of the *Study* shows that even the qualifying force of 'begin' is misleading. Farrer's external criterion is not so much tried and found wanting, as found difficult and never tried.

Why does Farrer dismiss this task so quickly? An aside in *Rebirth* suggests a disinclination for the unglamorous spadework of unearthing the literature surrounding the New Testament documents; there he pays a double-edged compliment to R.H. Charles for his work – or, rather, 'labours' – on Jewish apocalyptic:

> Nearly all the facts ... have been collected and piled to hand by ... admirable and massive learning which I have no pretensions to emulate. The next stage belongs to our generation ... We have not got to go down the mine and dig out the metal. (*Rebirth*, 9)

Farrer sees himself as a goldsmith, not a miner. Thus he gives up much too quickly, only for his 'understanding' of Mark to run unchecked. To this reader of Farrer, it feels as though a hunch about Mark's literary patterning breeds an impatience with combing the surrounding literary countryside, which *is* a painstaking task, and an uncomfortable one: if things fail to 'leap to the eye' it may be because the eye is looking for the wrong things.

Let us turn to the second range of possibilities for generic influence on Mark, the Graeco-Roman literature of which Beavis and Burridge make so much. Why does Farrer, himself a classical scholar,[23] have no time for influence from this source? When Farrer wrote the *Study*, W.L. Knox's work on a Hellenistic context for the Gospels had been available for some years,[24] and Farrer would not have been impressed by the form critics' insulation of the Gospels from the influence of Hellenistic sophistication by classing them as *Kleinliteratur*.[25] Part of his reluctance may stem from the then current assumptions, by Bultmann and others, about the prevalence of Gnosticism in Hellenistic culture; Farrer is not much taken with Bultmann![26] He does discuss (in the *Glass*) one instance of a literary marriage of Judaism and Hellenism, that of the pseudo-Sibylline Oracles, but they do not impress him. Read a page of them, he says, 'if you do not fall asleep in the middle' (*Glass*, 116). He cannot believe that the author of Revelation (his subject at this point) would choose, on deciding to be a poet, such a path of sterility as that of a sub-Homeric versifier. What, then, should John do? He would surely look to the lyrical character of contemporary prose writing, which, thanks to 'the popular rhetoric of his period', exhibited 'an ornate and musical style, with clauses carefully balanced in cadence and length'; fortunately, he would find this not unlike the rhythms of the balanced clauses of Hebrew poetry, even as it was felt through the 'jagged barbarity' of the Greek version (*Glass*, 116). In the case of 'manner' Farrer (again applying Burridge's mode/genre distinction) can see John deriving a little from Hellenistic culture, but then only in as much as it coincides with his ancestral literary heritage (*Glass*, 116). And what of the 'matter' of Revelation? 'Well, but so far as matter is concerned, St John is firmly attached to the Jewish tradition, and not the Greek' (*Glass*, 117). When he fills out these adumbrations in *Rebirth*, we find surprisingly little about the linguistic debt of Revelation to contemporary rhetoric. We do, however, find a reference to Mark:

> St John was making a new form of literature: it happens that he had no successors.
> St Mark performed the same unimaginable feat, and he was followed by others. The
> comparison is an interesting one, and students of St Mark ought to ask the same

23.   For Farrer the classicist, see Curtis, *Hawk*, 24f.
24.   Knox, *Elements*.
25.   That is, popular, 'non-literary' writings. See the discussions of the *Kleinliteratur* debate in Beavis, *Audience*, 27–29, Burridge, *Biography*, 7–11/7–11, and 12B (pp. 151–153) below.
26.   See Farrer's lampoon, 'Gnosticism', and his so-called 'Appreciation' for difficulties with Bultmann.

question as we are asking here abut St John. What did St Mark sit down to do? To us the idea of writing a memoir or a biography is perfectly familiar, and the literary men of the Hellenistic world had some notion of it too. But it is unlikely that St Mark had ever read such a work, and in any case his gospel had no resemblance to their efforts. (*Rebirth*, 306)

Rebirth appeared in 1949, two years before the *Study*. By the time of the second book, Farrer does not consider the question of possible connections between Mark and 'the Hellenistic world' worthy of discussion, or even denial. Perhaps Farrer the Christian averts his mind from the very thought that canonical writers might have owed dues to pagan 'barbarity'; for what has Athens to do with Jerusalem?

Austin Farrer's case shows what can happen if we ignore Burridge's warning about doing New Testament scholarship 'in a vacuum' (*Biography*, 254/247),[27] but Burridge himself is not entirely thorough about this. He writes that 'no matter how clear the results of our analysis might be, the idea that the gospels are βίοι would be untenable if no connection with Hellenistic literary culture was possible for their authors and readers' (*Biography*, 254f/247). Correct, but he then concludes that this connection is 'demanded ... by the generic features of the texts themselves' which appears to undo what he has just said. He does add that the connection is also demanded by the social setting of early Christianity, but there remains a slight impression of a hunch in a vacuum – 'the patterns look familiar, so it must be so' – which we find in a much stronger form in Farrer. The overall impression of Burridge's work is actually of something helpfully more modest: neither internal features nor social setting *demand* that the Gospels be seen as βίοι; each is a necessary condition, and together they offer sufficient conditions for the hypothesis to be maintained.[28] Burridge could have made the second, 'external' leg more sturdy, by more attention to audience definition, though he refers to others, Beavis included, who do this well (*Biography*, 251–254/243–246). It is the lack of a socio-literary leg which unbalances Farrer, and which he seems so uninterested in constructing. Further evidence is in his remark, made in 1949 in a letter to his father, about a

27. Brown's comment about 'Farrer's attempt to make the scriptures entirely self-contained' (made in relation to his sparing use of intertestamental Jewish writings, ('Human', 91) is pertinent here, also. Conversely, Collins finds Burridge cursory in his survey of Jewish literary scriptural models and herself urges the relevance of 'the biographical material in 1 & 2 Samuel and 1 & 2 Kings' (*Commentary*, 29). Farrer would approve!

28. Collins acknowledges the gravitational pull of the βίοι on Mark, but places it in the orbit of 'historical monograph', a *genus proximum* of Graeco-Roman biography:

Whether one defines Mark as a historical biography or a historical monograph depends on one's perception of where the emphasis in Mark lies: on the activity and fate of Jesus, or on God's plan for the fulfillment of history in which he played a decisive role. (*Commentary*, 33)

Her considered definition is 'eschatological historical monograph' (*Commentary*, 42f).

talk he gave in Cambridge, this time on scriptural typology: 'They could object nothing but generalities – Did people really think like this?' Two Jewish scholars present supported Farrer, but it was they and not he who said that '[n]othing would be more natural or *better evidenced*' (*Hawk*, 137, emphasis added).

Burridge contends, finally, that if a Gospel is a βίος, then it is the person of Jesus of Nazareth, whose life is portrayed, which is the key to interpretation. This statement seems a truism, until he sets beside it what he takes to be Norman Perrin's view, that 'the nature of a Gospel is not the ministry of the historical Jesus, but the reality of Christian experience' (*Biography*, 256/248). In fact, Perrin's position is more nuanced,[29] and Burridge seems to want something more like Bultmann's '[t]here is no historical-biographical interest in the Gospels' to represent the view he is rejecting (*Synoptic*, 372), though Bultmann is rather early to stand for what Burridge considers a *current* malaise in Gospel criticism. Burridge compares the Gospels with rabbinic literature, sees some resemblances between particular episodes, but sees nothing like a whole Gospel among the rabbinic writings; he feels this is probably because 'the centre of Rabbinic Judaism was Torah; the centre of Christianity was the person of Jesus' (*Biography*, 257/249).[30] Farrer here is quite close to Burridge, for in all his cyclical complexities he is clear that it is the ministry of Jesus that Mark is labouring to set forth, in short, recurring cycles of topics: 'Christ's action, according to our evangelist, constantly expresses the essentials of the Gospel' (*Study*, 34). What remains to be asked is the extent to which a first-century, Jesus-centred reading of Mark should be normative for every reader.

D. *Conclusion*

Burridge's book sets Mark on the very broad and varied canvas of Graeco-Roman biography, but still presents a rather different set of generic signals in the Markan text, and generic expectations in the Markan audience, from those of Beavis, since a βίος cannot also be a play (though it might display some similarities to drama). This may not give us much confidence in the feasibility of defining either the intentions of an author or the expectations of the original audience, yet Farrer

29.   Perrin's actual words are:

the nature of a Gospel is such that it must be held that the *locus of revelation* is not the ministry of the historical Jesus, but the reality of Christian experience; however it is also clear that there is *continuity* between those things. (*Redaction*, 75, emphasis added)

30.   Quoting P. Alexander, 'Rabbinic Biography and the Biography of Jesus: A Survey of the Evidence', in *Synoptic Studies*, 1984, 41.

shows the danger of not trying hard. In seeking to describe the activity of a historical author, he is, as we have seen, rash in dismissing the question of defining a historical audience, and heedless of those signals given or not given by the text. His imagination then becomes airborne on the thermals of misleading generic assumptions.[31] It may be in the end that the inscrutabilities of the authorial mind remain just that, and that the genre of a Gospel frustratingly straddles some categories and eludes others. Although no author writes out of nothing, perhaps we can never know, even in a provisional way, what sort of 'so-and-so' Mark thought he was writing. What Burridge (like Beavis) does achieve is some sense of the waters into which the stone of Mark's Gospel might have been dropped. We can know a little about the sort of ripples it would create in minds already accustomed to other sorts of literature. Even that will set limits to what we can say about its author. Burridge's 'almost trite'[32] statement that a first-century audience would see a Gospel as centred upon Jesus of Nazareth as a historically accessible life would call into question redactional readings which placed the burden of 'original meaning' entirely on the setting of the Markan community, though we have seen that Perrin's position is not quite this. It certainly places on their mettle those who see Mark as a work of fiction, unless they are doing no more than *laissez-faire* reader-response criticism. It might not even rule out Farrer's reading (Burridge's βίος-genre is, after all, 'a large room'[33]) though he cannot afford to assume that the structure and typological modes he describes were obviously part of the first-century literary landscape, especially when he also contends that Mark's Gospel is a new type of book.

Burridge's final remarks, however, reveal a presupposition which then casts a shadow over the preceding pages. He notes Graham Stanton's view that the biographical interest of the early church in Jesus should act now as a spur to evangelism, which should also be focused on the person of Jesus; he then himself concludes that 'this βίος nature of the gospel genre should also restore the centrality of the person of Jesus' (*Biography*, 258/250).[34] The centrality of the person of Jesus for whom? And for what? We presume he means its centrality for our, twenty-first-century, reading of Mark, but what *is* our, your, my purpose in reading Mark? Burridge has aimed, quite legitimately, to be faithful to the evangelists' intention,[35] but it now seems that he is also reading the Gospels as Scripture within the church. That too is legitimate, but it would help to

31. His last attempt to define the genre of Mark, as 'historico-theologico-parenetic', does not really help. Farrer admits that 'such a conjoint description gives us no positive guidance' ('Mind', 14f).
32. Tuckett, review of *Biography* (Review, 75).
33. Psalm 31.8.
34. Stanton, *Preaching*, 190f.
35. See e.g. *Biography*, 125f/121f, 149–152/145–147.

say this at the start, as Farrer does. As it is, he leaves the impression that he considers other readings of the Gospels as *illegitimate*.[36] But is there anything wrong in reading Mark, say, for evidence of agrarian society in the eastern Roman Empire, just as Burridge has read the *Agricola* as grist to his biblical-critical mill, rather than to be inspired by the virtues of a great Roman?

Nevertheless, a rounded reading of Mark will usually seek to lay bare the grain of the text as it might have been originally received or even conceived, and here even the most limited claims can provide a useful constraint. We return to the critical *via negativa*: a historically informed reading of a Gospel, especially as it asks what *sort* of writing the author was trying to produce, may not enable us to say what a Gospel is, let alone what it means, but we can be increasingly confident in saying what it is not. Farrer indeed speaks the truth when he says that Mark is neither a treatise nor a poem (*Study*, 301).

36.   See Watson, *Text*, for a better – because more candid – attempt to ascribe 'some form of normativity' to theological readings of the Bible (*Text*, viii). Burridge will go on, nonetheless, to make fruitful use of the normativity of Christocentric readings of the Gospels – within the enclave of belief – for an 'inclusive' approach to New Testament ethics. See his *Imitating Jesus: An Inclusive Approach to New Testament Ethics* (Grand Rapids: Eerdmans, 2007).

Chapter 12

THE PRE-HISTORY OF MARK

Naturally something is presupposed by St Mark's patterning of the tradition.
A Study in St Mark, 367

No author, we have seen, writes *ex nihilo*. In this section we shall look at the question of the historicality of the materials the writer of Mark used, the ways in which they were shaped, preserved and transmitted until the author took them up. These are the matters tackled by exponents of source and form criticism, and also by Farrer in his argument for Mark's typological use of the Old Testament. Our aim here is to ask in what way, and how adequately, Farrer is aware of this layer of historicality in his reading of Mark. Once again Beavis and Burridge will serve as foils to him. In the course of the comparison we shall also his discuss his contemporary Bultmann.

A. *Written Sources*

The *Study* is an exercise in final-form interpretation, though in the coda Farrer acknowledges the legitimacy of a concern for sources. On the penultimate page he speaks of how, in the quest for Christian origins, we 'have to separate between the tradition on which he [Mark] worked and the inspired labour he performed upon it' (*Study*, 370). Farrer himself spends little time on possible documentary sources. The index of the *Study* contains several references to '"source"-criticism' (*Study*, 391),[1] but 'source' is used here largely – and oddly – in the sense of Mark's text itself as a source for historical events. One exception is when he considers the possibility, advanced by some, of a documentary source behind the apocalyptic material in Mark 13. Characteristically, Farrer swats this aside by pleading his prime concern for the text of Mark itself, and arguing that the burden of proof lies not with him but with those

---

1.   See under 'Mark: Gospel of'.

who contend that 'a passage in a continuous book is a piece of old cloth
patched to a new garment. All I need to do is to show that the passage in
question results from the imaginative process which produces the whole
book' (*Study*, 361). Earlier, Farrer asks how far the Pauline writings
corroborate the Markan narrative (*Study*, 203–209), and in 'The Mind of
St Mark' he asks whether Paul's letters might be regarded as documentary
sources (e.g. 1 and 2 Thess. for the apocalypse of Chapter 13, 1 Cor. 11
for the Last Supper of Chapter 14); if they are, he says, then Mark has
extensively recast them, so the whole business is heavily conjectural: 'We
cannot claim to possess St Mark's Christian sources otherwise than as
St Mark has reproduced (or transformed) them' ('Mind', 16). This is a
restatement of his position as expressed much earlier, in the Preface to the
Study, where he says of the author of Mark that, 'whatever his materials
or sources, he dominated them' (*Study*, vi).

Since Farrer subscribes to Markan priority (*Study*, 268), and feels no
need to argue for it, his scanty references to classical source criticism are
unsurprising, indeed inevitable, and Beavis and Burridge follow him in
this. We have seen how much he has to say about Mark's typological
use of the books of the Old Testament, which – on his reckoning – are
documentary sources for Mark, though not in the same sense, he would
argue, as the Gospel of Mark is itself a source for Matthew. He can
say that 'St Mark does not quote the Old Testament much ... but he is
nourished on the substance of it, and so perfectly assimilates it that he
can write it into the matter of his own sentences' (*Study*, 321), but he is
anxious to reassure that, while – say – the Elijah cycle provides the model
for the form, the arrangement or the interpretation of Markan material,
the content comes from Mark's Christian inheritance.[2] When he comes
to treat of the author of Mark as a historian, he presents Old Testament
typology as part of a historiographical rationale (here Farrer talks just
of 'the men of the New Testament', but the context strongly suggests he
means by these people the New Testament authors and their audiences):

the men of the New Testament ... saw the history behind them as of finite length,
and Gospel history could obtain unique importance in relation to previous history
by being the retrospective epitome of its pith and substance. All that men had been
or done had prefigured Christ, and all they had prefigured, Christ did and was.
(*Study*, 185)

---

2.   This is at least true of the *Study*: see e.g. *Study*, 47, where parts of the Jesus
tradition 'remind' Mark of Old Testament texts, and *Study*, 367, where anecdotes about
Christ are 'related to' such texts. In *Matthew*, Farrer edges towards saying that Mark
invented material under the influence of Old Testament typological models, but never quite
goes the whole way (*Matthew*, 15–18).

B. Oral Sources

No such scantiness typifies his treatment of that other strain of pre-textual historical enquiry, form criticism. We have seen at many points already the acerbic pen he pokes at the form critics, not only in the *Study* but also in 'Mind'. This last led Drury, in a review of the collection (*Interpretation*) which includes this piece, to give as one of Farrer's achievements in these essays the demonstration that 'form criticism does not work' (Review, 136).[3] The earlier reaction to his assault upon form criticism in the *Study* was, however, not friendly.[4] Indeed, Eric Mascall's Foreword to *Interpretation* praises Farrer, eight years after his death, because

> he was convinced – and had the courage to say so – that many of the theories [of New Testament criticism] which it has become almost blasphemous to criticise were in fact ill-founded, implausible, and ham-fisted. (*Interpretation*, xiii)

Support, albeit implicit, for Farrer's heresies on form criticism awaited the emergence of mature redaction criticism.[5] We also find it in the two books we are here holding up for extended comparison with Farrer, and we begin with these.

Mary Beavis: Mark's Audience

Beavis notes the early post-1918 interest in the similarities between so-called 'pronouncement stories' and the *chria*-form, and between whole Gospels and βίοι, but claims that interest in both was arrested by the ascendancy of form criticism (*Audience*, 26f). She describes how, before this, Dibelius himself had looked at *chriae* but maintained the uniqueness of the Gospel 'paradigms' (pronouncement stories): *chriae* were literary devices, the paradigms pre-literary forms shaped by preaching (*Audience*, 27f).[6] Subsequently, she says, Schmidt and Bultmann insulated the Gospels from Hellenistic influence, except insofar as they might be regarded as *Kleinliteratur*. Once the Gospels were thus seen as accumulations of communal tradition, she says, it became all but impossible to absorb indications from a Gospel text that it might be the literary creation of an author, or even be literary in its parts (*Audience*, 37f).[7]

---

3.   Cf 'Mind', 22.
4.   Note e.g. the tone of McCasland's review of *Study* (see the Postscript to Chapter 5 above).
5.   For more explicit endorsement see Drury, *Tradition*, 76; for the persistence of source-based redaction criticism see Best, *Mark*, esp. 10–13.
6.   Dibelius, *Tradition*, esp. 152–64.
7.   Schmidt, 'Die Stellung'; Bultmann, *Synoptic*.

Beavis' difficulty with form criticism is twofold. First, there is the special pleading she detects in these attempts to preserve the generic 'purity' of the Gospels and in the determination to ignore similarities between the Gospels and other literary phenomena: for instance, both *chriae* and Gospel paradigms are unliterary or oral in their origin, since they began life as the remembered sayings of famous people, yet in both cases the *form* in which they have been transmitted to us is a written one (*Audience*, 27).[8] Secondly, there are what she believes to be three flaws in the form-critical principle itself: its reliance upon the questionable assumption that whereas orality implies vitality, writtenness implies the 'dead letter'; its taking of principles for the development of primitive literature (themselves more recently under attack) and applying them to the development of literature in the relatively sophisticated Judaeo-Hellenistic world; and its ignoring of the likelihood that the Gospel material developed over some four decades between the death of Jesus and the writing of the first Gospel, whereas the folk-tale methods underlying form criticism were conceived to trace development of literature over much longer periods (*Audience*, 28).

Beavis sides with Erhardt Güttgemans (one German scholar with whom Farrer might feel sympathy) who sees form criticism and redaction criticism as opposed methods, the one conceiving the Gospels

---

8.   On this transition in Mark, see also Kelber, *The Oral and the Written Gospel*, 44–139. Kelber questions the smooth evolutionary model of transition from oral units to written text (*Oral*, 90), and in stressing the creativity of the writer he has his similarities with Farrer. Kelber's aim, however, is to urge the disjunction between the oral and the written, and even the repudiation – implied in the evangelist's decision to write the Gospel – of the oral tradition and its (largely apostolic) tradents. His observations on the critical portrayal of the disciples in Mark (*Oral*, 97f) raise difficulties for Farrer's confidence about Mark's reverence for apostolic authority in the Jesus tradition (see p. 156, note 14, below), and Kelber quite properly draws a contrast between orality and textuality.

We can agree that, in the former, 'speaker and hearers co-operate in an effort to ensure a direct and immediate hermeneutical transaction'; we can also agree that, as the text floats away from its author, 'the co-operation ... is abolished' (*Oral*, 92); but can we be sure, with Kelber, that the very act of writing always constitutes such a seismic shift? Can we be certain that the process of Mark's composition did not have a quasi-oral 'dialogical' character between writer and audience (*Oral*, 92)? How can we know that the author was not in dialogue with his Christian congregation as he wrote, or that the text was not modified in the light of audience reaction during successive 'live' performances (as were the texts of some of Shakespeare's plays), perhaps even performed by the author himself? The quest for an 'original' text may then be no more sensible than the quest, which Kelber attacks, for 'original form' in 'oral speech' (*Oral*, 45f, cf Parker, 'Scripture').

Despite his warnings about the post-Gutenberg mentality, Kelber himself seems to be contrasting with orality some rather modern ideas of authorship, in which solitary writers deliver texts for publication, reproduction, and reading by a largely remote public; and even 'print-oriented' and 'chirographically-biased' modern biblical scholars have been known to try out chapters of forthcoming books in the seminar (see *Oral*, xv). Dewey well describes the 'original' text of Mark as 'just one textual rendition of a living tradition' ('Gospel', 158).

as transcriptions of oral tradition, the other as (in her words) 'works of creative literature'.⁹ She also supports Willi Marxsen, who is more cautious (as well he might be, writing in the infancy of redaction criticism), but who nevertheless maintains that '[t]heoretically, it would have been possible for redaction-historical research to have begun immediately after literary [source] criticism' (*Audience*, 28).¹⁰

Richard Burridge: What are the Gospels?

Burridge detects interest in comparing the Gospels with Graeco-Roman biography as early as Renan and Votaw, writing in the nineteenth and early twentieth centuries respectively, and he agrees with Beavis that the rise of form criticism choked development. The crucial factors for him are again the identification of the Gospels as *sui generis*, and as 'unliterary' *Kleinliteratur*, rather than 'literary' *Hochliteratur*, principles enunciated by Dibelius, endorsed by Schmidt and reproduced by Bultmann. Bultmann, he says, can barely bring himself to speak of the Gospels as a literary genre at all, so subordinate does he find them to the Christian communities' dogma and worship (*Biography*, 7–11/7–11).¹¹

Burridge endorses and adds to Beavis' objections to form criticism. He attacks the rigid distinction between *Hochliteratur* and *Kleinliteratur* (we have seen that he makes a good case for the flexibility of literary categories) which sees a Gospel not as 'the product of an individual author' but rather as a 'folk-book', produced without 'conscious literary intention' (*Biography*, 8f/8f). He also rejects the consequent atomistic tendency of form criticism, which precludes study of whole texts (even though the pre-literary origins of, say, the *Iliad* present no necessary bar to its study as a whole narrative), and the eclipse of the author, which then requires an implausibly active role for the community. This last is implausible because 'communities tend to be passive with regard to their traditions; the active innovations come on the part of the story-tellers – and thus we are back to the person of the author once more' (*Biography*, 14/13).

9.   Erhardt Güttgemans, *Candid Questions Concerning Gospel Form Criticism: A Methodological Sketch of the Fundamental Problematics of Form and Redaction Criticism* (Pittsburgh, Pickwick, 1979), 95–114.

10.   Quotation from W. Marxsen, *Mark the Evangelist* (New York/Nashville: Abingdon, 1969), 21f; ET of *Der Evangelist Markus* (1959).

11.   Ernest Renan, *Le Vie de Jésus*; ET, *Life of Jesus* (London: Kegan Paul, 1893); C.W. Votaw, 'The Gospels and Contemporary Biographies', *American Journal of Theology*, 19 (1915), 45–73 and 217–249; reprinted as *The Gospels and Contemporary Biographies in the Graeco-Roman World* (Philadelphia: Fortress Press, Facet Books, 1970); Dibelius, *Tradition*; 1f; Schmidt, 'Die Stellung', 55–76; Bultmann, *Synoptic*, revised edn, 371f, 374; Bultmann 'Evangelien', 1928; ET, 'The Gospels (Form)', in J. Pelikan (ed.), *Twentieth Century Theology in the Making* (London: Collins, Fontana, 1969), Vol. 1, 87, 89.

C. Evaluation: Farrer, Beavis and Burridge

Unlike Beavis and Burridge, Farrer does not mount a full-dress critique of the methodology behind form criticism. Nevertheless, there are obvious convergences, though – again unlike them – Farrer has no quarrel with the alleged generic purity of the Gospels, but rather with the *genus* to which they are held by form critics to belong. He would no doubt warm to the strictures of Beavis and Burridge about atomism and the antinomy between form and redaction criticism, and in fact his work shows that the bypassing of form criticism, which Marxsen believed to have been theoretically possible, had actually happened some years before.

We are familiar with Farrer's convictions about Mark as a literary whole, convictions which Beavis and Burridge share, and the consequent order of priority – wholes before parts – in study of the text. We saw how in the first chapter of the *Study* he describes the form critic's task, once Mark is disallowed as 'ready-made history', of seeking '*disjecta membra* of simple unadulterated tradition' (*Study*, 4). But then,

> what was the history of the '*disjecta membra*', the anecdotes and sayings, while they circulated orally and before St Mark strung them together in writing? Did they undergo much modification and, if so, of what sort? Did oral tradition introduce a characteristic bias, for which we must be on the watch? Form-criticism undertakes this difficult enquiry, looking at the form or shape of the traditional elements, and guessing at the forces which have thus shaped them. (*Study*, 5)

This is 'a laudable, though speculative, line of enquiry, and one with which we have no quarrel at all. All that we are concerned with here is a question of priorities' (*Study*, 21). Farrer puts himself for a moment in form-critical shoes:

> We want to see the Gospel as a compilation of virgin tradition, and so we want to reduce the role of the evangelist to that of a compiler, a contributor of 'ands' and 'thens'. But we cannot let ourselves off looking at the principles of arrangement that he does appear to follow. For it may be that his constructive activity goes further than we wish to allow; that (let us say) in making the traditional anecdotes illustrate theological topics under which he has grouped them, he has to modify their traditional wording a good deal, so as to make their connexion with those topics more evident. (*Study*, 5)[12]

Later, it seems he does have a quarrel with form-critical practice, if not with the hypothesis, for 'we cannot speak of the tradition as it existed before St Mark wrote; we can speak only of the way in which the literary form takes shape in the writing' (*Study*, 88). Farrer offers an example of what he sees as the misapplication of the form-critical method. The healing of the paralytic (Mk 2.1–12) is held by form critics to be a hybrid,

---

12.   See also *Study*, 11, 21f.

the fusing of two types of *pericopé*, the 'healing' and the 'dispute'. Rather than place it 'in an hypothetical series of pre-Marcan oral paragraphs' and complain that it does not fit, Farrer prefers to set it

> in the actual series of St Mark's paragraphs, where we find it fits perfectly. We cannot study the evolution of pre-Marcan oral stories because we have not got them. But we can study the evolution of the Marcan written story, for it evolves under our very eyes, as one paragraph elaborates upon another. (*Study*, 74)

In this case he sees 'dispute' as a germ contained in the previous two healings – in the shock of the crowd in the synagogue (1.27f), and in the orders of Jesus to the cleansed leper to observe the courtesies with the priests (1.44) – but now 'the dispute unfolds fully grown' (*Study*, 75). Farrer's contention is that, once you allow that his project of interpreting the Gospel as a whole is logically prior to other approaches, you see that form criticism is fundamentally flawed. It assumes an incoherence in the text which ought first to be demonstrated; and 'if St Mark is in fact after all a living whole, the work of the form-critics is, every line of it, called into doubt' (*Study*, 24). And if the form critic retorts that we must at least concede that Markan paragraphs do have a self-contained air about them? All that this proves for Farrer is that Mark chose to write in anecdotal form (*Study*, 24). Farrer advances a very similar argument in 'The Mind of St Mark':

> Suppose ... our concern is not with St Mark or with what he is at. Our overwhelming desire may be to reconstruct his Christian sources. For we want above all to collect evidence from which to establish historical fact about the human life of Jesus and about his teaching; and if we can work back from St Mark to his sources we come nearer to the fountain head. A most natural, indeed a laudable, line of enquiry, if a hazardous one. How are we to pursue it? ... It is only by seeing what St Mark does with the known factors that we can begin to conjecture how the unknown factor needs to be conceived or postulated ... But somewhat to our amazement we find another method commonly preferred. You start from the other end, with the invisible and unknown. You conjecture the form which the tradition must have taken in those pre-Marcan decades. It must, you think, have consisted of short, mutually independent, anecdotes or dicta; it must have dealt with a certain range of topics; and so on. Whatever, then, is in contradiction or in excess of your postulated rules will be editorial. ('Mind', 16f)[13]

Instead, we must begin with the act of composition, and remember that

> St Mark at every point is writing in view of three factors: ancient Scripture, his own developing narrative, his Christian sources. Of these the first two are observable, the third is not. It is the x in our equation. How are we to determine its value? How else than by working with the factors we can observe? It is only by seeing what St

---

13.   In both cases he also rebuts the form-critical approach by detailed example. See *Study*, 197, 'Mind', 20f.

Mark does with the known factors that we can begin to conjecture how the unknown
factor needs to be conceived or postulated. ('Mind', 17)

Having exposed form criticism's logical dependence on his own kind
of holistic study, and having then demonstrated that the crumbs falling
from his table will be meagre indeed, Farrer is largely content to starve
the form critic into submission, but he has a few methodological jabs
to deliver. Farrer is unconvinced, rather in the manner of Beavis and
Burridge, by the picture of units of tradition about Jesus floating in a
folkloric murk, aside from any connected story about the ministry of
Jesus, unchecked by eyewitness testimony. At one point this leads him
into burlesque.

Say he [Mark] was writing in Rome between AD 65 and 69. Had he never met an
apostle? Is it certain, after all, that he was not the John Mark of Acts, the man from
Jerusalem, the companion of Barnabas, Peter and Paul? Was there a special social
tabu in St Peter's entourage against ever talking about the sequence of events which
led from Christ's baptism to his passion? If one mentioned it, did the apostle turn
slightly green and suggest with embarrassment that one's proper course was to listen
to third- and fourth-hand recitations given in Church piecemeal by local elders? That
an apostle could scarcely misuse his superior knowledge to interfere with the growth
of a genuine Christian folk-tradition? (*Study*, 187)[14]

More soberly, Farrer describes the suspicion he (like Burridge) has of the
active role envisaged for Christian congregations in shaping the Gospel
traditions. If there is evidence of shaping and patterning, it strains his
belief to see it as the long-drawn-out work of 'the community mind
or any such mysterious agency' (*Study*, 367). He prefers as an agent
Burridge's story-teller, though Farrer calls him a preacher, who employs
in the writing of his Gospel 'a habitual way of handling anecdotes about
Christ and relating them to Old Testament texts. St Mark himself had
done plenty of it in the pulpit before he wrote his Gospel; who doubts
it?' (*Study*, 367).

Allow a degree of creativity to a writer, says Farrer (and of course
he 'soups up' the creativity by adding divine inspiration), and much of
the form critic's reason for insisting on the long germination of Gospel
traditions in 'the mind of the Church' disappears (*Study*, 358). After all,
Paul was capable of being quite sophisticated about Jesus quite quickly,
and Farrer's contention is that Mark's symbolic or theological shaping
takes place *in the writing*. 'To ask how long it took is to ask how long St

14.   Farrer's confidence in Mark's sitting at the feet of apostolic witness needs to take
account of Mark's unflattering portrayal of the apostles; Farrer himself notes the character
of the portrayal (see e.g. *Study*, 104, 117, 120). Kelber presses the point very hard, though
(of course) without reference to Farrer (*Oral*, 96–98). The closing words of the *Study* ask:
'Is it likely that the evangelist neglected as an authority what he built on as a symbol, the
apostolate instituted by Christ?' (*Study*, 371). We could as well ask: Would Mark have
deferred so much to the authority of any of those whom he was to depict as so perverse?

Mark worked on his Gospel. What do you say? Days or weeks?' (*Study*, 367).

D. Conclusion

For all the excesses of his exegesis, and despite the fun poked at form criticism (no doubt because, apart from believing it to be wrong, he found it aesthetically displeasing) we must credit Farrer with prescience in seeing, and nerve in saying, so early where the form-critical shoe would pinch. His argument about the priorities in exegesis concurs with that of Williams,[15] and we note that Farrer maintains his position even while admitting the legitimate desire of the historian to 'get back to Jesus'. Moreover his *historical* doubts about the role of Christian communities and Gospel writers in the form-critical scheme of things find their vindication in the more systematic critiques of Beavis, Burridge and their allies.

Is there anything left to say for form criticism, apart from some funeral sentences, or about Farrer's shunning of it, apart from some almost condescending words of congratulation? We can say that, unless one assumes that the evangelists took dictation as they followed Jesus or a disciple around, it remains 'a most natural, indeed a laudable, line of enquiry' to ask about the things concerning Jesus in the period between his death and the appearance of a Gospel, even if the results (as Farrer insists) are bound to be conjectural. If the particular methods of classical form criticism are questionable and its findings unconvincing, then (as in another context Farrer says against himself) '[b]ad practice should not discredit an art' ('Surface', 65). Moreover, Farrer's renunciation of the art and *all* its works makes his perspective on Mark the author too narrow.

Gerd Theissen, who more recently has assumed (though not uncritically) a form-critical mantle, has some illuminating observations about the practice of the art in his *Social Reality and the Early Christians*. He sees at its heart the desire to locate the *Sitz im Leben*, what he interprets as the 'real-life situation' of early Christian texts (*Social*, vii); this setting was in practice too narrowly defined by classical form critics, so that it became in effect a *Sitz im Glauben*, a *faith*-setting, but there nevertheless remains latent in the form-critical impulse an awareness that, just as texts such as the Gospels did not address a vacuum, nor did they *arise* from a vacuum (*Social*, vii, 4, 9f). We saw how a little more of a hearing for some of the aims of form criticism, and its sense of the need to be rigorous in asking what people used the Gospel material *for*, might have reined in the exuberance of Farrer's sometimes disembodied reading of Mark.[16] As it is, his commendably wide grasp of the literary and even the psychological

15. See 9A (pp. 104–108) above.
16. See 10A (pp. 113–117) above.

contexts of authorship is hampered by too narrow a grasp of its historical embeddedness.

Furthermore, while Farrer's point is very well made about the priority of the whole of a text over its parts, it is not inevitable that even the reader's best efforts will find the text seamless and unwrinkled. Farrer claims to manage this, but his gyrations prove more impressive than convincing. Beavis and Burridge have their difficulties too, which lead the former to multiply literary influences and the latter to set the boundaries of βίος very wide. The exposure of such wrinkles is part of the business of what is now called deconstruction.[17] A reader may stop at this point, and simply witness the text undermining itself. A historically sensitive reader, however, may wish to infer therefrom the limitations bearing on the author; and since one inevitably then asks what (apart from innate ineptitude) might have made the author's life so difficult, the reader may want to explore the possible pre-textual constraints which led, or forced, Mark to write as he did.

Some light may still be shed on these problems by traditional pre-textual approaches, on the grand scale by source criticism (though its usefulness in studying the earliest Synoptic Gospel is limited) and, on a more intimate scale, by a kind of form criticism now shorn of its over-confidence in reconstructing the hypothetical, and far more cautious of applying blanket principles of development to the peculiar settings of early Christian congregations. With these caveats, it might still point to the existence of some pre-textual, even pre-literary, traditions as an explanation for a wrinkled text.[18]

---

17.   This is what Moore calls the 'soft' style of deconstruction, which submits the apparent self-consistency of literary texts to stringent interrogation – uses 'against the edifice the instruments and stones available in the house' – which can result in a tottering or collapse of their internal logic (*Challenge*, 137, quoting Heidegger).

Moore contrasts this with the 'hard style', the 'utterly pitiless, no-holds-barred' deconstruction advocated by Jacques Derrida (*Challenge*, 136). In his more recent 'Deconstructive Criticism: Turning Mark Inside-Out', Moore offers an apparently non-combative description:

Literary texts are typically tied together by particular metaphors ... Deconstruction is characteristically interested in tracing the intricate interlacing of such metaphors with a view to untying them, thereby causing the text to disassemble into its constituent parts, so that its most basic operations are revealed. (*Method*, 106)

See also *Method*, 253, note 2: '[t]o deconstruct is to dismantle'.

For robust rejoinders to Derrida, see Tallis, *Saussure* (esp. 93f, 174f, 166–188), and Hirsch's attack on his 'decadent scepticism' (*Aims*, 146–148).

18.   On this 'second chance' for form criticism, see also Moore, *Challenge*, 164–167, a chance missed by Best, *Mark* (see p. 83, note 2). Despite claiming to treat the Gospel as 'story', Best proceeds by a historical-critical route heavily indebted to form criticism and arrives at the 'story', the final form of Mark, last of all. In the light of his title, he might have put his attachment to form criticism to better use by first attending to the story of Mark, and then using form-critical insights to account for narrative *aporiai*.

Postscript: *The Social Setting of the Critic*

Theissen also has pointed things to say about the *Sitz im Leben* of form criticism itself in the different decades in which it has been practised. Form criticism, he says, declared that 'biblical texts do not merely express theological concepts and are not simply utterances of authoritative individuals; they reflect the faith of simple men and women, and their common life' (*Social*, 4).

This placing of the wellspring of the Bible in 'the life of the people', and the possibility it presented for reading the Bible 'from below', reflects (in Theissen's view) the strivings of the liberal middle classes in Germany, at the end of the nineteenth century and the start of the twentieth, for greater freedom, and in particular the proposals for reformed church government that would be genuinely 'popular' (*Social*, 4). Conversely, Theissen detects from 1918 a 'neutralisation' of the social critique implicit in form criticism, because of the unease of bourgeois German church people (especially the clergy) with a secularised labour movement and the new world of the post-war German republic (*Social*, 10f). Theissen here is no reductionist, he does not unmask a supposedly 'objective' discipline of biblical criticism as a mere epiphenomenon of social conflict. Rather, his point is that

> knowledge never merely reflects the social world of the investigators and is never exclusively the 'objective' reproduction of the object that they desire to know. It is worthwhile creating a greater open-mindedness toward the object by thinking about one's own cognitive situation. (*Social*, 2)

We can see Theissen's aim here in terms of the logician's distinction between causes and grounds. Social (and indeed psychological) *causes* influence us when we adopt a particular conviction, but they need neither determine nor invalidate the *grounds* on which we argue for it, for 'we are quite well able to arrive at insights that run counter to the trends of our own social world' (*Social*, 2).

We have thought much about the grounds of Farrer's objections to form criticism; what of some of the causes? Of the alternatives posed by Theissen's description above, Farrer in his work on Mark leans towards the 'authoritative individual' as formative agent: not only is the author of Mark inspired, but he (surely) draws on acquaintance with the apostolic witness. '[T]he faith of simple men and women', 'the life of the people', these must denote the constituency at which the edifying text of Mark is *aimed* (*Study*, 140, 173), but this constituency can hardly be the chief agency in its *formation*; no, this is 'a mind of great power' (*Study*, 7). What aspects of his 'cognitive situation' may have helped Farrer incline to this view? The parallels Theissen draws in his study of form criticism are between a whole movement in biblical studies and no doubt widely documented stirrings in German church and society, so it is questionable whether his instruments, if turned on Austin Farrer, can be honed sufficiently to probe the cognitive situation of a single person holding unfashionable opinions. Our question is indeed finally unanswerable without having Farrer in the psychiatrist's chair to respond to it. And yet, there are elements in his personal circumstances, aside from his literary preferences, which chime with some of the notes he strikes in his scholarship.

According to Curtis' biography of Farrer, his early experience of the 'community mind' of the church was troubled. His family experienced a series of factious congregations in the Baptist churches which they attended and where his father ministered, as letters he received during 1924 show: 'from the time you were a little boy our church life has been spoiled and shadowed by split on split', writes his mother, while his father tells him that '[y]our mother and I have no more poignant regret than that our family experience of church life has been so unfortunate' (quoted in *Hawk*, 21f). This seems to have been part of what propelled Farrer from Baptist congregationalism to Anglican episcopalianism (idealistic though his hope of better things might seem!).[19] Curtis' account of the young Farrer's curacy in Dewsbury, Yorkshire (1928–1933), is of a clergyman not over-sanguine about leaving Christian thinking and nurture in the hands of the people; alas, 'laity will be laity', as he says in a weary letter to his father about Sunday-school teachers (*Hawk*, 69).[20] In 1959, Farrer the Oxford fellow preaches at Cambridge, an ambassador of an institution very successful at producing authoritative individuals, addressing another such institution. There he speaks of that rather populist notion, natural religion, as not 'a religion natural to Hottentots but a religion natural to that level of mentality and culture, which the graduates of our more respectable universities have attained' ('Religion', 20).

To repeat, the murkiest of causes do not in themselves invalidate good grounds for holding a certain point of view, and to build too much on these asides would in any case be fanciful psychologising. Nevertheless, if we take Theissen's principle that 'knowledge' sheds light on the world of the investigator as well as on the object of investigation, then we can point to aspects of Farrer's cognitive situation which are, at the least, unlikely to have led him in his Gospel studies to understate the significance of individual creativity and authority, or to exaggerate communal vitality and wisdom.

---

19.   See *Hawk*, 23f.

20.   Other pertinent moments in *Hawk* describe Farrer's fear of *étatisme* if Labour win the 1950 General Election, and his exasperation with the Church of England Liturgical Commission: 'They think that prose can be written in committee' (*Hawk*, 138, 154).

Chapter 12

MARK: A WINDOW ON EVENT?

Bare history is of inestimable importance ... if by history we are meaning a correct
account of the whole pattern and order of Christ's public life.

A Study in St Mark, 1

We come finally to the fifth sense of 'reading Mark historically', reading
the text with the intention of seeing it as a window upon historical
events. Though the *Study* is primarily an enquiry into what is written, not
what is written *about*,[1] Farrer is anxious to co-ordinate his claims in the
book with a robust view of the evidential value of Mark's Gospel in the
investigation of Christian origins, as his first chapter makes clear.[2] Since
Farrer considers this to be an important though subsidiary concern of his
study of Mark, and since it is of vital significance for his wider concern
in commending Christian faith, we shall spend some time examining
what he has to say about it; and the words 'history' and 'historical',
when they appear in this section, may be taken as shorthand for this
fifth stratum of historical reading. We shall then offer some evaluation of
Farrer's historical grasp in the *Study*, and note briefly the endorsements
and modifications in *Matthew*. We shall see that his treatment of Mark
raises in an acute form what is a problem for all historiography, the
question of whether narrative can ever give access to 'real' events. Beavis
and Burridge, our companions up to now, do not really address this
level; in their stead we shall revisit Kermode's *The Genesis of Secrecy*,
and also consider a contribution to the debate by David Carr, in his
article 'Narrative and the Real World'. This will lead to a more rounded
appreciation of Farrer's estimation of Mark as 'a history', in which we
shall also consider other work of his which bears on the question, apart
from his two books of Gospel exegesis. I shall argue that, in the *Study*,
he lets apologetic considerations blur his vision of the historian's task to a

1.   Kermode's distinction (*Genesis*, 118f), which he owes to Jean Starobinski's 'La
Démoniaque de Gérasa: analyse littérataire de Marc 5:1–20' (ET, *New Literary History*, 4,
1973, 331–356).
2.   See 4A (pp. 22–26) above.

disabling degree, whereas his thinking on these matters is elsewhere more rigorous, when he argues in a more philosophical mode.

A. Farrer and the Historian's Task

Farrer knows that writing history is never a straightforward business: the bald statement of a succession of facts or anecdotes is not history, for history requires 'continuity and development', both 'in theme' as well as 'in time' (*Study*, 2f). But can Mark offer such a history?

> To interpret St Mark historically may mean either of two things. It may mean that with good will and intelligence we can read him as history, that is, as actually exhibiting the sort of continuity and development which we have been talking about. Or it may mean that he supplies the sort of discontinuous evidence from which our historical wisdom can reconstruct an historical continuity not set forth by St Mark. (*Study*, 3)

He notes former Markan scholars' attempts to see the sequence between episodes in Mark as historically significant, but concludes that any such historical continuity was 'foisted upon' Mark (*Study*, 4). Eight years later, in his response to the criticisms of Helen Gardner, he digs himself in more deeply.

> If Miss Gardner wants, as she seems to want, a plain biographical answer to such questions [about the arrangement of Mark's material], all one can say is, that she is asking for the impossible. It might be agreeable to return to the days before Schmidt and Dibelius, if it could be done, but it cannot; of that method of exegesis we must say, *Conclamatum est*. ('Surface' 58)

The second possibility of interpreting Mark historically, as a source-book for history, is of course the great hope of form criticism, which he proceeds to despatch, though we should note here that in his reply to Gardner he gives credit to the great exponents of the discipline for their demolition work on naive notions of Gospel historicity. The crux for Farrer is whether the view of the Gospel he will advance, with its schematic patterning and riddling typology, can still leave room for the writing of the 'unconfused history' of Christian origins from the Markan sequence of events (*Study*, 370).[3]

Farrer has already told us that proper historiography exhibits thematic and chronological continuity, and he understands that the writing of such a narrative is a selective and interpretative act. He will argue that the evangelist has an historical awareness, but proceeds according to a different interpretative convention from our own. Farrer is hopeful of

---

3.   Cf Nineham's rebuttal of a similar attempt by Dodd (*Studies*, 223–239).

still commending Mark as the historian's friend, as long as the historian learns some 'docility'; for

> perhaps if we allow the evangelist to tell us his story in his own 'theological' or 'symbolical' way, and do not interpose with premature questions based on our own ideas of historical enquiry, we may be able to discern a genuine history which is communicated to us through the symbolism and not in defiance of it. (*Study*, 7)

We have seen that Farrer conceives the writer of Mark to be subject to a 'double control. He was controlled by the traditional facts about Jesus Christ and he was controlled by the interpreter Spirit who possessed his mind' (*Study*, 8). Farrer aims to disclose the latter, which must be a preliminary stage for the historian seeking the former, for 'it is only by the right analysis of St Mark's narrative that we are to arrive at the simple facts' (*Study*, 9). Once again, it is a matter of beginning with what you have, the text, and working backwards to what the text might imply.[4]

Mark the historian

We now look at some of Farrer's historical marginalia in the *Study*. Mark's Gospel for Farrer does indeed offer a window on event and the flow of events, but Farrer is concerned to make clear what he is claiming for Mark and what he is not. What, for instance, is implied by the cyclical character of Mark's narrative?

> We are not going to show that the history of Christ circles round and round. The history goes steadily forward to the inevitable end. What circles round and recurs is a series of topics which the forward march of the history constantly re-expresses. (*Study*, 34)

Does this mean, then, that Mark's sequence of events, great and small, might be historically accurate (as the 'early modern' scholars had hoped), but that Mark just draws out their significances in his cyclical presentation? Not exactly. Farrer prefers to speak of two sorts of pattern in the Gospel, the pattern of 'exposition' and the pattern of 'event'.

> The pattern of exposition belongs simply to the telling of the story and is no part of the events narrated ... Neither Christ nor St Peter supposed that only thirteen persons had been healed, or that among all the healings performed, thirteen had been marked with an asterisk of peculiar memorability. What they believed was something about the significance of all the healings in general. (*Study*, 182f)

On the other hand, the pattern of *event*

---

4. See further *Study*, 185, 370.

> is supposed by an historian to lie in the events themselves, as well as in his story about them. It is his business to draw it out, and make it visible, to exaggerate it, to stylise it, to make diagrams of it. There will be more or less artificiality in his representation of the pattern of event, but unless he believes the pattern to be really in the events in some sense, he is no true historian. A writer who is concerned to exhibit the influence of ideas on political action must believe that such an influence really operates and that the lines it takes are such as he indicates ... None of these men [who are true historians] supposes that he is simply playing a game of which he has invented the rules, and in which the facts of history are used as counters. (*Study*, 183)

This paragraph puts eloquently a 'realist' case in the debate about narrative and history, which we shall consider below. But it also shows Farrer's understanding that all historical interpretation is a synthetic exercise, which inevitably abstracts from the historical data, though the artifice of good historical interpretation will for him lie not in imposing regularity upon chaos, but in stressing regularities immanent in the flux.

All interpretation must proceed according to a certain principle, upon which the abstraction is made. What is Mark's?

> The pattern of event as St Mark understands it can be put in one word: prefiguration ... We ask ourselves how it is possible that St Mark should process his story with such elaborate artificiality, and the question merely shows that we are outsiders and have not understood him. Prefiguration is his form of historical thinking. (*Study*, 183)

Though he will acknowledge that this is an odd principle for the modern historian to follow, Farrer does not think it as artificial as all that.

> Prefiguration is an historical form, and not something else. It does not impose on events a pattern borrowed from somewhere outside the realm of events; it simply imposes on one stratum of events the pattern of a succeeding stratum. (*Study*, 183f)

He finds the principle to be not rigid but flexible, for the effect in the writing is that the former and latter events 'infect' one another, though he admits this approach belongs to 'history viewed as revelation' (*Study*, 184). It is part of a particular world-view (we might call it teleological), which looks towards the perfection of God's purposes in history, and 'it is unlikely that any historian would use it apart from theological belief' (*Study*, 184).[5] After all, 'St Mark's function is not simply to report the life and works of Jesus, but to become the instrument of the Holy Ghost interpreting the life and works of Jesus' (*Study*, 369). Farrer sees in Mark a perfect union of literary practice and historical method: the way Mark writes expresses the way he feels history goes, so '[e]verything becomes the seed of its own subsequent exposition or manifestation' (*Study*, 184).

---

5.   He omits to mention Whig or, latterly, Marxist historians, who *are* teleological. See E.H. Carr, *History*, 110f, 114f.

Modern, scientific historians will find Mark's method odd, because they work not with a teleological principle but with a principle of prior causation: 'History is for them a continuous chain fastened behind to the hidden origins of our race and stretching invisibly on before. No link in it is more than a single link' (*Study*, 185). This interpretative principle raises problems, he sees, for prefiguration in general and for the significance of Christ in particular, who can have no influence on what came before, and only a diminishing influence upon what lies after, as other events and influences arise and crowd in (*Study*, 184f). But Farrer is keen to dispel any absolutising notion that 'we' moderns write 'real' history, which describes things as they really are, while ancients like Mark had quaint schemes of interpretation which distorted the historical process. All historical interpretation has its artificiality, so that is no charge against Mark: 'You might as well ask how a scientist can be so elaborately artificial as to pattern all events in sequence of natural causation' (*Study*, 183). Prefiguration and cause-and-effect are alternative methods of synthesis, each a possible scheme of interpretation. So the question to ask of Mark or any historian 'is not whether he has used a method or scheme; of course he has. The question is whether he has used it in such a way as to force the facts, or, if he has, how far the forcing has gone' (*Study*, 185). This is not too difficult when there are other sources and authorities to consult, but for Farrer Mark's is the earliest Gospel, and Q is of no avail,[6] so there is only one criterion for judging Mark as history: 'Does St Mark tell a story which, as a story, makes sense?' (*Study*, 185f).

Now whether something seems to 'make sense' or not depends on the assumption upon which the enquirer proceeds. Farrer gives notice that his will be a 'Christian' judgement, though he trusts not a 'bigoted or antiquated one', and he knows that he has to defend his case for Mark's historical legitimacy in the court of historical interpretation as it is currently practised (*Study*, 187). He does this by attempting to demonstrate that the text of Mark, written on a prefigurative model, is nevertheless patient of interpretation as it stands according to the principles of prior causation. He does not himself give a name to this understanding to set against 'prefiguration', he just calls it 'another pattern – whatever we take to be the historical pattern of cause and effect' (*Study*, 187f).

Uneasy as we might be with the idea of one event *prefiguring* another, history being drawn forward from the end time, we do accept (if we follow Farrer) that one stage of history leads on to the next. We can therefore (he argues) follow Mark's succeeding cycles, write our 'historical interpretation of St Mark's rhythm', and then see whether it is plausible as history (*Study*, 188). This Farrer now does, surveying the

6. See his 'Dispensing'.

Gospel from Jesus' baptism up to the passion narrative (*Study*, 189–193).
We need not trace the whole story Farrer tells, but some examples will
help.

Reading Mark as history

Farrer discusses the visit of the Pharisees to the Herodians at Mark 3.6,
very early in the story. It has none of the 'political' consequences we
might expect (Jesus does not deliberately avoid the authorities thereafter,
and in Chapter 6 Herod takes notice of Jesus, it appears, for the first
time), but the conference of Pharisees and Herodians thematically
foreshadows the priests' bringing in of the secular arm to destroy Jesus in
Jerusalem (*Study*, 188). Farrer's verdict is that Mark 'places' the episode
'in a position of emphasis' to prefigure the Jerusalem arrest (*Study*, 188).
It is not clear from Farrer's words whether we are to understand that
Mark positions the episode *at this point in the story*, when he might have
placed it later on, or whether he has it here in its (traditional? historical?)
point in the sequence of events, but merely places it, so to speak, *in the
foreground*. Farrer's surrounding remarks about prefiguration suggest
that he means the former (it is indeed rather hard to put something in the
background of a narrative), but then Farrer himself has this story at the
beginning of Jesus' career when he attempts his *historical* interpretation
(*Study*, 190). The second example is the Caesarea Philippi confession
(Mk 8.27–38). Farrer has earlier described its literary character as that
of an 'epilogue' to the third double cycle, a 'prologue' to the last two
double cycles, and, with its reversal of the public-then-private sequence,
the start of a quite new phase in Jesus' teaching (*Study*, 104–107). Now
in its historical character it is the culmination of the northern sweep of
Jesus' ministry and the prelude to his move south to Jerusalem; first a
literary hinge, it is now also a historical/geographical hinge (*Study*, 191).
Finally, we note that the feedings of the multitude appear, as 'miracles',
in the historical summary, as does a terse account of the Transfiguration
(*Study*, 191). Farrer concludes:

> There is nothing new in the interpretation we have made: it is all implicit in the
> analyses of the foregoing chapters. We have done no more than collect together
> the historical fruits of those analyses. We say that the result is a sensible story.
> (*Study*, 193)

It is in the passion narrative that Mark is most accessible (and most
exposed) to the historians, for 'there alone', says Farrer, 'he gives us a
continuous system of causes and effects, and there alone he advances
into the public and political arena' (*Study*, 193). Farrer allows that the
narrative is not always correct in political detail (this was not Mark's
main interest) but that it is a single, continuous narrative, and free from

inconsistency or absurdity (*Study*, 194). He proceeds not by continuing his earlier exercise, but by 'untying knots' which students of the passion narrative have claimed to find in it (*Study*, 194–202; quotation, 194). Farrer can even contemplate that Mark misplaced the day of that year's Passover by twenty-four hours – '[h]e was concerned for the substance of events, he might err a day in chronology' – though probably he did not (*Study*, 202).

Farrer finds further support for Markan historicity in that Mark confirms virtually all Paul's (admittedly meagre) historical testimony, that the other Synoptic writers accorded the Markan history 'unique prestige' – 'there was nothing to set against it' (not much of a compliment!) – that even John, from Chapter 5 onwards, squares 'with what appears to be the Marcan chronology', and that even the earlier chapters of John (including an early visit to Jerusalem and an account of the Temple-cleansing) can be fitted into the indeterminate period in Mark between Jesus' baptism and his appearance in Galilee; for all of them 'the Marcan outline was history, and history was the Marcan outline ... there is only one history, and it is St Mark's' (*Study*, 205, 210, 215f, 220). He then turns to specific historical issues in Mark's account of Jesus. Thus on secrecy in Mark: 'did Christ reveal himself with the degree and sort of reserve St Mark describes? Well, what do you think? I find in myself no power to conceive otherwise' (*Study*, 246). Farrer, though, feels no need to claim that Mark gives Jesus' *ipsissima verba*, for 'a natural way of expressing some things to Roman Christians towards AD70 would have been an unnatural way of expressing them to Galileans in 29 or 30' (*Study*, 246). Again, Mark's teaching on the Son of Man is consistent, '[b]ut are his thoughts the thought of Christ?' (*Study*, 286). Whether or not the Son of Man was named in the High Priest's court, Mark is clear that this is what Jesus died for, so here too '[h]istorical seriousness must still govern the symbolical picture' (*Study*, 288). Once, when he detects clumsiness in the numbering of the disciples according to tribal typology, Farrer excuses Mark by saying that the schematic untidiness is only because he is being 'obedient to history' (*Study*, 314).

This has been a long trawl, and even then we have not documented all Farrer's historical asides. In *Matthew*, Farrer has a little to add. He stresses more firmly than in the *Study* the cleavage between the evangelists, with their prefigurative cast of mind, and modern readers – '[i]n this respect it really does seem plain that the Evangelists and their whole generation part company from us' (*Matthew*, 13). He can say that Mark, in giving his *ex post* exposition of events, can 'lay it on the lips of Jesus in the days of his flesh' (*Matthew*, 12), and thoughts such as this lead him to state, more firmly than in the *Study*, the implications of his account of Mark's Gospel:

> the enigma which is stated and progressively expounded in St Mark's Gospel is partly actual and partly artificial. It is actual in so far as it consists of the sheer

facts concerning Christ present in the world; artificial in so far as those facts are presented as physically symbolic or prefigurative ... If the artificiality is confined to the exposition, the factual statements which the Gospel contains are unaffected by it; St Mark merely places an artificially symbolical construction on the facts, in the comments he makes or records concerning the facts. But if the artificiality extends to the enigma, this means that the symbolism is written into the factual statements themselves; the story is so told as to bring out the symbolical qualities which the Evangelist sees in it. (*Matthew*, 13f)

In the latter case 'there is something artificial not only about the interpretation of the factual enigma but about the factual enigma as presented for interpretation' (*Matthew*, 15). Farrer does not, however, quite say whether the second is ever true of Mark, except perhaps in the case of number symbolism:

St Mark's numerical pattern does not falsify any historical fact, or even the meaning of any fact. Jesus did receive publicans and call Levi ... Jesus did institute twelve apostles, and he did heal twelve sufferers – indeed, he healed many more besides, but it is surely open to St Mark to choose out twelve, or rather, thirteen, for particular commemoration. (*Matthew*, 37)

Finally, in describing the conceptual gap between Mark and the modern reader, he implicitly casts some doubt on his attempt at historical interpretation in the *Study*:

the unity of St Mark's thought eludes us when we seek it on that straightforward historical level which is congenial to our own minds. We find that, after a strong beginning, marked by a swift forward movement and a sense of urgency, his story dissolves into a miscellaneous pile of healings and disputes and journeyings. (*Matthew*, 18)

What he hopes will 'restore' the unity of Mark is 'the element of artificial symbolism ... making visible the oneness of that factual enigma which is gradually unfolded as the Gospel proceeds' (*Matthew*, 18).

B. Evaluation: Farrer and Mark's History

To the person making historical enquiry of a 'scientific' nature (*Study*, 2), the divine presence assumed in the pages of the *Study*, especially in the doctrine of double control, comes as a shock. How can you be scientific about the Holy Spirit? The shock, however, can be mitigated. When, for instance, Farrer says that the control of the Spirit is 'visible and evident', it is not the control itself that he holds up to our view but the 'shaping and patterning' in which (he claims) it issues (*Study*, 9). Farrer's readers may agree or disagree with what he sees there, but at least conversation can begin. Very often his references to the Spirit's control or inspiration can be placed in mental brackets or 'translated' into terms of narrative design.[7] But is it not the narrative design, the shaping and patterning, which is the historian's great obstacle in trying to make use of Mark, after Farrer has finished with him? Farrer's position here is subtle. His defence of Markan historicity acknowledges a degree of artificiality in the Gospel's composition: it is not the detailed sequence of events which is of use to the student of Christian origins (that, on Farrer's strenuously theological reading of Mark, would make God into a puppeteer with a penchant for typology); rather it is the sweep of the Markan narrative which deserves the historian's confidence, and the very artificiality is but the effect of an essential part of the historian's craft. True history comprises fact and interpretation, and all interpretation has an artificiality about it. All historians mould as they interpret, and the real question is whether a historian's interpretative scheme does violence to the facts.

We look first at this 'argument from design', and we then return to the question of Farrer and the supernatural, for it cannot be entirely bracketed in the manner I suggest. In the course of our evaluation we shall follow some of its implications for the wider debate about narrative and history, but we shall see that Farrer's view of Mark as a divine book is so pronounced, that his observations about Gospel and history are hard to engage outside the enclave of belief, and belief of a certain kind.

Farrer begins with a strongly contrasting account of prefiguration and modern historical method, but as he moves towards rapprochement he blurs the distinction. Prefiguration, he says, imposes the pattern of later events upon the earlier, and sees each event as 'the seed of its own subsequent exposition or manifestation'; Mark thus 'feels ... the power of one historical phase to beget the next' (*Study*, 184). Now a scientific historian might happily use the seed image – 'the humiliation of Germany at Versailles sowed seeds that finally blossomed horribly in 1939' – and even talk of 'prefiguration', but the aim would be to place the pattern of later events upon the earlier in order to explain how the *later* events came to pass: to see, indeed, how the former begets the latter. Prefiguration, if it is to be a different historical method and not just a particular figure of historiographical speech, must view things the other way round, looking at the later events to see why the *earlier* things happened as they did. In effect (despite Farrer's words quoted above), God's future begets the past. In talking of prefiguration, Farrer sets it up as a distinctive historical method, but fails to distinguish it clearly from the 'scientific' approach.

---

7.   For instance, when Farrer discusses Mark's 'inspired choice' in not giving any resurrection appearances, the argument he advances derives from what he believes to be the inner logic of Mark's preceding narrative. Since the other evangelists, using their own, different logic, make the opposite choice and yet are also 'inspired' to do so, every appearance of the word can be struck out without harming Farrer's argument (*Study*, 179). The Farrer of the *Glass*, however, implies that Mark's position is preferable: 'The rest cannot be written' (*Glass*, 145). Hefling (*Ladder*, 79) takes this to be Farrer's considered position.

In the resulting confusion he understates the difficulty of the modern historian in handling Mark sympathetically, as we can see if we consider Farrer's own programme for interpreting Mark historically: he aims 'to take the Gospel as it stands, and see whether it tells a sensible story or not', and then 'to translate the pattern of prefiguration into another pattern – whatever we take to be the historical pattern of cause and effect' (*Study*, 187f).

In this attempt to show how Mark's prefigurative scheme can simultaneously exhibit the pattern of prior causation (*Study*, 189–193), we must judge Farrer unsuccessful. His 'historical interpretation of Mark's story' (*Study*, 189) does tell a 'sensible story', in that his sentences follow on one from another, but it fails to give a satisfactory sense of historical movement. Of course, we would not expect Farrer's historical interpretation to exhibit the same sort of onward thrust, even of inevitability, which a prefigurative frame of reference tends to give, for that sort of God-made 'inevitability' is the very stumbling-block for the modern historian. Nevertheless, history written according to the pattern of prior causation must have its own kind of motive power if it is to be convincing. Farrer knows this. He says that 'if … each anecdote started from the place where the last left off, we might still not have a history', for it would probably fail to reveal the influence of external circumstances, and the subject's (in this case Jesus') 'developing policy of action' (*Study*, 3). We find too little of those circumstances or that policy in Farrer's exposition.

To illustrate, let us consider the course of Jesus' southward journey from Caesarea Philippi to Jerusalem (Mk 10.1–11.11). Farrer tells us that he 'passed through Galilee … crossed North Judaea (that is, Samaria) into Peraea' and then 'took the second and final step of the southward journey when he left Peraea on the road through Jericho to Jerusalem' (*Study*, 192f). Mark does not tell us what route Jesus took across Galilee, but he does say that he then entered the districts of Judaea 'and' (following the most likely reading in a disturbed text) the far side of the Jordan (Mk 10.1). Farrer sensibly interprets these districts as Samaria and Peraea respectively. Now many Jews travelling from Galilee to Jerusalem crossed the Jordan and entered Peraea to avoid the more direct route through the apostate region of Samaria. Why then did Jesus first enter Samaria, a risky and significant thing to do but also the shortest route, then make an easterly detour by crossing the Jordan into Peraea, and finally cross back again to make for Jericho and Jerusalem?[8] When he is expounding what he takes to be Mark's 'symbolical' purpose, Farrer has no difficulty making sense of these meanderings: Jesus goes to the far side of the Jordan (Peraea) to stand in Moses' place and deliver a new Deuteronomy; and this has been prefigured in the Transfiguration, where Jesus appears

---

8.   See the helpful discussion of this passage in Hooker, *Commentary*, 235.

with Moses at his side, and God gives the disciples the same command Moses gave to the people when he told them of a prophet to come, 'listen to him' (*Study*, 113, Mk 9.7 cf Deut. 18.15). When he gives the 'historical fruits' of this exegesis, however, we do not sense 'the forward movement of events' (*Study*, 193),[9] but rather vagueness and wandering. A remedy would be to attribute the Moses motif to Jesus himself, who would then have made a deliberate detour as an expression of his own 'policy', but this Farrer does not do.[10] By Farrer's own definition, in his historical interpretation of this anecdotally cast narrative we still do not have 'a history'.

Farrer's difficulty stems from the quite different presuppositions underlying the prefigurative view of history. Prefiguration as a historical method finds its dynamic in the magnetic pull exerted from the future by the agency of God, and we shall see that the historical method as it is presently understood can never (as Farrer feels it should) find room for that.[11] Farrer's attempt to discern a conventional pattern of causation alongside a theologically motivated pattern of prefiguration is successful only with the rudimentary elements of the story – that Jesus' ministry began after his baptism, and probably after John's arrest; that he chose twelve disciples; that hostility from the religious authorities brought about his death; that his arrest and execution took a certain course – but now we are using Mark more as a 'source-book' than as 'a genuine history' in Farrer's full sense (*Study*, 3, 7). In *Matthew*, when Farrer describes the apparent dissolution of Mark into 'a miscellaneous pile of healings and disputes and journeyings' he appears to retreat from his position in the *Study* (*Matthew*, 18). If it is a retreat, it is judicious.

In the *Study*, meanwhile, Farrer seeks to soothe his reader: the study of Mark's compositional approach, his 'imaginative rhythm ... does not stand in the way' of historical enquiry, but is 'indispensable' to it (*Study*, 187). We may agree in the limited sense that, in seeking a historical understanding of the career of Jesus, we can only work from what we have, Mark's text. Farrer leaves it at that, however, as though the necessity of the study were a guarantee that its findings will be (for Farrer) benign, but there is still the strong possibility that the *results* of this study will indeed 'stand in the way' of our enquiry, by barring our

9.   Farrer has earlier seen Jesus' Peraean journey as, on the prefigurative view, foreshadowing the Gentile mission, while his historical account speaks of 'Jewish villages', and only of 'one occasion at least' when he ministered to a Gentile (*Study*, 149 cf 191).

10.   Later, he explicitly shuns this possibility with regard to numerology (*Matthew*, vif). See 13C (pp. 177–180) below.

11.   Roberts (*Apologetic*, 131) argues cogently that Farrer fails to see that he is here *assuming* a certain philosophy of history that needs to be argued for.

For the contrariness of the prefigurative paradigm, cf the tongue-in-cheek claim of David Lodge's character, Eng. Lit. scholar Persse McGarrigle, to have written a thesis exploring the influence of T.S. Eliot on Shakespeare (*Small World*, Harmondsworth: Penguin, 1984), 51.

route to the causes and the effects of occurrences among certain people in first-century Palestine. Farrer wants the modern historian to show respect for the rather different historiographical approach of Mark. The historian may retort that the respect due is (as Farrer says in another context) 'the respect of the physician for the disease' ('Appreciation', 214f). To such a historian, a writer like Mark will always look suspicious, and likely not just to force the facts, but even to offer as 'the facts' – the events and the relations between them – things which were not the case. The scientific historian may force things too, by using imagination to 'make sense' of raw or limited data,[12] but that only makes more evident the need to discuss the axioms, the 'creed', on which the business of a historian is founded. The need is acute when a different paradigm is proposed for consideration, but the Farrer of the *Study* chooses not to bring these matters into the open, though we have seen how, in *Matthew*, he seems to be more aware of the gulf between the two, and to move just a little towards acknowledging the possibility of the fictive in Mark.[13]

In the *Study* Farrer tells us that with historians it is by their assumptions that you shall know them: what makes sense as history will be different for the 'rationalist', who excludes all reference to the supernatural, or to the 'friendly Jew', who works on the assumption that Jesus never strayed from what might be expected of a 'self-taught Galilean rabbi moving on the fringe of orthodox Pharisaic circles' (*Study*, 186).[14] Farrer's own assumptions are 'Christian' (he is candid as ever), and he admits that his 'sensible story' will not impress those 'to whom no story makes sense in which the Christ of St Mark's and our faith intervenes' (*Study*, 186, 193). Farrer's axiom, then, is that Jesus of Nazareth is the incarnate Word of God, in hypostatic union with the Spirit which now guides Mark in the writing of the Gospel (he says as much, when he describes Jesus' prophecy in Mk 13 as the act of 'the incarnation of God' *Study*, 362; see also e.g. 8, 369): a large claim, sustainable perhaps, but not to be *assumed* in a study such as his, and not to be introduced as an extra piece on the board of historical enquiry. When describing rationalist and Jewish assumptions, Farrer is cautious, for '[p]roblems of an ultimate kind arise here into which it would be madness to plunge' (*Study*, 186). It might have been madness in a study such as his, *if* he had not made his own theological assumptions so integral to his interpretation. What he does instead is to leave their depths unplumbed, save to say that he hopes they will not prove 'bigoted or antiquated', and to set up as the only alternative the canons of evidence of the ultra-rationalist, which state

12.   We discuss below (see 13C, pp. 177–180) Kermode's thoughts about the 'fictiveness' of all historiography.

13.   See p. 150, note 2, above. Farrer does not, however, join with Kermode, as Jasper claims he does, 'in acknowledging the critical necessity of recognizing the fictive element in Scripture' ('Literary', 26).

14.   Geza Vermes is a present-day incarnation of the latter. See his *Jesus*.

that 'no man must be admitted ever to foresee that the course of action in which he is involved will lead to his death in a certain way', and such like (*Study*, 186, 193). There is a wide gap (and, as we shall see, at least one other possibility) between dogmatic rationalism and the dogmatic supernaturalism of Austin Farrer.

Dismissing his hard-boiled antagonist, Farrer turns to 'the Christian historian', who

> is not a man at war with his own believing heart. He does not as an historian strip away or discard the work of the Spirit on which a believer is fed ... He strips away, he discards nothing, but he assigns everything to its moment of occurrence. (*Study*, 370)

The problem is not that Farrer identifies such a person, but that he implies that here is a particular, even a privileged, *type* of historian. A Christian historian enjoys no more privilege among other historians than does a Christian banker among bankers. Farrer himself uses this analogy when, warning against impugning Mark's integrity by misunderstanding his task, he says that '[w]e cannot judge of the integrity of a banker except by understanding what the work of a banker is' (*Study*, 368). It follows that, if the Christian historian is to write the 'unconfused history' of Christian origins, the history thus written must be judged by the common understanding of what the work of a historian is (*Study*, 370). Instead Farrer offers us a picture of the historian which suggests, almost speciously, that any sense of tension between history and belief stems from some failing in the enquirer.

The limits of history

The historical method as presently understood has no place for God and the miraculous. This is not, or need not be, a policy of absolutism. It does not *ex hypothesi* deny these possibilities, but recognises its own limitations. It goes about its business by asking in a given case, 'What is likely to have happened here, given what usually happens in broadly similar circumstances?' The admission of miracle, or supernatural inspiration or any special action of God, all of which are by definition things that do not usually happen, completely overthrows the method. A non-controversial example will illustrate. Tacitus describes Agricola, as Governor of Britain, fighting a great battle in Scotland at a place called 'Mons Graupius' (*Agricola*, 29–38). Students of ancient history, lacking conclusive archaeological or documentary evidence, cannot be certain where this battle was fought. Instead they will make educated conjectures, using the information they do have about military bases in the area, sites of known marching camps, and the *likely* distance a Roman unit could have covered in a day or a week. Once allow, however, that a Roman legionary's speed or stamina could have been supernaturally enhanced, and historical enquiry is at an end, its chief criterion now superseded.[15] When Farrer puts miraculous feedings in his historical account of Jesus' ministry, the historian (Christian or other) is nonplussed. More alarming still for the historian is when Farrer, apart from invoking the Holy Spirit to 'explain' the presence of endlessly complex symbolism, can say that 'as historians we shall refer the working of the Spirit to the story of the Church, but the facts about Christ to the story of our redemption' (*Study*, 25). God is on both sides of the equation here, guiding the writing and also – because of the heavy theological freight in the word 'redemption' – being an agent of what is written *about*. Nevertheless, Farrer tells us we have 'no reason' for supposing that Mark's 'inspired' thinking 'is not being exercised upon, and sustained by, historical fact, or that it does not respect the articulations of fact with careful delicacy' (*Study*, 10). He compares his study of the composition of Mark to the study of an eagle's anatomy, with the history underlying Mark like the air supporting the bird: 'he is sustained by the air', and 'adapts his motions with fine appropriateness to its currents and pressures' (*Study*, 10). The bird disturbs the air as well, but Farrer passes over this. He cannot lose this game. If you admit the category of inspiration by God – and Farrer's God is powerful, benevolent and truth-loving – then you have the panacea; artifice can be squared with accuracy, divine agency with human autonomy; for with God all things are possible.

Part of the problem is the implied audience of the *Study*: 'Now we are Christians too; we share St Mark's belief in St Mark's inspiration' ... 'Our faith is in the joint utterance of Jesus and the Holy Ghost' (*Study*, 10, 369). Farrer does not seem to envisage anyone reading his book, or indeed Mark's Gospel, who is not a Christian, and a Christian at that who sees no need to set faith at arm's length from time to time, the better to refine it. If there is so little sense in the *Study* of the need for Christian faith to pay its intellectual way in the wider world, is Farrer after all a kind of Barthian, so convinced of the supernaturalism of Christianity that no accommodation is necessary to the demands of secular enquiry? Does he say, in effect, that if the world cannot stop its ears to the call of unregenerate reason (including the historical method), then so much the worse for the world? We know that, for all his hints of a biblical Barthianism, Farrer was unimpressed by Barth's complete programme,[16] and we have seen how the *Glass* is an elegant though implicit tribute to Aquinas, whose God does not abolish nature but perfects it.[17] Moreover,

15.   This is an ancient maxim. E.H. Carr quotes Polybius: 'Wherever it is possible to find out the cause of what is happening, one should not have recourse to the gods' (*History*, 74). Thucydides also writes his history without reference to the divine. Though Tacitus might refer to divine agency on occasion (e.g. *Annals*, XVI.16), he does not invoke it in the Mons Graupius episode.

16.   '[Farrer] used to ask à propos the extreme Barthian doctrine of the "wholly other": "How are you to tell God from the devil?"' (Nineham, *Use*, 175).

17.   See Chapter 2 (pp. 10–16) above for Farrer's Thomism in *Finite*.

if we turn to a work in which Farrer does address 'the world', his apologetic lectures published in *Saving Belief*, we see more Thomist naturalism in the picture of a God who 'makes the world ... make itself' (*Saving*, 51). We also see there what appear to be open arms extended to rationality:

> Can reasonable minds still think theologically? Is theology a science, or can it be made so? ... Think your way through your faith, and answers to your enquiries will keep tumbling in ... These happy discoveries will come to hand if we do our religious thinking like honest men, and in one piece with our thinking on other subjects. (*Saving*, 5)

What, then, of doing 'Gospel history' in the way other people do history (*Study*, 369)? From *Saving Belief* we discover that Farrer has a specific objection to the way history is usually done.

> Ought we to say that no alleged fact of Gospel history should be accepted, unless it would pass the rules of probability which secular history would employ? Surely not. The methods of sifting evidence, or of reconstructing continuous event, which secular history employs are just as proper in the field of Gospel history. But what of the criteria of probability? Secular history gathers its criteria from a flat-rate survey of humdrum humanity. But the man of discernment knows that whatever he is dealing with in Christ, it is not this. For anything we are to believe, there must, of course, be respectable evidence. But respectable evidence (in history) is seldom compulsive. There is much evidence for Christ's resurrection; but, to judge from the general level of history and, indeed, of biology, would any evidence suffice to prove that the dead should rise? ... To cut off the historical question of the resurrection and examine it by itself in an aseptic historical laboratory, giving your verdict on it without reference to your general estimate of the truth about Christ, would be nothing but a piece of intellectual cheating. It would not even be good history. History must allow for differences of level. On the dead level of human probability, it was not likely that Shakespeare should write his sublimest works. But he was Shakespeare and he wrote them. (*Saving*, 81f)

While Farrer is right to say that historians are on their mettle in the face of the unique, there is an incoherence in this parallel with Shakespeare. In assessing the playwright we do at least have his texts to work upon, but it is the very lack of 'hard' evidence for 'the truth about Christ' which gives rise to Farrer's remarks. Virtually all we have is the existence of the Christian church and its documents, a rather more ambiguous testimony to detailed claims about Jesus than is *Hamlet* to Shakespeare's genius.[18] It is hard to know what unambiguous testimony there could be. More generally, Farrer fails to grasp that the historians' workshop cannot contain any tools which will give purchase upon these other 'levels' Farrer wants to include, nor their vocabulary any words with which to describe what might be there. This is the more surprising when we hear Farrer, in a sermon of the same year (1963), making essentially this

18.   See Houlden, *Identity*, 56, for the inability of 'the facts' to compel belief.

point in relation to the limits of the natural sciences, as he arbitrates in a dispute between a scientist and a bishop.

> Who knows about *God's creation*? If by God's creation you mean the physical system God has instituted, then the scientist has a sort of knowledge about it to which no one else, and least of all a bishop, pretends. But if by God's creation you mean 'what the Creator's will intends and achieves', then that is not a subject on which a scientist has a syllable to say. In one sense, the supplier of artists' materials knows what paintings are, for they are certainly unquestionably paints and canvas. In another sense, he knows nothing about it. The painter knows, for he understands the game which is played with these substances. ('Colours', 63)

In *Saving Belief* and (implicitly) in the *Study*, Farrer seems uneasy with the idea that religious belief can still be rational if it goes beyond what rational enquiry can establish. This leads him to cavil at the practice of history and its limits as usually drawn, and to set up as the only alternatives either his dutiful acceptance or a programmatic scepticism. He leaves out of account a third way. Faith embraced with critical realism[19] will not deny *ex hypothesi* that quite exceptional events (say miracle or divine inspiration) occur, but it will be open to rational (including historical) enquiry. It will expect such enquiry to purge faith of its more fanciful claims, to probe belief in special providence in a case where convincing explanation can be found by other means; and it will acknowledge that, while rational enquiry can never in itself *compel* faith, it may, on the other hand, finally render that faith untenable. In John Robinson's words, 'though the historian can neither give nor directly take away the faith, he can indirectly render the credibility-gap so wide that in fact men cease believing' (*Trust*, 128). In the case, say, of the *Study*, critical realism will not use a credal wild card to win a trick in a historical game.

The best account of what Farrer is *actually* doing in his historical thinking in the *Study*, and a better remedy for what seems to underlie his unease in *Saving Belief*, comes in his rather unappreciative 'English Appreciation' of Bartsch's *Kerygma and Myth*. Farrer suspects that Bultmann is claiming in his essays that 'nothing but historical grounds ... can establish an historical belief ... in our minds' ('Appreciation', 220). Farrer distinguishes between belief in a historical *statement*, that is a statement that a thing occurred, and a particular *method* – the 'historical method' – used to establish grounds for such a belief. He claims that it is possible to believe the former on other grounds than those established by the latter, as when you trust somebody's word in the absence of evidence ('Appreciation', 220). On the virginal conception, Bultmann holds,

> and we will agree, that the sheer reasoning of scientific history would not oblige us to grant that the narratives of the virginal conception in SS Matthew and Luke, together with the allusions in St John, indicate the actual truth of the event referred to or

19.   For use of this phrase in the natural sciences, see Polkinghorne, *One*, 22f; and in biblical studies, see Wright, 'Pleasure', 309f, and *People*, 32–8.

described. But Bultmann assumes that if this is so we cannot believe in the virginal conception as a matter of historical fact ... on grounds of faith.

Farrer counters:

> What Christians find in Christ through faith inclines them at certain points to accept with regard to him testimony about matter of fact which would be inconclusive if offered with regard to any other man. The Christian who refused to take that step would be pedantic and irrational, like a man who required the same guarantees for trusting a friend which he would require for trusting a stranger. ('Appreciation', 220)

After all Farrer's manoeuvrings and special pleading in the *Study* and in *Saving Belief*, here is a subtle account of faith and rationality; his footing seems surer in this, a more philosophical piece. He acknowledges the autonomy of the historical method and its limits, and does not blame it for being limited, but suggests that there is more beyond. Is not the Farrer of the *Study* himself believing as history what he cannot prove on historical grounds, believing that God will somehow secure the historical necessities for the Christian gospel amid all the complexities of the Gospel of Mark? 'What the Spirit of [Mark's] ... inspiration does with his thoughts is but the tracing over of what Creative Power did with the events about which he thinks' (*Study*, 184). Does Farrer not simply trust God to look after the history because God is his friend?

C. Can Narrative Be History?

Although Farrer is aware of the artifice that inheres in any piece of historiography, he believes in the continuity between historical narrative and the events to which it refers: '[w]e desire to view the Marcan history as a history, that is, as a connected narrative' (*Study*, 186). In this section we take Farrer's account of Mark, as a usefully extreme example of literary elaboration struggling with historical transparency, to see what light it might shed on present perplexities over the possibility of any kind of narrative writing being a window on event. Our main partners here will be Frank Kermode and David Carr. Finally, I shall also suggest a way in which Farrer's reading of Mark may have some material contribution to make to the investigation of the origins of Christianity.

Artifice or fiction?

Kermode expresses well the establishment's difficulties with Farrer on Mark:

> the more complex the purely literary structure is shown to be, the harder it is for most people to accept the narratives as naively transparent upon historical reality ...

The [Christian? academic?] institution knew intuitively that such literary elaboration, such emphasis on elements that must be called fictive, was unacceptable because damaging to what remained of the idea that the gospel narratives were still, in some measure, transparent upon history. (*Genesis*, 62f)

Kermode and Farrer agree about what counts as history-writing: it cannot be just a 'pile of anecdotes ... mere continuity of time does not yield history' (*Study*, 2f); nor does mere 'chronicle', a stream of 'non-causal' statements (*Genesis*, 103); there must be relations between events that are not just temporal, but causal. In the Gospel narratives Kermode sees a different principle of relation at work, which he calls 'hermeneutic', and which resembles Farrer's account of prefiguration (*Genesis*, 106). Kermode sees it in the relation between, say, Mark and the Old Testament: 'the earlier texts are held to contain, possibly in a disguised or deceptive form, narrative promises that will later be kept, though perhaps in unexpected ways' (*Genesis*, 106). Farrer makes more of prefiguration within Mark itself, but the difference is not so great. Farrer speaks of prefiguration as 'history viewed as divine revelation', and Kermode of *pleroma*, fulfilment, but both are giving descriptions of narrative that is what Kermode calls 'teleologically guided', narrative written *from the end* (*Study*, 184, *Genesis*, 72, 118).

Kermode picks up the pleromatic thread in Mark while discussing the all-but-universal (and, he believes, futile) desire to find closure in any narrative, and he then directs his scepticism at historical narrative. He agrees with Farrer that the teleological paradigm is no less a 'form of historical thinking' than the ways of doing history currently in force: it has its 'artificiality', but so do they (*Study*, 183, cf *Genesis*, 107). Farrer says that 'the pattern of event is supposed by an historian to lie in the events themselves, as well as in his story about them'; so, though the historian will 'exaggerate' or 'stylise' the pattern, 'unless he believes the pattern to be really in the events in some sense, he is no true historian' (*Study*, 183). Kermode would assent to all but the last remark, for he sees that belief as self-deception. When we look at the characteristics of what usually passes among us for the writing of history, he says, we see that 'historians usually write narrative rather than explanation if they can' (by 'explanation' he means, we presume, the exposition of patterns), because narrative structure has a winning elegance, with that apparent coherence, that 'followability', which enlists the reader's co-operation (*Genesis*, 113). Beguiled by the narrative form, we delay the asking of awkward questions about it, and we certainly prefer not to see the alarming truth that this history writing shares all its pleasing characteristics with fiction; this is what 'history' is supposed to be like, so we accept it (*Genesis*, 117). Kermode now collapses the distinction between the paradigm of prefiguration and that of prior causation. As ways of doing history, they are for him just two forms of teleologically guided interpretation, different attempts to impose followability on an unfollowable world, and neither can be seen as altogether different from 'making fictions, or, *a fortiori*, from telling lies' (*Genesis*, 109).[20]

This is an alarming possibility. Many questers after the historical Jesus have long accepted that no Gospel can offer a reliable narrative of his ministry; but it is quite another thing to say that there is really nothing to choose between Mark's passion narrative (let alone the rest of the Gospel) and, say, Peter Hennessey's 'history' of post-war Britain, *Never Again*, as it trails its footnotes, its acknowledged sources, ascribed eyewitness accounts and the rest of what Kermode calls the 'metatextual announcements' about the text's credibility (*Genesis*, 116).[21] And Kermode goes further, for his position also means there is nothing to choose between Hennessey and a historical novel about the same period. A lot must change if ancient typological artifice and modern empirical rigour turn out to be just two teleological peas in the fictive pod. More alarming still: if we consider events (or 'alleged' events) during the time of this writing, is Kermode's implication that there will be nothing to choose between the story told by Robert Mugabe and that by, say, the BBC's Africa correspondent Orla Guerin when it comes to saying 'what really happened' in the Zimbabwean presidential elections of 2008 and their aftermath? Both will be cases of 'a narrative structure imposed upon events', each a differently futile claim to make sense of 'the unfollowable world' (*Genesis*, 117). This apparent nihilism may be morally repugnant, but repugnance is no proof of falsehood. We must look more closely at what Kermode is claiming.

It is not clear from *Genesis* whether he is saying that the whole enterprise of history, finding out about the past, is (like literary interpretation) irresistible but doomed, or whether it is just the doing of history by way of narrative that is in his sights. He sets 'narrative' against 'explanation' (*Genesis*, 113), but it is hard to see how a historian could undertake a project of any size without some recourse to narrative. He describes 'chronicle' as a (non-causal) alternative to narrative (*Genesis*, 103), but is that much less fictive? Does not the chronicling of human events any more complex than those found on a desert island entail *some* of the shaping and selection that are features of historical narrative? Kermode entertains the possibility that our narrative mentality is rooted in early experience of language, the followability and closure of subject-verb-object in intelligible utterance; on this reckoning, *all* history, any attempt to talk about the past, is indeed 'bunk'. Moreover, after he has said so much about the obscurity of narrative which keeps literary scholars in business, why does Kermode assume that readers of historical

---

20.   Kermode here sees historiography as a kind of 'game', something Farrer expressly rebuts. See *Study*, 183 and 13A (pp. 162–168) above.

21.   The passion narrative is one of Kermode's subjects here; see esp. *Genesis*, 109–113. Peter Hennessey, *Never Again: Britain 1945–51* (London: Jonathan Cape, 1992).

narrative find it so pellucid and satisfying? Patently they do not, for people go on writing historical narratives on subjects already covered by others, and still other people go on buying their books. Why would this happen unless previous attempts to tell 'what actually happened' were felt to be imperfect? The existence of four canonical Gospels (and the sometime existence of how many others?), at least two of which almost certainly modify Mark, suggests that this dissatisfaction with existing narratives of the past is no new thing.

There is a misleading all-or-nothing quality to Kermode's argument. Who doubts that the claim of a historical narrative to be 'a transparent account of the recognizable world' is overstated (*Genesis*, 101)? Who can object to Kermode's claim that '[t]he historian cannot write, nor can we read, without prejudice' (*Genesis*, 118)? This seems to Kermode a 'generally acceptable' view of history writing, but then three pages later he laments our difficulty in seeing the Gospels 'as stories, as texts totally lacking transparency on event' (*Genesis*, 118, 121). What is the force here of 'totally'? Are the Gospels useless, or worse than useless, for the historian trying to find out about Jesus? Would he use the same phrase of Macaulay, or David Starkey? Have we no possibility of a critical realism in approaching historical narrative, not expecting transparency but reasonably hoping for some illumination to get through? As Gardner says in riposte to Kermode: 'although no narrative is wholly transparent upon historical reality, all narratives are not therefore totally opaque, and ... there are ways by which we can test their degree of reliability' (*Defence*, 124). There are echoes here of Farrer's hypothetical total sceptic.[22]

We return to the sort of negative way advanced in the earlier discussions of meaning and genre;[23] for if we know that all narratives fail to tell us 'what actually happened', some may fail more than others. Critical realism, like Kermodian scepticism, needs to be argued for, however. With this in mind, and remembering that the *telos* of this protracted discussion is to weigh the contribution of *Austin Farrer on Mark* to the debate about narrative and history, we look at a recent argument for continuity between the two.

David Carr: 'Narrative and the Real World'

In *Citizens*, his account of the French Revolution, Simon Schama observes: 'Narratives have been described as a kind of fictional device used by the historian to impose a reassuring order on randomly arriving bits of

---

22.   Or even Hirsch's 'decadent' sceptic (*Aims*, 146–148; see p. 158, note 17, above). For a more tempered view, see E.H. Carr, *History*, 123.

23.   See 6A and 11D (pp. 62–72, 146–148), above.

information about the dead. There is a certain truth to this alarming insight' (*Citizens*, xvi).[24] In defending narrative, Schama invokes an article by David Carr, 'Narrative and the Real World'. It is Carr's case, pursued in conversation with Kermode and others, that we now examine and apply to Farrer's reading of Mark. Carr lists some famous claims for the discontinuity between narrative and reality:

> Stories are not lived but told ... Life has no beginnings, middles and ends ... Narrative qualities are transferred from art to life. (Louis Mink)

> The notion that sequences of real events possess the formal attributes of the stories we tell about imaginary events could only have its origin in wishes, daydreams, reveries. (Hayden White)

> [The narrative structure of beginning-middle-end applies] to ... story-events as narrated, rather than to actions themselves, simply because such terms are meaningless in the real world. (Seymour Chatman)

Barthes, he continues, contrasts art, which 'knows no static', with 'life', in which everything is 'scrambled messages'; and Ricoeur, though less extreme, sees the structure of the 'real world' as 'pre-narrative', and narrative as a 'synthesis of the heterogenous' (sic) which opens up to us 'the realm of the "as if"' ('Narrative', 118–20).[25] Carr summarises: 'the term "Narrative history" is an oxymoron ... [a] story redescribes the world; in other words, it describes it as if it were what presumably, in fact, it is not' ('Narrative', 118, 120).

Carr's theory is, rather, that narrative structure 'inheres in the events themselves', so that there is between them not only 'continuity' but 'community of form'. He argues that the 'real world' the historian seeks to describe is not physical reality, which may well be mere sequence, but human reality, the world of event, in which self-reflexive humans act and are acted upon; here at least other conditions obtain ('Narrative', 117–121). His thesis derives ultimately from Edmund Husserl, who, in his study of the human experience of the passage of time,[26] shows that it hinges on a retention of the past and an anticipation ('protention') of the future. If this is true of such a passive aspect of life as simply being aware, Carr says, how much more true it is of our active life; for here, far from

24. Simon Schama, *Citizens, A Chronicle of the French Revolution* (London: Viking Penguin, 1989).

25. Quoting Louis O. Mink, 'Narrative Form as a Cognitive Instrument', in R.H. Canary and H. Kozicki (eds), *The Writing of History* (Madison: University of Wisconsin Press, 1978), 145; idem, 'History and Fiction as Modes of Comprehension', *New Literary History*, 1 (1970), 557f; Hayden White, 'The Value of Narrativity in the Representation of Reality', in W.T.J. Mitchell (ed.), *On Narrative* (Chicago: Chicago University Press, 1984, 4–23); Chatman, *Discourse*, 47; Roland Barthes, 'Introduction à l'analyse structurale des récrits', *Communications*, 8 (1966), 7; Paul Ricoeur, *Temps et récit* (Paris, 1983, I, 113).

26. Edmund Husserl, *The Phenomenology of Internal Time-Consciousness* (1964; ET, Bloomington: Indiana University Press, 1964).

encountering life as structureless sequence, we embrace it in experience, hopes and plans: we operate on the principle of reviewing experience in order to devise means in the present of achieving our desired ends in the future. The heart of Carr's argument is that the memory-means-end structure of human action resembles the beginning-middle-end structure of narrative, and is bounded by the ultimate examples of those beginnings and ends within which texts define themselves, birth and death; in between these two is life, in which human action takes place, and the untidiness of action corresponds to the contingency and suspense we find in stories ('Narrative', 121f).

Narratives, says Carr, need a story-teller and an audience. The story-teller cuts out 'static', only offering functional data, and in doing so often provides surprises for characters and audience alike. The teller can do this by virtue of standing in what Carr calls an *ex post* position above and beyond the story, where the privileged knowledge of hindsight is available: only the story-teller knows all along how it will end ('Narrative', 123f). In 'real life' no-one knows how it will end, yet Carr's argument is that we behave as if we do, shaping our action by viewing it in the future-perfect tense, from the perspective of *having done it*. Human action, then, has a 'teleological' nature ('Narrative', 124). This, he concedes, is a 'quasi-hindsight', yet we try to reduce the unpredictability of the future by 'foreseeing' as much as possible, viewing the future selectively (pushing the 'static' to one side) and choosing our actions accordingly, and so the *ex post* state of affairs we imagine shapes our actual deeds in the present: 'we try to occupy the story-teller's position with respect to our own lives' ('Narrative', 126). We can perform this trick because we are self-reflexive beings, so that for instance, the narrative activity of saying 'what I am doing' can be addressed to myself, making me both the teller, the character and the audience, and this narration facilitates, is a constitutive part of, my action. This narrative activity, therefore, 'is practical before it becomes cognitive or aesthetic in history and fiction'; and Mink's distinction is quite false, for stories 'are told in being lived and lived in being told' ('Narrative', 125f).

Carr now applies this practical narration to the social aspect of human reality. He describes story-telling as a social activity, and story as that which constitutes a group, a 'we' with a shared sense of origin and destiny, a shared willingness to tell, inhabit and hear the same story. This is the first-order narrative activity, which is practical before it is cognitive or aesthetic; and though it may be formulated by only one or a few members of the group, it is accepted by others ('Narrative', 127f, 130). The second-order narrative is the cognitive and the aesthetic, and is what we describe as history or fiction: 'such narrative must be regarded not as a departure from the structure of the events they depict, much less a distortion or radical transformation of them, but as an extension of their primary features' ('Narrative', 131).

Carr observes that the second-order narrative, while retaining the same subject, the 'we' of the community constituted by the first-order narrative, may have a very different content; yet this 'literary' narrative retains the same *form*. He solidly rejects the notion that

> the narrative *form* is what is produced in these literary genres [of histories and fictions] in order to be imposed on a non-narrative reality – it is in envisaging new content, new ways of telling and living stories, and new kinds of stories, that history and fiction can be both truthful and creative in the best sense. ('Narrative', 131)[27]

To round off the tale, we can see Schama putting Carr into practice.

> As artificial as written narratives might be, they often correspond to ways in which historical actors construct events. That is to say, many, if not most, public men see their conduct as in part situated between role models from an heroic past and expectations of the judgement of posterity. If ever this was true, it was surely so for the revolutionary generation in France. Cato, Cicero and Junius Brutus stood at the shoulders of Mirabeau, Vergniaud and Robespierre, but very often they beckoned their devotees towards conduct that would be judged by the generations of the future. (*Citizens*, xvi)

Carr would do well to face the implications of the instability of narratives themselves for his argument for continuity (Kermode could help him there), but his scheme does not require total neatness in either stories lived or stories told, so this is no insuperable problem. Also (and this is not a criticism of Carr but of a possible misunderstanding of him), we should not allow the continuity of structure between narrative and the 'real world' to imply that every narrative has an equally good purchase on the events it purports to describe; that would be just an inversion of Kermodian total scepticism. Like Kermode, Carr accepts the resemblance of fiction and history; unlike Kermode, he does not conflate the two. Fiction and history each resemble the real world through community of form, while deliberately diverging in content. It follows that a given history cannot have the veracity or falsity of its content guaranteed simply by virtue of its possessing a narrative form. It will after all be possible to discern between the narratives of a Mugabe and a Guerin. Of great value is Carr's distinction between the natural and human worlds; once animals become self-reflexive, biology becomes history, and the denial of any impact of human thinking and choosing on the natural randomness of things begins to look no less an act of faith than any (quasi-)theological view of meaning and purpose.

27.   For a complementary approach to event as 'narratable', see Lash, 'Ideology', 100.

Farrer and Mark's narrative

What does Carr's thesis suggest about Mark and Farrer on Mark? First (if we revert to the historicality of the author), we can say that Farrer's insistence upon the accessibility of the authorial mind is bolstered a little by Carr's picture of the pervasiveness of the narrative form. If the human mind is constitutionally a narrative organ, then the writing of a narrative about the composition of a text may achieve some congruence with the text's composer. Of more immediate interest is a second line of thought. Farrer maintains not just that Mark and his first audience believed that they were about the business of writing and reading history, but that the Gospel does communicate 'a genuine history' (*Study*, 7), which is a matter not just of story-teller and audience, but of actors too. Let us grant that the shape and character of the Markan narrative as Farrer describes it is even broadly in accord with what the writer intended. If a pattern of prefiguration, of prophecy and fulfilment, is the way Mark sees and 'explains' these events, if that is the manner of his second-order narrative, to what extent might it have been the manner of the first-order narrative practised by the people of whom he writes, as they reflected on the past and shaped their future action?

Both they and Mark lived in a mental and narrative world saturated by the Jewish Scriptures (if 'Scripture' is not anachronistic for some writings at this stage) and such other works as made up first-century Jewish literature. These writings contained history, prophecy and apocalyptic: heavy hints about how Jewish people, and indeed the Jewish people as a whole, should tell and live the beginning, middle and end of their story. They also contained figures of such an authority as would impress itself on the minds of any who felt called by God. If Cato, Cicero and other heroes of the Roman Republic stood at the shoulders of the revolutionaries of 1789, no less would Elijah, David, the Patriarchs, and Farrer's other typological favourites loom over John the Baptist, Jesus and the disciples. Here is a way in which Farrer might still help take us beneath the synchronic matter of text.

We still cannot say that Mark's chronology or sequence is historically transparent, or even perhaps particularly translucent; nor can we have any more confidence than before that we have 'what really happened' when we read of the rending of the Temple veil (Mk 15.38), or of things done by people who do not inhabit a Jewish narrative world (Pilate, for instance). Nor does this line of enquiry take us any further in assessing the miracle stories historically. Where Farrer may help us is in offering an admittedly speculative picture of the way in which certain Jewish persons' minds might work at significant points in their religious 'career'. If a *writer of* history like Mark can give off typological signals to indicate the significance of a character or episode, might not an *actor in* history, inhabiting a similar milieu, behave in a similar way? Could a Jewish religious virtuoso of the time avoid acting thus?[28] Once others detected such signals from Jesus, they would see therein signs of how he was shaping his story, how he wanted to be understood. For instance, at Mk 3.13 Farrer describes a typologically pregnant moment, the choosing of the Twelve. This Jesus does after going Moses-like up a mountain, and although Farrer cannot show any very close resemblance between the choosing of the disciples and the giving of the Sinai covenant to the tribes of Israel, the mountain setting and the common number of twelve are enough to establish the point that Mark wants it – and, we might suggest, Jesus wanted it – to be seen as a confirming signal of the appearance of someone to embrace and reconstitute Israel, a prophet like Moses (*Study*, 81, cf Deut. 34.10). Farrer does not press this symbolic continuity in the *Study*, and in *Matthew* he rules it out, at least in respect of numerology (*Matthew*, vif). Another example is Jesus' triumphal entry into Jerusalem (Mk 11.1–10). In the *Study*, Farrer does not pursue the prophecy of the Lord's Anointed coming from the Mount of Olives and riding on an ass (Zech. 9.9, cf *Study*, 345); he does, however, in a sermon, preached three years earlier. And, as is fitting in preaching on 'the mind of Christ', he sets out the historical possibility:

> Did Jesus ride into Jerusalem on an ass, with the circumstances of an arranged triumph? Well, Zechariah had prophesied that Sion's king should come to her riding on an ass. This being so it is very possible that theological stylisation has exaggerated the chance ride of a footsore man into a messianic triumph ... On the other hand ... Christ may have deliberately wished to fulfil Zechariah's oracle. But did he? Can we see him do it? Is it a proper part of his life and action; especially of his final invasion of Jerusalem? Only as we answer this question, shall we decide whether he sent for the ass and headed the triumph, or not. ('History', 43)

D. Conclusion

Our aim has been to see what contribution Farrer's work on Mark might make to the project of exploring the history of Jesus. He is astute in setting out the synthetic nature of a historian's task, but in the *Study* he wholly underestimates the gap between the prefigurative and the cause-and-effect methods, a failing he does a little to make good in *Matthew*. This inadequacy is compounded by pervasive neglect, not of his credal presuppositions, but of the disabling effect they have upon his perspective at this our fifth level of historicality. He does indeed introduce what from one point of view appears to be (in Houlden's phrase) 'a major fresh obstacle ... the powerful imagination of the evangelist' ('Scholarship',

---

28. Harvey follows a similar line in *Constraints*. This way of thinking need not be seen as only for the virtuoso: does not Farrer speak of how 'we go on cheerfully treating everything in heaven and on earth as a parable of everything else' ('Surface', 55), as indeed we do?

203), but what he offers as the fruits of that imagination, for all that they seem to us to be literary elaborations or fictions, may paradoxically give some access to the narrative world not just of writer but of 'actor' too. Other difficulties remain in using the Gospels to establish the character of Jesus' ministry but, at the very least, we should not assume that the presence of typology in Mark *inevitably* makes Jesus more remote than he was before. Kermode is seized by the narrative and interpretative conventions that operate in different epochs and cultures. Carr shows how such conventions do not banish the possibility of a qualified realism about historical narrative, as people live as well as tell their stories. In so far as Farrer gives us a glimpse of a first-century Jewish narrative mentality, his work can make a contribution to the study of Christian origins, though not quite in the manner he would have envisaged.

Chapter 14

MARK AS HISTORY: CONCLUSIONS

'History' can signify a number of things. When applied to a text, which is a notation not a commodity, it must denote an aspect of reading. We have identified five levels of historicality, overlapping but still usefully distinguishable, at which we might read Mark. Farrer himself has some awareness of historical reading as a stratified activity, though it is coloured by his pervasive theological consciousness.

Level 1: The Historicality of the Reader

Reading at this level is a self-reflexive activity – 'What makes me read Mark as I do?' – and a useful brake on self-delusion. In Part II we considered Farrer's own historical rootedness as a reader of Mark. We have now investigated signs of Farrer's *awareness* of his place in history, finding a definite sense of his own distance as a modern from the mental and instinctual world of the author whose mind he is seeking. Farrer has much less of a sense of the confines imposed by his own Christian belief and his calling as a public ambassador for Christian faith, but he stands out among apparently more 'objective' exegetes by giving his readers – more from candour than self-suspicion – abundant material for making due allowances.

Level 2: Defining an Original Audience

Any attempt to distinguish between different readings of Mark on grounds other than those of personal preference demands criteria which require a sense of the original audience. For an interpreter who, like Farrer, seeks the author's intention, the attempt to define an original audience is at the same time an attempt to place the author in some intelligible social context. As such it inhibits the worst excesses of the interpreter's self-projection upon the author. Farrer does this best in a subsidiary argument about the date of writing; otherwise he is content with general assertions about first-century 'Jewishness', and even claims that Mark's original audience would not have grasped some of the subtler aspects of composition which he has grasped. This leaves Farrer's mind dangerously unfettered.

Mary Beavis' *Mark's Audience* makes good and highly significant claims for the pervasiveness of rhetoric (especially the *chria* form), even among the moderately educated in the Roman Empire, and for Mark as a text written to be heard rather than read. If Mark's audience was aware of rhetoric, this helps Farrer's case, as quite sophisticated aspects of a text would then be intelligible to them, even if they could not pore over the scroll itself. Another suggestion of hers, that the Gospel may well have been heard by non-Christians, presents a difficulty for Farrer, whose thesis requires an audience of church *cognoscenti*. Beavis' work further exposes Farrer's lack of interest in defining for Mark a rounded context of intelligibility. While she pays little attention to Jewish influence on Mark, she does point up Farrer's all but complete neglect of Hellenistic literature, a neglect perhaps explained by his too-easy acceptance (itself religiously prompted?) of Mark as generically unique. Beavis rebuts claims of uniqueness, but her range of influences on the Gospel does not lead to a well-focused picture of the genre of Mark. She does, however, show the chastening effect of seeking an audience when one is, like Farrer, seeking the author.

Level 3: The Quest of the Historical Author

Lacking external information about an author, we can only speak of the historicality of the author *implied in the text*, and then of generalities of milieu. The best route (if there is any route) to such an author lies through the original audience. Indeed, attention to the original audience of a text all but inevitably leads to inferences about the person who wrote it, hence the virtual fusion of some material relating to this and the previous section. The author is the goal of Farrer's quest, but his scanty treatment of the Markan audience leads him to treat the author too much as a disembodied mind, a mind remarkably like his own. Farrer claims that Mark was a preacher, but does not adduce much evidence. When he claims to detect processes in Mark's mind which escaped not just the audience but perhaps even the author his account becomes uncheckable and implausible.

Richard Burridge's *What are the Gospels?* makes genre its point of entry. Genre for him is a system of textual signals which prompt expectations in the audience essential to the understanding of the text and the intention of the author. Particularly helpful is his distinction between genre and mode, whereby a text can remain in one genre but, in borrowing traits from others, move through a number of modes. Such a distinction would have sharpened Beavis' focus. Burridge's expansive survey of Graeco-Roman βίοι provides a generic home for the Gospels that is plausible but only limitedly useful, because of the very width of the genre as he describes it. Also, his case for the Gospels' apologetic and polemic purpose is insufficiently grounded.

Burridge's approach shows how Farrer could have paid more attention to the generic signals from the text before he treated Mark as 'poetry', and how the genre/mode distinction might have saved him from this category error. The limits set by Burridge are very broad, but even these are effective in ruling out some readings. Moreover, in Farrer's easy dismissal of the possibility of external criteria for the generic character of Mark, there are hints of a disinclination for the painstaking work required. Burridge, however, (like Beavis) makes little of Old Testament models,[1] where Farrer's antennae are extremely sensitive. Burridge's closing remarks – that as the Gospels are βίοι of Jesus, so the person of Jesus should be at the centre of *all* our readings of the Gospels – look like Farreresque credal prescriptivism. But Burridge's creed, unlike Farrer's, is largely covert.

Level 4: The Pre-history of Mark

The implied author occupies the narrowest of seams between the strata above (the audience) and below (the pre-textual materials). If Farrer is brash in drilling through from above, he is at his most effective here, at the pre-textual level. An advocate of Markan priority, he has little to say of documentary sources, but much to say of oral traditions as form criticism describes them, and argues with great force for the priority of whole texts over their parts, corroborating the order of priorities we advanced in Part II. Support for Farrer comes from Beavis and Burridge, who regret the insistence of form criticism on the pre-literary character of the Gospels, and the importing of questionable principles of development designed to elucidate folk-tale. If Farrer's attempts to prove the full coherence of Mark are unconvincing, and indeed if the findings of Beavis or Burridge are sometimes too various, a reformed form criticism might still be helpful in probing the pre-history of a wrinkled text. Gerd Theissen (moving back to Level 1) offers a sketch on the historical rootedness of form criticism itself, from which we advanced some tentative observations about aspects of Farrer's own church experience which might have added bite to his critique.

---

1.   A judgement shared by Collins, as we have seen. See p. 145, note 27, above.

Level 5: Mark – A Window on Event?

Farrer believes it vital to preserve the possibility of reading Mark as a text giving access to external events it purports to describe, and in the *Study* gives considerable space to this, in what is primarily a literary study. He sees genuinely historical narrative as an interpretative, synthetic exercise, which proceeds from a certain principle of causation. Mark's is the principle of prefiguration, which Farrer acknowledges to be foreign to the modern historical method but which he believes can yield a narrative still patient of the latter. His attempt to demonstrate this is less than successful, because each interpretative principle is based on a quite different axiom: prefiguration requires the agency of God, 'scientific' history excludes it from its calculations. Farrer's retention of the miraculous within his historical thinking presents insuperable problems for engagement with a scientific historical method. The latter does not deny the possibility of such events but is analytically incapable of comprehending them. While seeking to extend the historical method to cater for the exceptional, Farrer is himself holding historical beliefs on *non-historical* grounds, a possibility which elsewhere he himself allows.

Kermode and others believe that all historical narrative, whatever its interpretative principle, is fictive. Kermode's apparent and unwarranted belief that any distortion of event by narrative amounts to total derangement (by means of arrangement!) leaves no space for the qualified realism advocated by Carr. A psychologically grounded continuity between the narrative form and human action restores the possibility of finding evidential value in narrative, Mark's Gospel included. Farrer's picture of Mark must greatly limit that Gospel's contribution as a history, however, though his account of the typological mentality might yet shed some light on the narrative instincts of the actors in the events Mark describes, even of Jesus himself.

Literary Implications

We ended Part II with some unresolved questions about the range of possible reading strategies and the status of their claims. We noticed the setting up of fierce alternatives, so that the only recourse from transcendent, Hypostatized Content seemed to be either interpretative anarchy or institutional control. The dilemma (for those who are not happy with *laissez-faire* reader-response criticism or arbitrary constraint) is about how to adjudicate between different conceptions of what a given text means. Having established the performative nature of all texts, we have seen how each performance has an ineluctable historicality about it, since all readers and audiences inhabit a certain place and time. In the case of readings of narrative, it should be possible to assign each to one or more of the five levels of historicality we have explored. This eases some of the problems of meaning, as it acknowledges that the significances of a text change according to the level at which it is read. Readings which seek the author, or the author's materials, or the author's historical subject, are obviously conducted at Levels 3, 4 and 5 respectively; but what of those more consciously 'literary' readings, which go under the names of reader-response and narrative criticism?

A reading which reflects only that reader's response, with no attempt to register the interpretations of others, operates simply on the first level of historicality; it is a kind of autobiography. Readings which attempt to describe the response of the ideal or implied reader are more complex. Since texts are performative, we cannot accord them significance apart from particular instances in which they are read, by us or by others; but here is the problematic figure of a reader who, being ideal and so imaginary, *could never perform a reading*. If I seek in my reading to describe the implied reader, a little self-interrogation ('Why am I reading this text in this way?' a Level-1 activity) may clarify who this figure really is that I seek. It may actually stand for me, giving my reading the apparent imprimatur of 'the text itself' (perhaps so that I can persuade you to read the text as I read it), but really masking another instance of Level-1 reading.[2] Or, the implied reader may stand for the audience to whom I think the text was originally addressed. This places my reading immediately in the realm of Level 2, and requires of me some patient historical work as I explore the original setting. If I seek to stay hermetically sealed in the 'story world', I can only speak of what *I* read there.

A Divine Exception?

There may be one exception to this maxim that all meaning is historically appropriated. If, with Farrer, I believe that God inspired the writing of Mark, then I believe that there is in the fullest sense a transcendent meaning, that which God accords it.[3] We praise Farrer for holding his *a priori* beliefs and readerly aims up to scrutiny, but we have not yet fully scrutinised these influences on him, and the harm sometimes done by his belief about the evangelist's inspiration. He does not wish us to forget that in Mark we are studying an inspired work, a book of Holy

2.   Moore notes that implied readers with their 'correct' responses, reflect critics at their most well-behaved (*Challenge*, 106f). We might call this biography of the critical *superego*. For an overtly autobiographical reading see Moore's *Perspective*: 'I have tried to write a book on the Gospels that would not be bound to the ingested body of a dead Father (Mark or Luke) ... but would be moored more to my own body instead' (*Perspective*, 157).

3.   Even here there is a puzzle of historicality, if a timeless God is to engage with time-bound humanity and its creations.

Scripture. To pursue the mechanics of divine inspiration would quickly take us beyond the limits of this enquiry, but we must look more closely at what Farrer sees as this consequence of inspiration: the significance of Mark as a canonical text for Christian faith. For Austin Farrer, *this* is the Mark that ultimately matters. But what must Scripture then be, within the terms of Farrer's scheme? And what evidence is there for it to be so? These questions we consider in Part IV.

PART IV

MARK AS SCRIPTURE

[I]f you read the Bible other than as the word of God, you will yawn over most of it.
'The Inspiration of the Bible', 9

We are now familiar with, if not weary of, the observation that Austin Farrer's convictions about Mark (or rather 'St Mark') as an inspired sacred text set the tone for his debate, sometimes cloud his judgement, and always make it easy for readers of Farrer to keep in mind the motives which jostle with the grounds on which he advances his theories. Our task now is to change our vantage point, so that Farrer's treatment of Mark as Scripture is neither subsidiary nor a distraction (if it has ever been that), but at the centre of the picture. Our path at this closing stage of the journey will take two turns.

First, we shall look at the reasons which may have made Farrer so uncompromising in his insistence on the canonical identity of Mark, and this will lead us into a very brief discussion of Farrer's more renowned work, in philosophical theology. Here I shall argue that the grit at the centre of Farrer's theological pearl is the question of the manner of God's action in the world, and that it is in this light that he approaches his biblical studies.

Secondly and consequently, we shall return to Farrer's thoughts about inspiration, as the typical mode of God's influence upon human beings and *a fortiori* upon the Gospel writer. Here I shall argue that Farrer's taking of Mark as a worked example of inspiration is a legitimate thing to do: it is in essaying the 'horizontal' task of literary analysis, while not making clear the philosophical assumptions on which the analysis rests, that his work falters.

Thirdly, we shall consider the extent to which Farrer succeeds in co-ordinating the three senses which press upon his work: his sense of divine action, his sense of poetic creativity and human rationality, and his sense of biblical authority. Here I shall argue that Farrer largely accepts the canon as an axiom, and does not examine the problem of inspiration in the canon's formation, when this is what his account of the inspired *writing* of canonical texts requires. A coda to this third phase will be some thoughts about how the insights of Austin Farrer may be brought to some resolution, which may help his – and my – fellow Christians (perhaps others too) to make good use of biblical texts.

Chapter 15

SCRIPTURE AND THE ACTION OF GOD

An evangelist ... was caught between two forces and subject to a double control.
A Study in St Mark, 8

If a hill has three paths to its top, one wooded, one muddy, one rocky, each giving different views on the way, the condition of the people who reach the hilltop, their footwear, the photographs they have taken on the way up, their feelings about what sort of a walk it is to get up this hill will partly depend on the route they have taken. Austin Farrer had taken an unusual route up to the writing of his weightiest contribution to Gospel studies, and quite a different route from that of most of the Gospel specialists who first read the *Study*. Houlden explains:

> Part of the difficulty in placing Farrer's biblical work arises from the fact that it by no means represented the whole of his mind. It was an outcrop, albeit a vital one for him as a Christian theologian, of other operations. The central question of all his work... was the mode whereby divine and human action are related. ('Scholarship', 202)

Though Farrer's earliest published writing was biblical,[1] his first book, *Finite and Infinite*, was a dense piece of pre-theological philosophical speculation. Here his broadly Thomist programme of understanding (God's aseity, infinity and essential otherness) requires all talk of God's being and action to be analogical, conducted with reference to known finites. God is then in a certain sense unknowable, but does things in the finite world as a primary cause acting through secondary causes, acting in such a way as not to overwhelm or manipulate creatures. This is the foundation of what Farrer calls his 'rational theology' (see e.g. *Finite*, 1–3, 43f, 299f). He sees this engagement of the infinite with the finite supremely in the Incarnation, as the book's closing words (written during the fall of France) demonstrate:

> Rational theology will not tell us whether ... [the occupation of Paris] has or has not been an unqualified and irretrievable disaster to mankind and especially to the men

1. 'Categories'.

who died. It is another matter if we believe that God Incarnate also died and rose from the dead. (*Finite*, 300)

Ask how the subject of the last sentence – the events and the interpretation of the events – is to be apprehended, and the route to his biblical work is clear.

Scripture and Images of God

Farrer's conceptual bridge from philosophical theology to Bible is the *Glass*, where a coalescence of the necessity of analogical understanding of God with that for God's action in the world (*in primis* in Jesus) to be interpreted before it can have significance issues in the requirement for some trustworthy means of apprehending that action: 'Christians suppose such mysteries to be communicated to them through the scriptures' (*Glass*, 35). As we now know, he considers the central function of the Scriptures to be the provision of controlling images as the means of right interpretation. He comes to the Bible as one already exercised, not just Christianly but – though Farrer would make no separation – *professionally*, as a scholar, by the problem of speaking rationally about God's existence and action. He identifies the Bible as the place to find the thing his hypothesis requires, and so approaches biblical texts with a quite particular line of questioning: if God is to act in a certain way; and if it is the books of the Bible which are to function as the organs for the images which control human apprehension of God's action, and feed human contemplation of God's presence; then what sort of writings are they? Farrer himself is of course less tentative: 'Anyone who has ever felt, even in the least degree, the power of these texts to enliven the soul and open the gates of heaven must have some curiosity about the manner in which the miracle is worked' (*Glass*, 36).

This is a biblical agenda that will sit awkwardly with the ways of scholars habituated to the canons of historical criticism. The same hilltop, but a different path.

The question 'What sort of book?' we have already asked as a question about genre. In the *Glass*, Farrer asks it as a question about the process of inspired composition, as he explores Mark as a treasury of images, for the substance of Markan truth 'is in the great images … in the figure of the Son of Man, in the ceremony of the sacramental body, in the bloody sacrifice of the Lamb, in the enthronement of the Lord's Anointed' (*Glass*, 146).

In the *Study* he asks it again, though this time with much less stress upon the manner of God's action than on the 'poetical' process in which it issues. It is odd that Farrer, amid all his confessions of faith, makes little reference to the fundamental themes of the *Glass* which underpin all his detailed thinking in the later book. More fullness here would have lessened the confusion of readers taken aback by bald statements about the 'joint utterance of Jesus and the Holy Spirit' (*Study*, 369). Farrer's failure to identify the parentage of his study of Mark within his wider scriptural and philosophical concerns must be counted a formal weakness of the *Study* and an obstacle to its intelligibility. It feels as though he does this because, in assuming that his readership is Christian, he can also assume that they accept that Mark must be read as Scripture, and that they know what Scripture is for. We now ask 'What sort of book?' as a question about Mark's scriptural identity.

Chapter 16

FARRER AND THE CANON

> If the biblical books had not been taken to express the apostolic mind, they would not have been canonized.
>
> *The Glass of Vision*, 53

People, says Farrer, are inspired to do different things, and a Paul or a Mark, as a scriptural author, is inspired to reveal God. This is the function of the canon of Scripture for Farrer: it is above all an organ for the setting forth of revelatory images, and it is for the assisting of that revelation that an author like Mark receives his especial inspiration. We know a lot about what Farrer thinks of certain canonical texts; but what of the canon itself?

In his article 'Origen *Redivivus*: Farrer's Scriptural Divinity', Charles Hefling describes Austin Farrer's biblical work as being a precursor of the canonical criticism of Brevard Childs.[1] This is a misleading comparison if taken any distance. Both Farrer and Childs are concerned for the integrity of the final form of the text over against its pre-history, and both read a given biblical text in the light of its near and distant canonical neighbours; but beyond this they diverge. Farrer's interest in Mark is in the creative processes of the author as they are discernible in the text at the moment when, so to speak, the ink dries, while Childs' often-repeated emphasis is upon what he calls the 'canonical shaping' of a text, its post-authorial life as a text among scriptural texts. In fact, Farrer's biblical work is remarkable for its lack of attention to the formation of the canon of Scripture. Sometimes the topic of the canon appears in an aside; more often it is an implicit influence upon him as he approaches some other question.[2] He appears to acknowledge it as a providential datum and then moves smartly on.

Hefling nevertheless has some good things to say in drawing out the implications for the canon of Farrer's pronouncements. 'Naturally,' says

1.   See e.g. Childs *Scripture, Canon* (and for Childs on Mark, *Canon*, 86–90).
2.   This is surely the root of what Brown sees as Farrer's attempt to treat the two Testaments as self-contained, free of outside influence of any consequence ('Human', 91).

Farrer, speaking of the gestation of the Gospel traditions which issue in Mark, 'the process of reflection upon the paradoxical complex of things the faith contained took time'; he then adds 'and indeed I do not see any signs of its being completed' (*Study*, 366f). Farrer here surely refers to the uncompleted reflection practised by successive generations of readers of Mark, but Hefling sees a bearing here upon the formation of the canon as well, for 'if the process of reflection, which began with choosing, using and combining images, continued as the choice, use, and combination of texts; and if the first stage is revelation – then, what of succeeding stages?' ('Origen', 48). He finds Farrer's answer in 'Revelation': 'The Church believes that she has been inspired, or guided, to canonize what is required for the understanding of the revelatory events' ('Revelation', 107). He buttresses Farrer's case from the philosophical discussion of revelation in *Faith and Speculation*. There Farrer talks of the moveable 'point of punctuation' between divine disclosure and human response. For instance, Isaiah's prophecy is the human response to the datum of the looming of the Assyrian armies, yet itself becomes a divine datum, 'thus says the Lord', to which the Israelites must respond (*Speculation*, 98f). Hefling extends this tendency for God's disclosure to gather human response to itself, and sees in it an argument for the continuance of revelation as the church moves from Gospel making to canon making ('Origen', 48). He sees another seed in the *Glass*: 'Development is development, and neither addition nor alteration' says Farrer, while stressing that '[t]he first and decisive development is the work of the Apostolic age' (*Glass*, 42, 'Origen' 49).

To repeat, Farrer's interest is much more with the inspiration evidenced by particular biblical writers, and Hefling's thoughts are extrapolations from this; but the exercise is a sound one. If, as Farrer says, revelation consists in 'the self-giving of the divine mind to man', if this is 'fully actualised in ... Jesus Christ', if Jesus begins the communication of his 'human-divine mind', and 'by that beginning lays down the lines of *all* further development' (*Glass*, 41f, emphasis added), then we should expect some consistency between Gospel making and canon making. Both must be inspired, so that the human response of gathering authoritative writings together becomes itself gathered into God's address to humanity.

Hefling's article is largely affirmative of Farrer, and he leaves the matter here, though observing that Farrer's assumptions 'are, perhaps, a little too obviously orthodox for many' ('Origen', 49). His closing paragraphs, however, which attempt to defend Farrer against charges of his hostility to historical examination of the New Testament, show the strain of Farrer's position over history and canon. Hefling quotes words from Farrer's 'Infallibility and Historical Revelation'. Here he offers a canon (that is, a yardstick) of Christian doctrinal development: it must be measured 'by the standard of Christian origins; and "Christian origins" can only mean in practice the evidences we have for Christian origins; and they come down pretty nearly to the New Testament writings' ('Infallibility', 158). Hefling could also have quoted Farrer's call for church dogma to submit to the 'historianship' of the 'fallible' historian, whose work is 'endlessly corrigible' ('Infallibility', 158). The picture of the New Testament as evidence requires no more than that it be a collection of primitive writings (perhaps just an arbitrary collection) which we accept as authoritative because it is the best we have got. This is a far cry indeed from the 'joint utterance' of Jesus and the Holy Spirit, and from the confident 'Christian historian', as it is from Farrer's reluctance to separate the 'informative' from the 'inspired' in Scripture, and his abhorrence of 'fencing-off of non-inspired areas' in the Bible (*Study*, 369f, *Glass*, 52). Indeed, the Farrer of the Bampton Lectures seems almost to rule out the treatment of Mark simply as evidence: 'Inspired image and historical memory are so fused in this oldest of our gospels that it is virtually impossible any more to pull them apart' (*Glass*, 53). It may be that 'Infallibility', a very late piece, shows a shift in Farrer's position, though he himself denies that he has changed his mind over the relation of faith and history ('Infallibility', 161). It may be significant that this scientific rigour is here being deployed against what he sees as the 'infallible fact-factory' of Roman Catholicism and so presents Farrer at his most critical and 'Reformed' ('Infallibility', 158, 164), but there is certainly not enough here to cause us to revise our impression of Farrer's estimation of the New Testament documents as writings with an evident divine radiance. It remains for us to ask whether the history of the formation of the canon has the character we should expect, the story of an inspired church discerning which of its writings were inspired. This is what Farrer's position requires, for special (i.e. scriptural) inspiration needs not only a means of coming to pass, but a means of being recognised for what it is. It must not only be done but be *seen to have been done*.

A. Inspired Canon Making?

This is a question about the primitive church's competence in verification: what criteria of discernment might there be to distinguish, for instance, 2 Peter from *The Shepherd of Hermas*? Farrer does not tell us, but his essay 'Inspiration' addresses the question of verifying particular occurrences of revelation, and he tells us that the guarantee lies in 'the convincingness of the communication' ('Inspiration', 44). Following Hefling's method, we extrapolate from the local to the general and say that the same principle of convincingness must apply to the reception of an inspired book. But convincing to whom? What counts as 'convincingness', and why? Farrer is (to use his own terms) *'believing* enough' to accept the inspiration of Scripture, but his programme requires him to be *'tough* enough' to claim the same kind of privilege for the drawers-up of the canon as he does for the canonical writers, for it is they who must have verified that certain documents had this mystical quality ('Inspiration', 45). If Paul's inspiration was to speak the mystery of God, theirs was to discern the mystery (cf 'Bible', 10). Farrer generally takes this privilege for granted, but we have seen that he does once specifically claim it ('Revelation', 107).

What consistency now requires of him is that he continue the process described in 'Inspiration' and 'ask ... after the control under which it took shape ['it' now being the New Testament canon]; for we cannot suppose it to have taken shape idly or casually' ('Inspiration', 42). This Farrer does not do, and when we do it for him, we see a rather messier picture than is comfortable for the vigorous view of scriptural inspiration which he holds. We see, for instance, the *Muratorian Canon* omitting 1 Peter, the uncertainty over the *Apocalypse of Peter*, the *Shepherd of Hermas* and the *Apocalypse of John* (*Muratorian Fragment*, Eusebius, *HE*, III.3.6, 25.4). We see the late Western acceptance of Hebrews, the long absence of any mention of 2 Peter, the lack of evidence for the Fourth Gospel being used by other than (so-called) heretical Christians before the later second century (when its virtues are praised by, for example, Irenaeus, III. II.II/8). We see the preponderance of Paul, which may not exactly make for a balanced representation of the apostolic age. We see all the troubles over Marcion.[3] Farrer's sharp words about 'the community mind' of form criticism return, for in the development of the canon we see what is in some ways a similar pattern, only here we *can* see it, we do not have to conjecture. At some moments what we see might even resemble the machinery that later manufactured the Marian dogmas, which Farrer pleads should not be 'held incorrigible' ('Infallibility', 164).

Someone might object that we wrong Farrer here, because he does not defend the whole of the Bible, or even the New Testament, equally. Does he not speak of a mixture of 'divine gold and human clay', and say that 'a doctrine of the unchallengeable inspiration of the whole text is a burden which our backs will no longer bear' ('Bible', 12, *Glass*, 52)? Indeed, he seeks a strategy for getting at what Luther called the 'matter' of Scripture, 'a doctrine ... as causes us to look for the right things in Scripture: above all that we should look for the life-giving inspired word'; after all, '[t]here is a great deal else in Scripture' (*Glass*, 52). Yet this appears on the very page where he inveighs against any 'fencing-off' of the more inspired from the less. Farrer also produces *A Short Bible*, a sort of 'canon-within-a-canon', yet even here he is constrained to talk of God as 'the true author of both Testaments' (*Short*, 10). It is hard, in the face of almost contradictory assertions, to escape the view that Farrer sees the difficulties of a uniformly inspired Scripture but shrinks from the consequences. And having offered no criteria to enforce the crucial distinction he makes between canonical inspiration and its lesser poetic cousin, he ignores the process of forming the canon (the evidence for

3. See von Campenhausen, *Formation*, esp. chapters IV–VII, and Barton, 'Canon'.

which he surely knows) in which such criteria must (on his reckoning) have been at work.

We return once more to the question of what is controlling him, so that he can be so penetrating and suggestive as he broods on how human imagination might collaborate with divine inspiration, yet so unwilling to pursue its implications. John Drury thinks he knows:

> The criterion is the ecclesiastical fixing of the bounds of Holy Scripture, and Farrer is arguing from that canon for a quite different kind of inspiration inside the Bible from any to be found outside it: which looks more like a clergyman beating the bounds than anything ordinarily practised or understood in historical literary criticism. Indeed, his own major biblical work, which might be described as radical redaction criticism ahead of its time, was something of an invitation to ignore those ancient bounds because it presented us with the understandable (if dauntingly complex) human imaginative processes of the NT writers. And this is the difficulty of Farrer ... (Review, 135)

B. The Curse of the Canon?

Farrer's work on the possibility of inspiration remains full of insight and profundity, and the problem which trips him up is a real one for those who, like him, do much of their living and thinking within the ecclesiastical bounds: why should they, when they speak of divine disclosure, continue to regard the Apocalypse as crucially different from, say, the *Four Quartets*? Farrer by his success and his failure points up a continuing difficulty for Christians over their handling of Scripture. This is the difficulty John Barton addresses in his own Bampton Lectures, *People of the Book?* Barton is a critical admirer of Farrer, but he feels the arbitrariness of the distinction Farrer felt compelled to maintain. He is content to have a canon with fuzzy edges.[4] He commends the authority of the Scriptures in terms of testimony. Part of this is their special evidential value as Christianity's 'authentic documentation' (*People*, 43), but here he does not fully answer Farrer's insistence that we need evidence but also interpretation ('controlling images') to know why the contingent events surrounding Christian origins are of universal and salvific importance. Barton's position nevertheless has the virtue of a certain pragmatism which can preserve Farrer's insights yet not deny their implications. If we wish to make a case for the blessing of the canon for Christian people, prompted by Farrer and Barton, it could proceed thus.

---

4.   In 'Canon', he recommends distinguishing between 'scripture', meaning sacred texts, and 'canon', 'a closed and defined corpus' of such texts ('Canon', 104).

C. A Way Forward

As far as the New Testament is concerned, we know about Christianity's first-century origins only what the second and third-century churches wanted us to know. No doubt they excluded documents which would have enhanced any church lectionary, while they included some (2 and 3 John?) whose content it is hard to see as necessary to salvation. Here, then, is Barton's fuzziness. If we follow Farrer's line of controlling images, there is fuzziness here too, when so central an image in Mark as the Son of Man has so minuscule a role to play in the New Testament outside the Gospels. If we use all the criteria which Farrer seems to apply – subject matter, proximity to Jesus and quality of perception (inspiration) – then not all writings in the New Testament meet all the criteria.

This means that we must deny the canon makers pure and infallible discernment; but we would not expect to find it in a world which God makes to make itself. Nevertheless, though the New Testament could have been differently composed at the margins, it contains enough writing with 'theological class'[5] to be sufficient to the cause of furthering growth in grace and to be the springboard for developing Christian reflection. It is a 'good enough' canon of Scripture. We can see those compiling the canon in terms similar to those Farrer uses to describe the process of inspiration in the minds of the writers whose work they weigh up: in both cases there must be a mixture of 'divine gold and human clay' ('Bible', 12). We may also allow a distinction between the canonical writers and the mass of poetic minds for the unmysterious reason that they have (or most of them have) a close proximity to the events and the primal interpretations on which Christian identity finally rests.

If the canon makers are, like the Pope in Farrer's eyes, fallible, are the results of their labours corrigible? The logic of the argument compels us to say Yes,[6] though pragmatism suggests No. The Bible is not sacrosanct except in so far as the churches have regarded it as such, but there is in these fragmented days a virtue even in that modest affirmation, in agreeing upon the boundaries of Scripture that *have been* (though even here there is again some blurring), as long as we can continue to see the Scriptures containing enough to be 'good enough' for their task. It is at this point that claims, for instance, about the irredeemably patriarchal cast of the Scriptures have their force. Even Dennis Nineham, with the keenest sense of the Bible's remoteness, sees its images as 'primordial', and the culture of the West as so imbued with them (different considerations might apply elsewhere) that they have a potency for articulating Christian faith which no new set of images could attain (*Use*, 249).

---

5.   Houlden's words (Review, 67), quoted by Barton (*People*, 60).
6.   Farrer himself admits the formal possibility of a revaluation of Scripture in the face of 'necessary refusals of the modern mind' ('Appreciation', 214f).

Chapter 17

MARK AS SCRIPTURE: CONCLUSIONS

For one whose thinking shows such breadth and connectivity, and whose creed is never concealed, Farrer disappoints and surprises by the lack of an explicit statement of the philosophical assumptions underlying the *Study*. His failure to follow through the consequences of his thinking for the early church's construction of the canon is equally disappointing but less of a surprise, when the evidence we have is of a less charmed development than is implied by Farrer's story of the creation of the texts themselves. It seems to be an abyss into which Farrer declines to look; though if he were to look, on our reckoning of his wider theological reflections he could still sustain a Christianly plausible position.

CONCLUSION

Conclusions are not of much profit ...

The Glass of Vision, 146

We have attempted a critical examination of the work of Austin Farrer upon the Gospel according to Mark from literary, historical and scriptural perspectives. Comparative study with other critics has identified significant connections and instructive contrasts between his and more recent work within the 'literary paradigm' of Gospel studies, despite the widespread neglect of his work and his own insistence upon the privileged nature of Mark as an inspired, canonical text. This has been the prime aim of this enquiry, which is chiefly a contribution to the study of the work of Farrer himself. Arising from this, however, are some observations about the wider practice of Gospel interpretation.

We saw in *The Glass of Vision* Farrer's literary instincts and philosophical cast of mind laying the foundations for his exegesis in *A Study in St Mark* and subsequent writings. We found his smaller-scale exegesis in the *Study* to be considerably more successful than his case for the overall shape and detailed coherence of the Gospel. A major error of his was to treat Mark as poetry rather than as prose narrative, though his work is not unique in creating difficulties through a consideration of genre which does not have sufficient historical grounding (Rhoads and Michie's original *Mark as Story* faltered here too). Writing at the dawn of scepticism about authorial intention, Farrer believed firmly that it was a catchable quarry, but his speculations demonstrate the hazards, not least because of his flimsy treatment of the audience such an author might reasonably have addressed. Even so, his picture is preferable to that presented at first by Rhoads and Michie, as they attempted to work with authorial intention while trying to stay quite within the story world (a position improved in their later collaboration with Dewey). More compelling is his argument for the study of whole texts (whether or not they exhibit 'wholeness') to precede the study of their parts or antecedents. We found good support for this among other critics we considered (Drury, Beavis and Burridge). Overall, Farrer emerges more creditably than his neglect, then and now, would suggest.

We argued that historical attentiveness can ease some of the problems of consciously 'literary' readings of Mark, since every text is a notation, without substance apart from its 'performance' by readers, who inhabit space and time. Beavis and Burridge demonstrate that much can be achieved in defining an original audience, not least the possibility of saying something testable about the author, and about the genre of the text, an essential consideration for all but the most subjective of readings. Despite the unison of Farrer, Beavis, Burridge and Drury on the infirmities of form criticism, enquiry into the pre-history of a text can still be valuable, especially once consideration of the whole has shown up flaws and incoherences. Farrer is anxious to bolster Mark's prestige as a Gospel that gives access to the events surrounding Jesus, but his work fails to show that a richly allusive narrative written according to the principle of prefiguration can be transposed into the key of prior causation, in which the tunes of 'scientific' history are played. The total scepticism of Kermode and others about narrative historiography cannot, on the other hand, be sustained. It is well rebutted by Carr's argument for the narrative consciousness of humans acting in society. This does not rescue Farrer, however, except in the light he may shed on a typological mentality in first-century Judaism.

One level of historicality in reading concerns awareness of one's own motives as reader. Here Farrer is exemplary in making clear his aims and presuppositions: he is a Christian writing for other Christians to elucidate divine revelation through the inspired, indeed scriptural, writing of a canonised saint. While critics aim, commendably, to do their work *sine ira et studio*, none can achieve it, and an early confession provides essential information as the critics' own readers weigh up their work. Kermode's use of Farrer shows that profitable conversation is possible even across the sacred/secular divide. Nevertheless, we noted at various points how Farrer's Christian allegiance to Mark as Scripture swayed his reasoning, and how overall it led him to presume in favour of wholeness and coherence.

Direct attention to this third aspect of Mark in Farrer's work revealed that his exegesis proceeds from a particular philosophical interest in, and a broadly Thomist view of, God's action in the world: it is God working on Mark's mind by means of double agency which produces the Gospel. Farrer's failure to make clear at least this aspect of his presuppositions in the *Study* no doubt accentuated the puzzlement caused by that book. We found a second failing in the absence among his published work of a case for the action of God in inspiring the formation of the canon of the New Testament. This is what his scheme requires if Mark is to have been seen for what (in Farrer's mind) it is. Evidence of the process of canon-making is not too friendly to what Farrer would need to demonstrate, while he himself sees its product as a prompting more for gratitude than for investigation. We saw, however, that a messier process and a fuzzier product would blend with Farrer's wider thinking about God's action in the world, while still being adequate to their task within the church.

Such pragmatism Austin Farrer would no doubt have seen as lacking in 'toughness'. This is an irony when, as Drury suggests in his deeply perceptive review, Farrer's own instincts about the fecundity of human imagination married to divine grace seemed to lead in the direction of rich plurality rather than buttoned-up neatness.

> He was the discoverer of wholeness where other men put asunder. He knew about the co-habitation of fact and interpretative imagination, of ideas and their verbal expression, of Old Testament and New. He understood how nuance, tone and twist are not the throw-away wrapping of revelation but its stuff; and how inspired writers are a kind of sleepwalkers, unconscious of all the riches of allusion in their work. But where a possible wholeness might blow a hole in the traditional bounds of orthodoxy he prefers to divide ... The man who drew so much truth and beauty from the fullness of Catholic tradition found that his search for that truth and his sense of that beauty led him to places where sacrifices are necessary. And there, understandably, he demurred. (Review, 135f)

BIBLIOGRAPHY

1. Works of Austin Farrer cited

Books

(Some elements have been reproduced in works cited under 'Collections' below.)

Finite and Infinite (Westminster: Dacre Press, 1943; 2nd edn, London: A & C Black, 1959; page references are to 1st edition).

The Glass of Vision (Bampton Lectures, 1948; Westminster: Dacre Press, 1948; 'Images and Inspiration', part of Lecture III, reproduced in Loades and MacSwain, *Truth*, 20–36).

A Rebirth of Images, The Making of St John's Apocalypse (Westminster: Dacre Press, 1949).

A Study in St Mark (Westminster: Dacre Press, 1951).

St Matthew and St Mark (Edward Cadbury Lectures, 1954; Westminster: Dacre Press, 1954).

A Short Bible (London: Collins, 1956; Introduction reproduced in Loades and MacSwain, *Truth*, 3–13).

Said or Sung (London: Faith Press, 1960).

Love Almighty and Ills Unlimited (Nathaniel Taylor Lectures, 1961; London: Collins, 1962).

Saving Belief: A Discussion of Essentials (London: Hodder & Stoughton, 1964; Chapter 1, 'Faith and Evidence', reproduced in Loades and MacSwain, *Truth*, 168–184).

Faith and Speculation (Deems Lectures, 1964; London: A & C Black, 1967).

The Triple Victory (London: Faith Press, 1965; Chapter 1, 'How to Read St Matthew', reproduced in Loades and MacSwain, *Truth*, 47–59).

A Science of God? (London: Bles, 1966).

Collections

A Celebration of Faith (J.L. Houlden (ed.); London: Hodder & Stoughton, 1970).

The End of Man (Charles C. Conti (ed.); London: Hodder & Stoughton, 1973).

Interpretation and Belief (Charles C. Conti (ed.); London: SPCK, 1976).

The One Genius, Readings Through the Year with Austin Farrer (Richard Harries (ed.); London: SPCK, 1987).

Austin Farrer: The Essential Sermons (J.L. Houlden (ed.); London SPCK, 1991).

The Truth-Seeking Heart: Austin Farrer and His Writings (Ann Loades and Robert MacSwain (eds); Norwich: Canterbury Press, 2006).

Individual Articles, Papers and Sermons

'A Return to New Testament Christological Categories' (1933), *Theology*, Vol. XXVI, (1933), 304–318.
'On Credulity' (1947), reproduced in *Interpretation*, 1–6; *Truth*, 190–195.
'History and the Gospel' (1948), reproduced in *Celebration*, 36–45.
'The Inspiration of the Bible' (1952), reproduced in *Interpretation*, 9–13; *Truth*, 14–19.
'An English Appreciation' (1953), in Bartsch, *Kerygma*, 212–223.
'On Dispensing with Q' (1955), in Nineham, *Studies*, 55–88.
'Revelation' (1957), in Mitchell, *Logic*, 84–107.
'On Looking Below the Surface' (1959), reproduced in *Interpretation*, 54–65.
'On Religion, Natural and Revealed' (1959), reproduced in *Celebration*, 19–25.
'St Mark' (before 1960), *Said or Sung*, 95–99; reproduced in *Essential*, 65–68; *Truth*, 60–64.
'Inspiration Poetical and Divine' (1963), reproduced in *Interpretation*, 39–53.
'Mary, Scripture and Tradition' (1963), reproduced in *Interpretation*, 101–125; *Truth*, 65–78.
'The Painter's Colours' (1963), reproduced in *Celebration*, 63–66; *Essential*, 1–4.
'Infallibility and Historical Revelation' (1968), reproduced in *Interpretation*, 151–164; *Truth*, 81–93.
'The Brink of Mystery' (date unknown), reproduced in *End*, 10–14.
'Gnosticism' (date unknown), reproduced in *Interpretation*, 138–148.
'The Mind of St Mark' (date unknown), reproduced in *Interpretation*, 14–22.

2. *Secondary Literature*

Alter, Robert and Frank Kermode, (eds), *The Literary Guide to the Bible* (London: Collins, 1987; repr. Fontana, 1989; page references to 1989 edn).
Anderson, Janice Capel and Stephen D. Moore, (eds), *Mark & Method: New Approaches in Biblical Studies* (Minneapolis: Fortress Press, 2nd edn, 2008).
Barthes, Roland, *Image-Music-Text* (Stephen Heath (ed. and trans.), London: Fontana, 1977).
— 'La mort de l'auteur' (1968; ET, 'The Death of the Author', in *Image-Music-Text*, 142–8).
Barton, John, 'Canon' (in Coggins and Houlden, *Dictionary*, 101–105).
— *People of the Book? The Authority of the Bible in Christianity* (Bampton Lectures, 1988; London: SPCK, 1988).
Barton, John (ed.), *The Cambridge Companion to Biblical Interpretation* (Cambridge: Cambridge University Press, 1998).
Bartsch, H.W., *Kerygma and Myth: A Theological Debate* (1953; ET, London: SPCK, 1972).
Beavis, Mary, *Mark's Audience: the Literary and Social Setting of Mark 4.11–12* (JSNT Supplement Series, 33; Sheffield: Sheffield Academic Press, 1989).
Beck, Brian E., *Reading the New Testament Today* (Guildford: Lutterworth Press, 1977).
Berlin, Isaiah, *Against the Current, Essays in the History of Ideas* (London: Hogarth, 1979).
Best, Ernest, *Mark: The Gospel as Story* (Edinburgh: T&T Clark, 1984).
Bilezikian, Gilbert, *The Liberated Gospel: A Comparison of the Gospel of Mark and Greek Tragedy* (Grand Rapids: Baker, 1977).
Booth, Wayne, *The Rhetoric of Fiction* (Chicago: Chicago University Press, 2nd edn, 1983).
Brett, Mark, 'Four or Five Things to do With Texts: A Taxonomy of Interpretative

Interests', in Clines, Fowl and Porter, *Dimensions*, 357–378.

— 'The Future of Reader Criticisms', in Watson, *Open*, 13–31.

Brown, David, 'God and Symbolic Action', in Hebblethwaite and Anderson, *Divine*, 103–122.

— 'The Role of Images in Theological Reflection', in Hebblethwaite and Hedley, *Human*, 85–105.

Bryan, Christopher, *A Preface to Mark* (Oxford: Oxford University Press, 1993).

Bultmann, Rudolf, *Die Geschichte der synoptische Tradition* (1921, 2nd edn, 1931; ET, *The History of the Synoptic Tradition*, Oxford: Blackwell, rev. edn, 1972).

Burnham, Frederic (ed.), *Postmodern Theology: Christian Faith in a Pluralist World* (New York: Harper & Row, 1989).

Burridge, Richard A., *What Are the Gospels? A Comparison with Graeco-Roman Biography* (Society for New Testament Studies Monograph Series, 70; Cambridge: Cambridge University Press, 1992; 2nd edn, Grand Rapids: Eerdmans, 2004; page references to both edns).

Butterfield, H., *Writings on Christianity and History* (Oxford: Oxford University Press, 1979).

Campenhausen, H. von, *The Formation of the Christian Bible* (1968; ET, London: A & C Black, 1972).

Carr, David, 'Narrative and the Real World', *History and Theory*, 1986, 116–131.

Carr, E.H., *What is History?* (Harmondsworth: Penguin, 1964).

Carrington P., *The Primitive Christian Calendar* (Cambridge: Cambridge University Press, 1952).

Carroll, Robert P., 'Poststructural Approaches', in Barton, *Companion*, 50–66.

Chatman, Seymour, *Story and Discourse: Narrative Structure in Fiction and Film* (Ithaca: Cornell University Press, 1978).

Childs, Brevard S., *Introduction to the Old Testament as Scripture* (London: SCM Press, 1979).

— *The New Testament as Canon* (London: SCM, 1984).

Clines, David J.A., David M. Gunn and Alan J. Hauser (eds), *Art & Meaning: Rhetoric in Biblical Literature* (JSOT Supplement Series, 19; Sheffield: JSOT Press, 1982).

Clines, David J.A., Stephen E. Fowl and Stanley E. Porter (eds), *The Bible in Three Dimensions: Essays in Celebration of Forty Years of Biblical Studies in the University of Sheffield* (Sheffield: JSOT Press, 1990).

Coggins, R.J. and J.L. Houlden (eds), *A Dictionary of Biblical Interpretation* (London: SCM, 1990).

Collins, Adela Yarbro *Mark: A Commentary* (Hermeneia series; Minneapolis: Fortress Press, 2007).

Crossan, J.D., *Four Other Gospels: Shadows on the Contours of the Canon* (Minneapolis: Winston, 1985).

Culpepper, Alan, *Anatomy of the Fourth Gospel: A Study in Literary Design* (Philadelphia: Fortress Press, 1983).

Curtis, Philip, *A Hawk Among Sparrows, A Biography of Austin Farrer* (London: SPCK, 1985).

Dalferth, Ingolf, 'The Stuff of Revelation: Austin Farrer's Doctrine of Inspired Images', in Loades and McLain, *Hermeneutics*, 71–95.

Dewey, Joanna, 'The Gospel of Mark as an Oral-Aural Event: Implications for Interpretation', in Malbon and McKnight, *New*, 145–163.

Dibelius, M., *Die Formgeschichte des Evangeliums* (1919; ET, *From Tradition to Gospel*, London: Ivor Nicholson and Watson, 1934).

Drury, John, Review of Farrer/Conti, *Interpretation*, *Theology*, Vol. LXXX (March 1977), 134–137.

— 'Mark', in Alter and Kermode, *Guide*, 402–417.

— 'Mark 1.1–15: An Interpretation', in Harvey, *Alternative*, 25–36.
— *Tradition and Design in Luke's Gospel: A Study in Early Christian Historiography* (London: SPCK, 1976).

Eaton, Jeffrey C. and Ann Loades, *For God and Clarity: New Essays in Honour of Austin Farrer* (Allison Park: Pickwick, 1983).

Eco, Umberto, *The Limits of Interpretation* (Bloomington: Indiana University Press, 1990).

Fish, Stanley, *Is There a Text in This Class? The Authority of Interpretive Communities* (Cambridge, MA: Harvard University Press, 1980).

Forsman, Rodger, 'Revelation and Understanding: A Defence of Tradition', in Loades and McLain, *Hermeneutics*, 46–68.
— '"Double Agency" and Identifying Reference to God', in Hebblethwaite and Anderson, *Divine*, 123–142.

Fowl, S.E., 'The Ethics of Interpretation, or What's Left Over After the Elimination of Meaning', in Clines, Fowl and Porter, *Dimensions*, 379–398.

Fowler, Robert M., 'Reader-Response Criticism: Figuring Mark's Reader' in Anderson and Moore, *Method*, 59–93.

Gardner, Helen, *The Business of Criticism* (Oxford: Oxford University Press, 1959).
— 'The Poetry of St Mark' (from the Riddell Lectures, 1956), in Gardner, *Business*, 101–126.
— *In Defence of the Imagination* (Norton Lectures, 1979–80; Oxford: Clarendon Press, 1984).

Gaventa, Beverly Roberts and Patrick D. Miller (eds), *The Ending of Mark and the Ends of God* (Essays in Memory of Donald Harrisville Juel; Louisville: John Knox Press, 2005).

Goulder, Michael, *The Evangelists' Calendar, a Lectionary Explanation of the Development of Scripture* (Speaker's Lectures, 1972; London: SPCK, 1978).
— 'Farrer the Biblical Scholar', in Curtis, *Hawk*, 192–212.
— 'The *Fram* Abandoned', in Goulder and Hick, *Why*, 1–30.
— 'A House Built on Sand', in Harvey, *Alternative*, 1–24.
— *Midrash and Lection in Matthew* (Speaker's Lectures 1969–71; London: SPCK, 1974).

Goulder, Michael and John Hick, *Why Believe in God?* (London: SCM, 1983).

Harries, Richard, '"We Know on Our Knees …" Intellectual, Imaginative and Spiritual Unity in the Theology of Austin Farrer', in Hebblethwaite and Anderson, *Divine*, 21–33.

Harvey, A.E., *Jesus and the Constraints of History* (London: Duckworth, 1982).
— 'Rabbis, Evangelists – and Jesus', *Theology*, Vol. XCII, July 1989, 244–251.
— (ed.), *Alternative Approaches to New Testament Study* (London: SPCK, 1985).

Hauerwas, Stanley and L. Gregory Jones (eds), *Why Narrative? Readings in Narrative Theology* (Grand Rapids: Eerdmans, 1989).

Hauge, Hans, 'The Sin of Reading: Austin Farrer, Helen Gardner and Frank Kermode on the Poetry of St Mark', in Loades and McClain, *Hermeneutics*, 113–128.

Hebblethwaite, Brian, 'Farrer as Theologian', *New Fire*, Vol. VII (Autumn 1983), 390–395.

Hebblethwaite, Brian and Douglas Hedley (eds), *The Human Person in God's World: Studies to Commemorate the Austin Farrer Centenary* (London: SCM Press, 2004).

Hebblethwaite, Brian, and Edward Henderson (eds), *Divine Action: Studies Inspired by the Philosophical Theology of Austin Farrer* (London: T&T Clark, 1990).

Hefling, Charles C., Jr, *Jacob's Ladder: Theology and Spirituality in the Thought of Austin Farrer* (Cambridge, MA: Cowley, 1979).
— 'Origen *Redivivus*: Farrer's Scriptural Divinity', in Eaton and Loades, *Clarity*, 35–50; reproduced in Heine and Henderson, *Captured*, 149–172.

Heine, David & Edward Henderson (eds), *Captured by the Crucified: the Practical*

Theology of Austin Farrer (London: T&T Clark, 2004).

Hirsch, E.D., *The Aims of Interpretation* (Chicago: Chicago University Press, 1976).

— *Validity in Interpretation* (New Haven: Yale University Press, 1967).

Hooker, Morna D., *The Gospel According to St Mark* (Black's New Testament Commentary, London: A & C Black, 1991).

Horbury, William and Brian McNeil (eds), *Suffering and Martyrdom in the New Testament* (Cambridge: Cambridge University Press, 1981).

Houlden, J.L., 'Austin Farrer's Biblical Scholarship', *New Fire*, Vol. VII, (Winter 1982), 201–205.

— *Bible and Belief* (London: SPCK, 1991).

— 'History, Story and Belief' (Inaugural Lecture, King's College, London, 1988).

— *Jesus, A Question of Identity* (London: SPCK, 1992).

— Review of Curtis, *Hawk*; *Theology*, Vol. LXXXIX, January 1986, 67f.

Jasper, D., *Coleridge as Poet and Religious Thinker* (London: Macmillan 1985).

— 'Literary Readings of the Bible', in Barton, *Companion*, 21–34.

Jeanrond, Werner, 'After Hermeneutics', in Watson, *Open*, 85–102.

— *Text und Interpretation als Kategorien theologischen Denkens* (1986; ET, *Text and Interpretation as Categories of Theological Thinking* (Dublin: Gill & Macmillan, 1988).

John, Jeffrey, 'Making Sense of Scripture', in John, *Living*, 44–65.

— (ed.), *Living Tradition* (London: Darton, Longman & Todd, 1992).

Kee, Howard Clark, *Community of the New Age, Studies in Mark's Gospel* (London: SCM Press, 1977).

Kelber, Werner, *The Oral and the Written Gospel: the Hermeneutic of Speaking and Writing in the Synoptic Tradition, Mark, Paul, and Q* (Philadelphia: Fortress Press, 1971; 2nd edn, 1983 (page references to 1971 edn).

Kermode, Frank, *The Genesis of Secrecy: On the Interpretation of Narrative* (Norton Lectures, 1977–1978; Cambridge, MA: Harvard University Press, 1979).

— *The Sense of an Ending: Studies in the Theory of Fiction* (Oxford: Oxford University Press, 1966).

Kessler, Martin, 'A Methodological Setting for Rhetorical Criticism', in Clines, Gunn and Hauser, *Art*, 1–19.

Kingsbury, Jack Dean, *Conflict in Mark: Jesus, Authorities, Disciples* (Minneapolis: Fortress Press, 1989).

Knox, W.L., *Some Hellenistic Elements in Early Christianity* (London: British Academy, 1944).

Lash, Nicholas, 'Ideology, Metaphor, and Analogy', in *Theology on the Way to Emmaus* (London: SCM Press, 1986, 95–119; reproduced in Hauerwas and Jones, *Narrative*, 113–137).

— 'What Might Martyrdom Mean?', in Horbury and McNeil, *Suffering*, 183–198.

Lewis, H.D., *Our Experience of God* (London: Allen & Unwin, 1959).

Lightfoot, R.H., *The Gospel Message of St Mark* (Oxford: Oxford University Press 1950).

— *History and Interpretation in the Gospels* (Bampton Lectures, 1934; London: Hodder & Stoughton, 1934).

— *Locality and Doctrine in the Gospels* (London: Hodder & Stoughton, 1938).

Loades, Ann and Michael McLain (eds), *Hermeneutics, the Bible and Literary Criticism* (London: Macmillan, 1992).

Loughlin, Gerard, 'Making it Plain: Austin Farrer and the Inspiration of Scripture', in Loades and McLain, *Hermeneutics*, 96–112.

Lyotard, Jean-François, *La Condition Postmoderne: Rapport sur le Savoir* (1979; ET, *The Postmodern Condition: A Report on Knowledge*, Minneapolis: University of Minnesota, 1984; Manchester: Manchester University Press, 1984).

McCasland, Vernon, Review of Farrer, *A Study in St Mark, Journal of Biblical Literature*, 72, 1953.

Malbon, Elizabeth Struthers, 'The Major Importance of the Minor Characters in Mark', in Malbon and McKnight, *New*, 58–86.

Malbon, Elizabeth Struthers and Edgar V. McKnight (eds), *The New Literary Criticism and the New Testament* (Sheffield: Sheffield Academic Press, 1994).

Martin, R.P., *Mark: Evangelist and Theologian* (Exeter: Paternoster Press, 1972).

Mink, Louis, 'History and Fiction as Modes of Comprehension', *New Literary History* 1 (1970).

Mitchell, Basil, 'Austin Marsden Farrer', in Farrer/Houlden, *Celebration*, 13–16.

— (ed.), *Faith and Logic* (London: Allen & Unwin, 1957).

Moore, Stephen D., 'Deconstructive Criticism: Turning Mark Inside-Out', in Anderson and Moore, *Method*, 95–110.

— *Literary Criticism and the Gospels: The Theoretical Challenge* (New Haven: Yale University Press, 1989).

— *Mark and Luke in Poststructuralist Perspectives: Jesus Begins to Write* (New Haven: Yale University Press, 1992).

Morgan, Robert, with John Barton, *Biblical Interpretation* (Oxford: Oxford University Press, 1988; 2nd edn, 1989; page references to 1989 edition).

Myers, Ched, *Binding the Strong Man, a Political Reading of Mark's Story of Jesus* (New York, Maryknoll, 1988).

Nineham, D. E., 'Cultural Relativism', in Houlden and Coggins, *Dictionary*, 155–159.

— 'Dr Dodd's Thesis Examined', in Nineham, *Studies*, 223–239.

— *St Mark* (Pelican New Testament Commentary, Harmondsworth: Penguin, 1963; 2nd edn, 1969; page references to 2nd edn).

— *The Use and Abuse of the Bible* (London: SPCK, 1976).

— (ed.), *Studies in the Gospels* (Oxford: Blackwell Press, 1955).

Parker, D.C., 'Scripture is Tradition', *Theology*, Vol. XCIV (January/ February 1991), 11–17.

Perrin, Norman, *What is Redaction Criticism?* (London: SPCK, 1970).

Peterson, Jeffrey, 'A Pioneer Narrative Critic and His Synoptic Hypothesis: Austin Farrer and Gospel Interpretation', *Society of Biblical Literature 2000 Seminar Papers*, 39 (2000), 661–671.

Polkinghorne, John, *One World: the Interaction of Science and Theology* (London: SPCK, 1986).

Polletta, G. (ed.), *Issues in Contemporary Criticism* (Boston: Little, Brown, 1973).

Powell, Mark Allen, *What is Narrative Criticism? A New Approach to the Bible* (London: SPCK, 1993).

Rahner, Karl, *Über die Schrift Inspiration* (1961; ET, *Inspiration in the Bible*, Edinburgh: Nelson, 1961).

Räisänen, Heikki, *Beyond New Testament Theology: A Story and a Programme* (London: SCM Press, 1990).

Rhoads, Donald and David Michie, *Mark as Story: An Introduction to the Narrative of a Gospel* (Philadelphia: Fortress Press, 1982).

Rhoads, Donald, Joanna Dewey and David Michie, *Mark as Story: An Introduction to the Narrative of a Gospel* (Minneapolis: Fortress Press, 2nd edn, 1999).

Ricoeur, Paul, *Essays in Biblical Interpretation* (Lewis S. Mudge (ed.); London: SPCK, 1981).

Roberts, T.A. *History and Christian Apologetic* (London: SPCK, 1960).

Robinson, J.A.T.R. *Can We Trust the New Testament?* (Oxford: Mowbray, 1977).

— 'Hosea and the Virgin Birth', in Robinson, *Twelve*, 1–11.

— *Twelve More New Testament Studies* (London: SCM Press, 1984).

Rogerson, John, 'Wrestling with the Angel: A Study in Historical and Literary Interpretation', in Loades and McLain, *Hermeneutics*, 131–144.

Rorty, Richard, *Consequences of Pragmatism* (Essays: 1972–1980; Minneapolis: University of Minnesota, 1982; Brighton: Harvester, 1982).

Sanders, E.P., *Paul and Palestinian Judaism* (UK Edition, London: SCM Press, 1977).

Schmidt, K.L., 'Die Stellung der Evangelien in der allgemeinen Literaturgeschichte', in Hans Schmidt (ed.), *Eucharisterion: Studien zur Religion und Literatur des Alten und Neuen Testament* (Göttingen: Vandenhoeck und Ruprecht, 1923).

Schweizer, Eduard, *Das Evangelium nach* Markus (Commentary, 1967; ET, *The Good News According to Mark*; London: SPCK, 1970).

Scroggs, R. and K.I. Groff, 'Baptism in Mark: Dying and Rising with Christ', *Journal of Biblical Literature*, 92 (1973), 531–548.

Slocum, Robert Boak, *Light in a Burning-Glass: A Systematic Presentation of Austin Farrer's Theology* (Columbia: University of South Carolina Press, 2007).

Smith, Morton, *Clement of Alexandria and A Secret Gospel of Mark* (Cambridge, MA: Harvard University Press, 1973).

Smith, Stephen H., *A Lion with Wings: A Narrative-Critical Approach to Mark's Gospel* (Sheffield: Sheffield Academic Press, 1996).

Stanton, Graham, *Jesus of Nazareth in New Testament Preaching* (Society for New Testament Studies Monograph Series, 27, Cambridge: Cambridge University Press, 1974).

Steiner, George, *Real Presences: Is There Anything in What We Say?* (London: Faber & Faber, 1989).

Tallis, Raymond, *Not Saussure: A Critique of Post-Saussurean Literary Theory* (London: Macmillan, 1988).

Taylor, Vincent, *The Gospel According to St Mark* (London: Macmillan, 1952, rev. edn, 1966; page references to 1966 edition).

Telford, W. (ed.), *The Interpretation of Mark* (London: SPCK, 1985).

Theissen, Gerd, *Social Reality and the Early Christians: Theology, Ethics, and the World of the New Testament* (Minneapolis: Fortress Press, 1992).

Thiselton, A.C., 'On Models and Methods: A Conversation with Robert Morgan', in Clines, Fowl and Porter, *Dimensions*, 337–356.

Tracy, Thomas F., 'Narrative Theology and the Acts of God', in Hebblethwaite and Henderson, *Divine*, 173–196.

Troeltsch, E., *Die Absolutheit des Christentums* (1929; ET, *The Aboluteness of Christianity*; London: SCM Press, 1972).

Tuckett, Christopher, Review of Burridge, *Biography*, *Theology*, Vol. XCVI (January/February 1993), 74f).

Vermes, Geza, *Jesus the Jew: A Historian's Reading of the Gospels* (London: Collins, 1976; SCM Press, 1983).

Via, Dan O., *The Ethics of Mark's Gospel: In the Middle of Time* (Philadelphia: Fortress Press, 1985).

Wadsworth, Michael, ed., *Ways of Reading the Bible* (UK edn, Brighton: Harvester, 1981).

Watson, Francis, *Text, Church and World: Biblical Interpretation in Theological Perspective* (Edinburgh: T&T Clark, 1994).

Watson, Francis (ed.), *The Open Text: New Directions for Biblical Studies?* (London: SCM Press, 1993).

Weeden, T.J., 'The Heresy That Necessitated Mark's Gospel', *Zeitschrift für die neutestamentliche Wissenschaft*, 59 (1968), 145–158, reproduced in Telford, *Interpretation*, 64–77.

— *Mark – Traditions in Conflict* (Philadelphia: Fortress Press, 1971).

Wiles, Maurice, *God's Action in the World* (Bampton Lectures, 1986; London: SCM Press, 1986).

Williams, J.G., *Gospel Against Parable: Mark's Language of Mystery* (Sheffield: Almond, 1985).

Williams, Rowan D., 'Postmodern Theology and the Judgment of the World', in Burnham, *Pluralist*, 92–112.

Wimsatt, William and Monroe Beardsley, 'The Intentional Fallacy', 1946, reproduced in Polletta, *Issues*, 194–206.

Wright, N.T., 'Taking the Text With Her Pleasure', *Theology*, Vol. XCVI (July/August 1993), 303–310.

— *The New Testament and the People of God* (London: SPCK, 1992).

Young, Frances, 'Allegory and the Ethics of Reading', in Watson, *Open*, 103–120.

— *The Art of Performance* (London: Darton, Longman & Todd, 1990).

Ziesler, John, 'Justification by Faith in the Light of the "New Perspective" on Paul', *Theology*, Vol. XCIV (May/June 1991), 188–194.

Index of Biblical References

INDEX OF AUTHORS